AF505438

Dowry & Inheritance

Dowry & Inheritance

Edited by
SRIMATI BASU

Series Editor
RAJESWARI SUNDER RAJAN

Dowry & Inheritance
was first published in 2005 by

**Women Unlimited
(an associate of Kali for Women)
K-36, Hauz Khas Enclave, Ground Floor,
New Delhi- 110 016**

© 2005, this collection Women Unlimited
© 2005, individual essays with authors

ISBN: 81-88965-22-7

Cover design: Visual Vibe

All rights reserved

Typeset at Print Services, B-17 Lajpat Nagar Part 2,
New Delhi 110 024, and printed at
Raj Press, R-3 Inderpuri, New Delhi 110 012

Contents

Series Note

Issues in Contemporary Indian Feminism is a series that is premised on the need for an overview of the substantial writing available on a variety of issues in Indian feminism. Each individual volume will relate to an issue of some moment, specifically one on which there has been a wide variety of views and positions. The mapping of these complex and often contentious issues—around 'feminism' itself, caste, dowry and inheritance, censorship and media representation, to name the topics of the first few volumes—is intended to serve as a point of entry and guide to what might be unfamiliar territory to some; to those closer home, themselves perhaps participants in these debates, they would indicate some of the shifts in the direction various feminist debates have undergone.

With these volumes we hope to construct a long overdue archive of writings relating to gender issues in India. The materials have been selected from a large mass of several decades of feminist writing scattered in journals and books, pamphlets, manifestos, speeches and official documents. By bringing them within the covers of a single volume, we hope to provide handy reference to otherwise hard to access resources. The series is therefore particularly intended to serve the needs of research scholars, teachers in Women's Studies courses, and activists. These collections will at the same time, we hope, bring to prominence a substantial, complex and important body of feminist writing that is closely related to the issues tackled by the women's movement in India. Viewed in this way, it becomes evident that these engagements, at once topical and far-sighted, make a major contribution to global feminist theory.

The editors of the individual volumes are experts in their areas. Their introductory essays will provide an overview of the debate/discourse on each topic, identify its landmarks, and offer a distinctive perspective on the theoretical tendencies that determine its frames of reference. The selections are based on implicit criteria, such as the influence a work may have exerted on subsequent thought or policy, its representation of a prominent trend, the contribution it makes to a particular debate, or its intrinsic 'merit'. Every volume includes a select bibliography at the end.

Rajeswari Sunder Rajan
Series Editor

Acknowledgements

With hope for new generations of feminists who will not need lavish displays at weddings to mark personhood and community.

First and foremost, my deepest thanks to Rajeswari Sunder Rajan for visualizing the project and inviting me to it, providing sage advice and mediating confusion, and always, for being an inspiration in scholarship and kindness. Thanks also to Ritu Menon for supporting the project and taking it out into the world, and to Rosamma Thomas for her careful and engaged attention to countless editing tasks across continents. We are very grateful, too, to the authors and publishers who gave us permission to reprint their work.

Myriad people have been inordinately generous in helping me locate and format the texts that went into writing this book. I would like to thank, in particular, the staff of the Center for Women's Development Studies (New Delhi); the library and support staff at the School of Women's Studies, Jadavpur University (Kolkata); Anjum Katyal of Seagull Theatre Quarterly; Joyanti Sen at Sachetana (Kolkata); the library staff at Depauw University. I thank the Faculty Development Committee at DePauw University for the Summer Grant and the Professional Development Grant that partially funded me for the project, and Carol Cox, Terri Collins and Krista Dahlstrom in Sociology/Anthropology and Women's Studies at DePauw University for their cheerful and efficient help with copying, collating and mailing.

Friends and family have been an essential part of the journey, in their vigilant search for resources and careful feedback of my writing, as well as the succour and joy they provide. Sylvia Vatuk, Geraldine Forbes and Mrinalini Sinha were very kind in agreeing to read draft versions of the introductory essay, Kathryn Ward in bibliographic generosity and sharing fieldwork resources, Jashodhara Bagchi and Sudha Kulkarni in putting me in touch with women's organizations in Kolkata and Mumbai, Meryl Altman in both careful reading and cross-fertilization around our very different research projects. Thanks to Veena Oldenburg not only for numerous fascinating conversations about dowry and inheritance, but for putting me in touch with Women's Feature Service, which allowed me to highlight some of the issues developed here. Brinda Bose, Kinsuk Mitra, Bishnupriya Ghosh, Nirmalyo Ghoshal, Anuradha Paul, Anubha Chatterji, Ashok Ravat and Naseem Ahmed have provided all kinds of concrete help and not least, the most intriguing of conversations and warmest of moments across decades. My parents, Sujata Basu and Tapas Basu, have enthusiastically supplied both sustenance and labour, but perhaps even more importantly, habits of contemplating practices and ethics, wealth and well-being. And to Tiku Ravat, partner and co-conspirator, thank you for thinking with me, and for sharing the passion and pain around these issues and so much more.

Carbondale, Illinois, USA.
October 2004

The Politics of Giving: Dowry and Inheritance as Feminist Issues

SRIMATI BASU

At a Bengali Hindu wedding, the institution of the *tattwa*—the formal display of gifts between the marrying families—never fails to turn my stomach. It is a rare wedding where pride of place is not occupied by a roomful of cellophane-wrapped trays of clothes for the couple, clothes for a wide circle of relatives, linen, houseware, make-up, sweets, spices, fish ... I even saw a container of Glenlivet single malt whisky as part of a recent display! It is possible to hire a professional *tattwa* designer these days to make this display 'artistic'—clothing shaped into fantastic silhouettes; bamboo or styrofoam sculptures; jewel-like accoutrements. People inevitably hasten to tell me that I am misreading *tattwa* as 'dowry' in the same sense as 'dowry deaths': as opposed to that terrible greedy and materialistic stuff, this phenomenon is cast as an authentic celebration of cultural traditions, a fundamental component of wedding ceremonies.

It is, of course, possible to read this as a celebration of women's artistic traditions: I remember women from my grandmother's generation fashioning intricate huts built from whole *garam masala* (spices), carriages from jicama fruit, bride and groom figures from *lauki* (gourd) and *baingan* (brinjal). The gifts for the wider family may also, of course, be seen as symbolic markers of the most sacred of anthropological moments: the establishment of relations of affinity/alliance. I am repeatedly told that *tattwa* is meant to be scrupulously reciprocal, although current expectations seem to be for brides' families to give more stuff, nicely set up by the rhythm of ritual in which grooms' families give first and set the standard to be surpassed.

Can this phenomenon possibly share a signifier with the kerosene-doused burning, beaten woman, and her family, rendered destitute through her marriage? These are the commonest associations with the word dowry, which is seen to mark Indian women's ultimate vulnerability and their families' disproportionate burden. We are scarcely even surprised at news about gruesome deaths—a headline such as 'Harassment for dowry claims another life—two-year-old cries for mother'[1] acknowledges the prevalence of the phenomenon even as it makes a sensationalist pitch. Sometimes the surprise is only in the extent of prevalence—dowry demands could be made of a practicing woman lawyer in Mumbai,[2] dowry deaths could happen among the Kolis—'Dowry Claims First Koli Victim,'[3] dowry is rising in working-class communities and among non-Hindus (Pati 1993); it is related to urban migration and is rising among the urban poor in Delhi (Luthra 1983). C.S. Lakshmi (in an article included in this volume,) reports an incident of a father selling his kidneys in order to acquire a capital fund for his three daughters' marriages (1989). Barbara Miller sees dowry as one prime motivator of female infanticide (1981). That is, multiple forms of violence against women (and their families) coalesce around dowry as an over-determined signifier, a sort of clearing-house cause for a complex range of forms of sexual violence.

I realize I could try to be an assiduous cultural relativist about what 'dowry' means, but it seems to me that the juxtaposition of so-called 'dowry violence' with institutions such as *tattwa* (substitute the form particular to your community here) illustrate the problematic of dowry and inheritance for feminist analyses particularly well. Can we read *tattwa* as a celebration of women's material culture, as artistic expression of the domestic realm to be preserved and admired, and yet separate this from the plethora of gifts through which it is expressed? Where does one draw the line between 'gifts' in accordance with community norms and 'dowry'? Why is this area so vulnerable to violence and extortion? Questions of women's agency are critical here as well: in what ways do women participate, and what do they express through such participation? If dowry or bridewealth is seen as a form of inheritance or functions de facto as a form of inheritance, then the gifting is encoded with both material and emotional meanings. Moreover, how might this spill over to affect de jure inheritance practices and women's access to a fuller share of both natal and affinal resources? Also, weddings, and particularly institutions such as *tattwa*, may be interpreted as being primarily focused on status displays, and we may need to put class-based consumption (and women's participation in it) rather than gender at the centre of the equation.

Feminist debates over dowry and inheritance have taken place over these sorts of contested questions. There is, obviously, little disagreement about whether extortionate dowry demands and dowry related murders are a good thing. Rather, conversations have centred around the definitions and significance of dowry and inheritance: the connection between dowry and bridewealth norms as alleged measures of women's status; the putative role of dowry as a form of inheritance; the relationship between inheritance and women's empowerment. Feminist interventions have dealt with questions of slippery definitions and concepts in legal formulations and social and cultural measures, and with fundamental theoretical questions regarding the centrality of gender vs. class and agency vs. structure, foregrounding women as both actors and victims. This essay will lay out some of these strands by way of evaluating proposed strategic actions: should we abandon dowry in all forms? Should only some forms be boycotted? Are we against dowry, or merely dowry-related violence? Is dowry to be substituted for inheritance? How do feminists respond to the solidification of class hegemonies through dowry and inheritance?

Protests against dowry demands and dowry murders have also been one of the most prominent faces of the Indian women's movement (organizing around inheritance rights has been comparatively eclipsed as an issue despite the obvious connection). Dowry (or the dowry/ inheritance dialectic) is one of the primary associations with Indian feminism in European/American feminist contexts; inevitably also linked with violence, it is seen as the central focus of the Indian women's movement. As Uma Narayan's marvellous critique suggests, dowry gets read as a peculiar Indian problem of 'culture': dowry murder is frequently conflated with *satidaha* (widow immolation), and Indian women are invariably depicted as voiceless victims of a harsh patriarchy, dowry being its synecdoche (1997).

Few parallels are drawn with problems related to marriage as an institution or women's access to financial resources, or violence against women in ways that affect women in the US or Europe. Radhika Parameswaran's reading of the *Dallas Observer*'s coverage of Aleyamma Mathew's death exemplifies Narayan's argument: here, an Indian Christian woman's death due to domestic violence and alcoholism was reconstructed, using images of bride burning, spices and traditional food, which led to an obscure attribution of the causes of the tragedy to Indian patriarchal culture (1996). Parameswaran frames the essay with an episode from her Feminist Theory class in the US where the librarian introduces the class to the journal *Manushi* by saying, "I read this two or three times a year when I feel bad or depressed. After reading this, I feel much better about my own situation" (1996: 69). Indeed, bride burning images may be depicted as the sine qua non of women's oppression that allow European/American feminists to feel vindicated, both in their condemnation of patriarchy and as affirmation of the superiority of their culture/politics. Narayan argues that the obfuscation of 'cultural causes' is an impediment for feminist theorizing and activism on a global scale: 'the ways in which issues emerge in various national contexts, and the contextual factors that shape the specific issues that are named and addressed, *affect the information that is readily available for such connection-making*, and hence our ability to make connections across these contexts' (1997: 86). Yet studying dowry as an institution, paying attention to patterns of resource exchange and the cultural/emotional coding of these exchanges, can be seen as being central to feminist theoretical concerns about the economic/ ideological workings of patriarchies and class systems, of femininity as a cultural marker, issues of women's agency, and the intractability of legal provisions.

Marriage payments: an index of culture and status

The prospect of mentioning dowry boycott as a solution seems a little surreal when we consider dowry and bridewealth in broad cultural scope. The exchange of gifts at marriage, whether as dowry or bridewealth,[4] is so ubiquitous that it is regarded as fundamental to human culture. Here, Levi-Strauss' work on kinship is the critical text: marking a radical shift from a concern with lineage and descent as being central to kinship, to questions of alliance and affinity (relationships between disparate groups through marriage), he postulated that cultural connections between groups are established and strengthened through marriage.[5] The so-called 'incest taboo', the fact that each culture has groups of people who are not permitted to marry/have sexual relations with each other (importantly, the particular categories differ from culture to culture) was read by Levi-Strauss in terms of directives towards exogamy or marriage outside one's particular group (again, group is defined in various ways), and much of *The Elementary Structures of Kinship* (1949) lays out patterns of these 'rules' of marriage partners. Influenced also by Marcel Mauss' (1967) contention that gift-giving marks ongoing relationships between groups and hence is a primary building block of culture, Levi-Strauss argued that women and bridewealth were the most significant of 'gifts' exchanged between cultural groups, and delineated marriage as the site where the gift of women travelling in one direction and bridewealth travelling in a counter direction was put into play between groups, the combination helping to cement intergenerational exchange.

v

Levi-Strauss' argument is almost too pat as a target of feminist critique. As Gayle Rubin points out in the richly complex essay, 'The Traffic in Women', his schema may be read as a trafficking cycle where human culture is founded upon the transfer of mute, acquiescent women as goods equivalent to bridewealth. It is significant that women, rather than men, are seen to be exchanged, because men as a group gain from it in ways that women do not:

> If it is women who are being transacted, then it is the men who give and take them who are linked, the woman being a conduit of a relationship rather than a partner to it. The exchange of women does not necessarily imply that women are objectified, in the modern sense, since objects in the primitive world are imbued with highly personal qualities. But it does imply a distinction between gift and giver. If women are the gifts, then it is men who are the exchange partners. And it is the partners, not the presents, upon whom reciprocal exchange confers its quasi-mystical power of social linkage. The relations of such a system are such that women are in no position to realize the benefits of their own circulation. As long as the relations specify that men exchange women, it is men who are the beneficiaries of the product of such exchanges—social organization (1997: 37).

Rubin challenges Levi-Strauss' idea that the exchange of women/ bridewealth is a 'prerequisite of culture'.

> 'If his analysis is adopted in its pure form, the feminist program must include a task even more onerous than the extermination of men; it must attempt to get rid of culture and substitute some entirely new phenomena on the face of the earth. However, it would be a dubious proposition at best to argue that if there were no exchange of women there would be no culture, if for no other reason than that culture is, by definition, inventive' (1997: 38).

She argues, rather, that kinship systems should be analyzed in terms of the concrete rights and forms of power that are obtained, and in terms of the specific ideologies of sexuality that undergird this system and the ways in which they are maintained. This, then, takes the question of marriage exchanges away from the obfuscating rubric of 'culture' and links it to political economy, class and other hierarchical structures—the 'sex/gender system' of each cultural group is constitutive of these other systems. Challenging nexuses of power and privilege thus entails reinscribing forms of gender and sexuality.

In a critique of definitions of dowry and bridewealth, Laurel Bossen points out that anthropologists have tended to make female motivations and transactions invisible: it is typical to 'consider... only what men do to get brides, but not what women do to get husbands, or other men, and how they gain access to men's economic contributions' (1988: 129). Even if the most simplistic assumption that women are commodities exchanged like bridewealth is avoided by adopting the perspective that 'certain types of rights in women (labour, sexual, reproductive) are being transacted, not women themselves', it is still common to 'treat women either as a passive, homogeneous category, or as analytically anomalous and unpredictable', to forget the evidence that 'women often reject, veto or nullify the agreements made between men, making men scramble to restore economic order when women disrupt their arrangements' (1988: 133). Bossen's analysis thus casts women as subvertors and transactors, as agents acting within material relations, beyond Rubin's critique in which they are still seen as being acted upon and rendered homogeneous.

As these arguments indicate, the equivalence between marriage payments and the 'value' of the humans being 'exchanged' has become a staple of anthropological and feminist inquiry. The central question here is what the dowry or bridewealth is a payment for: a mere token exchange to mark the establishment of affinal relations? A display of the givers' wealth that brings them social status? An acknowledgment of the receivers' status and the payment required to become their kin? Compensation for the labour value of a person from the family which can now benefit from their labour? Incentive to the family taking on an economically unproductive liability?

Appreciation for a groom's current market value? One or more of these criteria come into play, depending on individual and group resources, monetization and other forms of status, and ritual and symbolic domains. Of the 563 societies listed in Murdock's *Atlas of World Cultures*, 24 or four per cent are associated with dowry systems, 226 with bridewealth, and 63 with brideservice (Harell and Dickey 1985: 105). Goody's classic article on the subject succinctly points out that dowry and bridewealth may co-exist in a particular wedding transaction, and that it is therefore simplistic to visualize the two forms as 'mirror opposites' (1973: 6).

It had been a frequent working premise (Boserup 1973, Goody 1973, Schlegel and Eloul 1988) that bridewealth cultures were associated with higher status for women because they were an acknowledgment of the loss of women's labour power, while dowry cultures were associated with lower status for women because they saw women as economic liabilities rather than assets; but an overview of research indicates that this is far too simple a formula.[6] In an innovative foray into anthropology, Papps used the tools of economic analysis to postulate that 'brideprice is the discounted value of part or all of the wife's share of marriage output, and that the value of this share must at least equal the bride's possible earnings in alternative households...in a full analysis one has to consider not only the value of the bride to her husband and to her own family, but also her value to all other potential husbands' (1983: 204). That is, the focus here was on equivalence between bridewealth and the bride's provision of particular services including domestic work, sex and children. However, Kressel has argued that the very equation of bridewealth and loss of women's labour power is framed from a partial perspective:

> The sons' brides who move in take the place of the household's daughters who marry out, while the profit from the daughter's brideprice is offset by that paid for the son's wife. This explanation, therefore, has always been questionable, and the question becomes more pointed with increasing frequency of neolocal[7]

residence. Here the contribution of women's work to the household economy decreases, while we often see a rise in brideprice' (1977: 441–442).

Kressel points to the emergence of bridewealth payments among Northwest Coast American Indians, and to his own ethnographic findings among sedentarized Bedouin in two Israeli towns where bridewealth payments varied widely depending on the degree of kinship between marrying families and their class status, to iterate that bridewealth in these cases is related to 'social differentiation': 'brideprice conventions are determined in relation to, and as a measure of, social distance' (1977: 449). Mulder measured bridewealth among the Kenyan Kipsigis in the context of increasing education for women and men and greater prevalence of consumer goods, and found that bridewealth norms had changed across generations, but 'recovering' value for women or building alliances through marriage were both important goals:

> ... either educate a daughter and marry her to an educated groom for a high bridewealth, or *lower* the bridewealth asked of a high ranking wife-taker so as to increase the chances of attaining an economically secure marital position for the daughter and the potential political benefits associated with having well-situated affines (1995: 587).

Similarly, Watson's study of a Hong Kong lineage found that people from different classes pursued different strategies: among peasants, a system similar to bridewealth prevailed, while the landlord class had a form of dowry that was used to cement relationships with powerful affines, which in turn helped them consolidate class status over the peasants (1981). Several of these examples demonstrate the strengthening of political and class alliances or the building of alliances with emergent powerful groups through marriage, in what might be regarded as an extension of Levi-Strauss' claim.

Rubin's critique of Levi-Strauss should also be recalled in this context: the above studies are typical of many others which look at class and status benefits from the point of view of 'the group', males by default, and assign little valence to what women might gain or seek. In contrast, Maya Unnithan-Kumar's research on Girasia women in Rajasthan (from which an excerpt appears in this volume,) provides a stringent critique of theories that bridewealth correlates with higher status for women, by demonstrating that women may act as mere tokens of transfer within a strongly patriarchal distribution of resources. Among the Girasia, she contends, 'brideprice' is

> not so much a recognition of a woman's contribution to the household, nor a payment for the loss of a productive member, but a compensation to the father and his agnatic group for past expenditure on her maintenance.

As one father explained, "I have not fed and clothed her so that she may work in another's field" (1997: 196). Girasia women have no control over marriage payments, and no rights to any part of the brideprice or affinal (and in practice, natal) property. Moreover, their labour is ideologically devalued and their sexuality controlled by their natal family. Patterns of negotiation between fathers and first, and subsequent, husbands show them to be 'markers of the transfer of wealth' (1997: 205). In effect, Unnithan-Kumar argues, they are perhaps worse off than upper-caste Hindu women because they may have no control on marriage payment decisions for the next generation when they are non-monogamous, and they have precarious rights to maintenance in the affinal family: 'Hindu wife-givers buy the maintenance rights of their daughters through dowry. Among the Girasia a woman's labour buys her right to maintenance, but only as long as she is seen to be working' (1997: 206). Unnithan-Kumar's research is an important reminder that bridewealth is not a proxy for women's high status; rather, access to productive resources and capital fund and control of labour might be seen as some of the most significant criteria.

It is critical to remember, in the Indian context, that the alleged emergence of dowry to replace customary bridewealth payments[8] is not necessarily a marker of women's declining status. An energetic debate over this issue arose in the early 1980s, framed by concerns about women's declining labour force participation rates and men's rapid insertion into the salaried sector. Some researchers documented a distinct change in practices involving the cessation of bridewealth and/ or its replacement with dowry, correlated with new, lucrative economic opportunities for grooms.[9] A related argument is that by Kishwar (1987), who argued that in a time of rising land acquisition among the Ho, wealthier families were reluctant to pay bridewealth to poorer families, while poorer families were willing to forego bridewealth in order to make alliances with wealthier families. As Indira Rajaraman (included in this volume) says in the discourse of economics,

> Employment in the organised sector, and access to such employment through acquisition of appropriate skills, is largely restricted to males. Such males as do gain entry receive, relative to their unorganised sector counterparts, a remuneration that is generally higher and less variable. It is inevitable, therefore, that marriage to such males would be highly desired, and that the resulting competition could result in a dowry where none existed before. For example, in an endogamous group consisting of weavers, say, eking out an uncertain livelihood and among whom the payment of a brideprice upon marriage is customary, the lone male who has achieved employment in say a government office may be able to command a spouse at a zero brideprice. His desirability might be such that he can even get one at a negative brideprice. At that point, a dowry comes into being. (1983: 275).

Rajaraman follows the notion of bridewealth-as-labour-compensation, calculated as the value of women's economic compensation in the paid labour force and her unpaid labour contribution in terms of housework and child care, minus the cost of maintaining her—as per this formula, dowry emerges as an option to replace bridewealth only when the unpaid labour contribution is believed to be less than the cost of her subsistence and the paid labour contribution is less than unpaid labour minus maintenance (1983: 276).[10] Rajaraman contends, moreover, that the emergence of dowry need not necessarily be an oppressive institution because it may simply reverse the flow of compensatory payments uniformly; systemic hardship is most likely to arise only when conspicuous consumption in wedding celebrations becomes prominent. Unnithan-Kumar's argument that dowry is not necessarily worse for women's status may be usefully reflected on here, but by focusing on the economistic argument of dowry/ bridewealth as a compensatory fund, Rajaraman completely misses myriad cultural factors related to alliance encoded in the payments. Can bridewealth or dowry be studied exclusively as 'labour values' with no connotations of class status or political negotiation? Can such a transition really only reverse the flow of money with no corresponding reflections in patriarchal relations? Critiques of Rajaraman have taken issue with her methodology of labour force statistics and challenged the claim that there is a widespread reversal of marriage payments, but they have also emphasized the domain of cultural practices. Sambrani and Sambrani (1983) and Aziz (1983) postulate the opposite question by way of refutation: why do educated urban women still require dowry at marriage rather than bridewealth?[11] Aziz further reverses the paradigm to focus on the value of 'acquiring a groom and then evaluating the utility index of the bride and her family' (1983: 603) rather than on compensation for the bride. In an article included in this volume, Randeria and Visaria (1984) demonstrate that payments are not just about the value of labour compensation on the basis of ethnographic data in Gujarat, where multiple payments occur over several generations in both directions, and bridewealth and dowry-like payments coexist among lower castes, both having increased substantially in the previous decade.[12] Parry (1979) also found that bridewealth was on the increase among the Rathi *biradari* in Kangra. It is thus most fruitful to see bridewealth as situated within a nexus of status needs, of which labour and maintenance compensation may, at best, be one factor, and to draw no correlation with women's 'value'.

Dowry as power and subordination

Can we associate dowry unequivocally with women's extreme subordination? Here, too, multiple systems of status are being negotiated: as with cultures where bridewealth is common, marriage is often a primary means of displaying wealth and status (Srinivas 1984, Paul 1986). Dowry may help cement favourable community ties helpful for the economic expansion of both families (Heyer 1992, Bradford 1985). Marriages are also significant instruments for negotiating boundary changes in caste status. A particular caste may seek to 'sanskritize' or adopt practices associated with the highest caste groups by integrating dowry practices, or a high caste may maintain its superior status by not allowing other castes to integrate dowry practices (Luthra 1983, Rajaraman 1983, Sambrani and Sambrani 1983, Srinivas 1984). The ritual status assigned to dowry is of critical importance here: the payment of a *dakshina* or token gift to the groom's family along with a gift of the virgin daughter or *kanyadan* is associated with the highest form of Brahmin marriage, while bride-wealth is associated with the inferior *asura* form of marriage (Tambiah 1973, Srinivas 1984).[13] As M.N. Srinivas (included in this volume) points out, Brahminical groups thus made their practices hegemonic and exclusive:

> One way of looking at classification of marriages by the Brahmin law-givers is to regard it as an attempt to impose the Brahminical ideology of *kanyadan* on a country where most people, including many Brahmin castes, but excluding the richer sections of hypergamous castes, practiced brideprice. That extremely popular form of marriage was dubbed *asura* and condemned as unsuitable for Brahmins (1984: 19).

Referring to Manu's injunction against an 'erudite father' accepting brideprice or *kanyashulka* because that would make him 'the seller of his offspring', Sukumari Bhattacharji emphasizes Manu's logical flaw that

> while the practice of paying dowry to the groom is present in palpable or incipient forms, there is no text forbidding the groom's father from accepting it; no one calls the transaction a 'sale' which, in reality, it was. (1991: 507).

Srinivas argues that hypergamy, the practice of wife-givers seeking grooms from a superior grade (caste, class or economic advantage), and the resultant 'status asymmetry between affinal groups' or superiority assigned to the groom's family, is at the heart of dowry practices; the hierarchy created between groups can become the conduit for extortionate demands, and the material and ideological dependence and subservience for women enshrined in the ideology of *kanyadan* exacerbates their vulnerability as well.[14]

The notion of hypergamy may become associated with marriage even when caste is not an issue. Tambiah's revised formulation of the significance of dowry is that it is aimed at increasing the resources and status of the groom's joint family, from which the couple and thence the woman may ultimately derive a share (1989). My ethnographic work confirmed this focus on the groom's family: 'at the wedding, *both* families' expenses seem to be directed toward increasing the assets (through gifts) and status (through hospitality) of the groom's family, which is supposed to be the 'joint family' into which the bride merges, and whose continued prosperity makes it less likely that the daughter will turn to the natal family for help or property shares later. Simultaneously, the bride's family also enhances its own position/status by displaying due propriety in ceremonies and prestations' (Basu 1999: 96). Grooms' family expenses went mostly into hospitality for their neighbours and colleagues, and gifts for the bride. There was a token of reciprocity of gifts that symbolically marked the establishment of kinship, but 'the weight is overwhelmingly on the bride's family in terms of having to give more, on more occasions, and more expensive things' (1999: 95).[15] Dowry may serve as a conduit for improving the groom's family's economic situation: a recent AIDWA report records an example from Orissa where girls who had been promised jobs and were engaged to be married on that condition, remain single because the jobs have not come through in ten years; in another case, a Dalit activist from Lucknow reports that men in the community say 'we can't get jobs, but we can get dowry to start our work' (2002: 3–4). On the other hand, Pnina Werbner in her study of Pakistani Muslim immigrants in Britain argues that, in some contexts, dowry may be the means of reversing status asymmetry:

> The logic of dowry is the logic of contradictory messages. The daughter given as a bride is a "pure gift" and as such a representative of a species (pure virgins) most worthy to be given as tribute to a king or family of superior status. Since she is given as "tribute", her passage defines her family as inferior, whether they are inferior or not. The wife-givers' prestations which accompany the bride (and which are formally directed to the *descending* generation) are, however, contrary to appearance *non*-tributary; they deny the inferior status implied by the simultaneous gift of the daughter. The wife-givers' wedding prestations are unilateral, freely given, asserting the high status of the wife-givers by creating a never-to-be-repaid debt' (1990: 277).

In either case, Srinivas' contention that gender norms form the bedrock of these transactions is significant, but importantly, these gender norms are constituted through and play out caste and class negotiations, indicating one of the critical areas of difficulty with treating dowry as a problem where gender is foregrounded.

Srinivas also reminds us to be wary of relying on alleged scriptural concepts in characterizing contemporary dowry. Status asymmetry is clearly not a primary criterion any more, as seen in the case of south Indian Hindu communities, (which typically contracted marriages with those equal in rank) enthusiastically adopting dowry practices (1984: 8). Moreover, it seems specious to equate the amount and kinds of goods habitually sought at present with scriptural sanctions to give a small *dakshina* gift along with the principal gift of the bride, plus some *stridhanam* which was to be the woman's exclusive property:

> Modern dowry is entirely the product of the forces let loose by British rule such as monetization, education and the introduction of the organized sector. The attempt to equate the huge sums of cash, jewellery, clothing, furniture and gadgetry demanded of the bride's kin by the groom's to *dakshina* is to legitimize a modern monstrosity by linking it with an ancient and respected custom, a common enough and hoary Indian device (Srinivas 1984: 13).

The categories of dowry items documented by researchers—clothing and jewellery for the bride, clothing and jewellery for affines, household goods for general use, even land or a house or cars, plus huge entertainment expenses[16]—conforms with a part of Rajaraman's argument (1983), that expenses of the ceremony are likely to be most extortionate to families, although the first two categories can also have inordinate expenses. However, vilifying 'modern excesses' as the primary problem is also an incomplete assessment. Romila Thapar (1987) and Sukumari Bhattacharji (1991) refute claims that the advent of Islam, and later, of European colonizers, caused a decline in women's status; there is enough textual evidence of women's subservience in Vedic times and increasingly, in the second half of the first millenium A.D. An 'ancient and respected custom' in a starkly patriarchal milieu was not weighted in favour of women's equitable subjectivity. Thus, rather than revisiting 'traditional' meanings of dowry, a fundamental challenge to symbolic systems is required.

One of the 'ancient and respected customs' often referred to as a putatively positive original form of contemporary dowry is the idea of *stridhanam*, gifts at marriage (jewellery or other valuables) which were to be regarded as the bride's own property. Sukumari Bhattacharji designates the categories that constituted *stridhanam* in ancient texts—'*pana*, with which the bride was purchased; *yautuka*, gifts given to the girl at marriage by her relations and friends, and *saudayika*, gifts given to the bride or to the couple, either at her or his place, by the respective friends and relations', plus a portion of the mother's *stridhanam* and a sort of penalty paid to an earlier wife when the husband married again (1991: 507)—but is careful to point out that readings of scholars such as Yajnavalkya might suggest that there were several extenuating circumstances in which the husband could claim and use this property. The notion of *stridhanam* as incipient property also corresponds with Goody and Tambiah's formulation of dowry as a 'pre-mortem inheritance', as a fund acquired at marriage and controlled partly by the woman (1973): the idea fits well in European milieus where families alienated land and other productive resources upon a daughter's marriage, and where this practice faded away as married women began to be able to own their own property; but the equivalence with inheritance portions in the Indian context is not very tenable. Even if it is not exactly an inheritance portion, the question of whether the dowry (at least minus gifts of clothing and jewellery to affines) is the bride's capital fund or not is still highly contested.

Veena Oldenburg (an excerpt from her book is included here) contends that dowry among Punjabis had commonly functioned as a property fund for women, 'one of the few indigenous, woman-centered institutions in an overwhelmingly patriarchal and agrarian society', put together by the bride's female relatives over numerous years, paid for through a complex system of community reciprocity called *neonda* (2002: 9–10; 90). The colonial concern about rising dowry payments, infanticide linked to Hindu concerns about not being able to pay dowry, and the attempt to control marriage expenses to diminish the impoverishment attributed to dowry, were all scapegoating attempts that cast Hindu culture as the problem and justified colonial paternalist domination. Oldenburg not only refutes the evidence that infanticide was a high-caste Hindu problem, and that dowry was suddenly extortionate, but turns the culpability back upon the colonial state and argues that the growing impoverishment had a far greater correlation with colonial land and revenue policies and the suppression of modern industry, and increasing son-preference correlated highly with the colonial construction of males as property owners and the creation of lucrative wage jobs in the military (2002). Dowry thus has a long history as an overdetermined signifier of impoverishment.

The question of whether any *stridhanam* goods are under the bride's control has also been raised by many researchers, and the gap between 'usage' and 'control' has become a murky issue. Ursula Sharma contended that in practice dowry goes 'with' the bride rather than 'to' her (1976). Unnithan-Kumar suggests that when the bulk of dowry is consumable goods rather than a cash brideprice, as is the norm among the Girasia, then it becomes correspondingly harder for a bride to retrieve or set aside a separate share (1997). On the other hand, Pnina Werbner found that among British Pakistani immigrants, who were of course in a very different economic and cultural context than the examples above, brides' property rights were usually validated:

> It is said that if a husband takes away his wife's jewellery he takes away her most precious thing, since this is the jewellery she expects to pass on to her own daughter when her time comes to marry ... A girl expects to be consulted about the disposal of all the property and cash she brings with her from her native home. She thus derives her status within the new household from her control over these resources, as well as her independence in matters of clothing and adornment (1990: 278).

There are thus a range of experiences depending on class and community, but overall, although dowry is often construed as intended for the bride's welfare, it cannot be assumed that it is necessarily going to be controlled or even appropriated by her.

However, Werbner's research results are an important reminder that women's subjectivities with regard to the taking and giving of dowry are complex. Gayle Rubin critiques Levi-Strauss for visualizing cultural exchange in terms of 'the traffic in women', but Rubin, in turn, may be said to cast women as passive victims of these exchanges and to pay little attention to their agency in the transaction. Similarly, much of the research on dowry ignores the ways in which women involve themselves in dowry exchanges as brides, mothers, mothers-in-law, sisters-in-law etc., in both the giving and taking of it. Perhaps the toughest problem is that of brides themselves. Kishwar reports that many young women wrote to her about the emotional value they attached to dowry, as well as its status as the only substantial transfer of resources from the natal family, and sees this as an opportunity to interrogate what dowry has come to stand for:

> Instead of dismissing the refusal of young women to say "no" to dowry as a sign of their low consciousness or lack of awareness, we would do better to examine why they are not willing to give it up (1999: 12).

Kishwar's findings are reiterated in a survey of single women undertaken for the AIDWA report, where women of poor families opposed dowry because of their families' potential ruin,

> but a fairly substantial section of urban young middle class women felt that dowry was 'inevitable'; that their parents would not listen to their objections; others were of the opinion that since they would not inherit anything from their parents, at least in this way, they would get some of what they felt was their due (2002: 6).

Parminder Bhachu, who studied East African Sikh women in Britain, argued that putting together an elaborate dowry from their own earnings, over which they exercise substantial control, was a substantial point of empowerment (1993).[17] Among the families I interviewed, marriage payments and expenses were entirely within the realm of doxa as custom, but demands were seen as crass and unacceptable; while the implicit standards of giving were quite clear, grooms' families benefitted morally by not making explicit claims and were rarely deprived in the process (Basu 1999). In Ranjana Kumari's study based on dowry harassment cases reported to authorities, 60 per cent of families had paid, despite there being no explicit demands; 79 per cent had paid 'voluntarily' rather than 'under pressure', 35 per cent had given dowry 'for the girl's happiness', 12 per cent as a 'status symbol', and 22 per cent because of 'social pressure' (1989: 44–45). These findings correspond with those of many others who report that it is the demand that is the focus of ire; otherwise women are interested in dowries, especially in items for themselves and the conjugal home, reading it most often as a transfer of resources rather than a marker of hypergamy or gender subordination.[18]

Marking women's (and brides' families) participation, is not however, tantamount to raising a sort of 'blame the victim' standard in bemoaning the entrenched quality of dowry,[19] or women's 'false consciousness' in colluding with an instrument of their degradation. As critiques of 'false consciousness' show, there is not likely to be a magic moment where the veil of ideology is ripped aside—rather, one could visualize women's identities as being constituted through these ideologies, a deep-rooted process of associating dowry and marriage with notions of family, intimacy, or love, of ritual gifts with profound emotional bonds. The association of conspicuous consumption with status and emotion is a further complicating factor; given that prosperity and class are marked through wedding displays, women (especially from middle-class and elite homes) may not be enthusiastic collaborators in proposals to have dowry-less weddings.

It is these troubling moments of agency, such as women's allegiance to dowry as marker of love and esteem, that pose the most difficult challenges for feminist politics about what should be the means and who should be the focus of reform. Like feminist critiques of the subservience of housewives or of the ubiquity of make-up and hair removal to look 'normal', critiques of marriage and dowry may be seen as out-of-touch, patronizing scolding that ignores 'real' women's desires. And indeed, it seems essential that feminist critiques should be smart about the ways in which women involved in these processes make sense of them, at the very least to enhance the understanding of powerful, metonymic signifiers and the ways in which systems of subordination are held in place. However, a hard-hitting feminist politics aims to not just validate feelings but to radically question the workings of patriarchy and class hierarchies. And there is no getting away from the fact that the contemporary phenomenon of dowry marks a profound space of gender-based dependence and hence, vulnerability to multiple forms of violence. I have dwelt on the academic terrain of marriage payments at length to provide some sense of the complex and contradictory evidence about the meanings and purpose of dowry and bridewealth, and the issues that must be tackled by feminist interventions in the realm of social mobilization, law and popular culture in trying to connect the domains of marriage-payments with assault and murder.

Interventions: cultural and legal

The legal realm is often seen as the most concrete means to seek solutions to gender equity, whether with regard to family law, labour or violence. The hope is that instituting a law signals recognition of a social problem, acts as a deterrent and, in the ultimate instance, as a punitive instrument. In practice, cultural behaviours often adapt, finding a way around legal loopholes (Agarwal 1994, Basu 1999, Kishwar 1999, Menon 1999), leaving the law to be an ideological marker of censure, or at best a site where feminist discourse may be worked over and negotiated (Kapur and Cossman 1996). Dowry laws are, par excellence, an example of such slippery legal terrain. The amended Dowry Prohibition Act (1984) makes the giving and taking of dowry 'as a condition of marriage' punishable by law, while excluding 'voluntary gifts'. Suicides and murders attributed to dowry have a special apparatus of evidence and arrest: Section 498A of the Indian Penal Code relating to 'cruelty' which may drive a woman to suicide, or 'harassment' related to 'unlawful demands for property', Section 304B of the Indian Penal Code and Sections 113A and 113B of the Evidence Act relating to presumption of dowry deaths for unnatural deaths within seven years of marriage carrying a term of seven years to life; Section 174 of the Criminal Procedure Code relating to compulsory post-mortems for women dying within seven years of marriage and Section 32(1) of the Evidence Act (relating to the weight given to dying declarations in assessing the guilt of the accused). But the execution of these legal provisions does little to address the social mechanisms through which dowry flourishes.

A fundamental illustration of the kinship and religious politics within which dowry is encoded is seen in legislative attempts to define 'dowry'. A case in point is the definition of 'dowry' in the Dowry Prohibition (Amendment) Act (1984):

> Dowry means any property or valuable security given or agreed to be given either directly or indirectly (a) by one party to the marriage to the other party to the marriage, or (b) by the parents of either party to a marriage or by any other person to either party to the marriage or to any other person, at or before any time after the marriage in connection with the marriage of the said parties, but does not include dower or *mehr* in the case of persons to whom the Muslim Personal Law (Shariat) applies.

Moreover, customary forms of *stridhan* are also explicitly exempted. One immediately notices that it is impossible to unhook the idea of extortion from the notion of 'customary gifts', and to define 'in connection with the marriage' (which is an improvement over 'in consideration of marriage') with any specificity. Alongside caste councils that worked in local languages, the colonial State sought to curb 'extravagance' in marriage because of its link to impoverishment (needless to say, with no apparent recognition of their own role in the said widespread impoverishment), in measures such as the Sindh Leti Deti Act of 1939, but Ranjana Sheel (included in this volume) argues that attempts to identify dowry as a 'social evil' were quite lukewarm (1999: 161). After Independence, legislation to penalize giving and taking dowry was undertaken in two states under the Bihar Dowry Restraint Act (1950) and the Andhra Pradesh Dowry Prohibition Act (1958), but despite stringent and specific criteria, the measures were reportedly failures because of the difficulty of proving that gifts were 'in consideration of' marriage. The two Acts also relied on brides' parents to lodge complaints (Sheel 1999: 162–163).

The Parliamentary debates provide vivid examples of resistance to the ban on gifts at marriage: most legislators objected virulently to the 1959 Joint Committee's suggestion to ban all gifts (a modification of the original proposal to set an upper limit of Rs. 2000), revealing an understanding of dowry as an indubitable element of Hindu marriage and a protective gesture towards women. Ranjana Sheel delineates some of these discourses:

> The plight and the untold misery of young girls, some members observed, underlined and justified the need for gift-giving or dowry which protected the interests of girls all over the country. In fact, Pandit Thakur Das Bhargava of Hissar demanded the abolition of the Bill if its intentions were to abolish the system of dowry itself. Other members regarded dowry as an 'ancient custom' which had provided 'security' and 'protection' to women. As such it was a mark of affection for the daughter. Thus it was 'not always an unmitigated evil'. What made this custom objectionable was the recently introduced 'new phenomenon' of dowry demands. The Speaker of the House excluded the *stridhana* which was given out of love and affection to the daughter from dowry the evil … . Dowry as such was not an evil till the demands went 'beyond the reasonable financial competence of the other party' … . Marriage, which is 'the starting point' for a girl's life must thus be accompanied by gift-giving. The shastric recommendation of the high spiritual merit of *kanyadana* in a Hindu marriage, which required the bride to be properly ornamented and clad in riches, was also brought in the discussion to justify dowry. (1999: 168–169).

A couple of women members pointed to the central issue that this legislation was about—setting radically new social standards—rather than business as usual. Parvati Krishnan questioned linking gifts of love with marriage when love could be expressed through gifts at any point in a woman's life, and objected to the suggestion of having a graded scale based on availability. Subhadra Joshi and Renu Chakraborty also argued for delinking marriage and gifts and pointed to brides' lack of control over dowry items. But the prevailing discourse was one of retaining 'tradition' and conveying symbolic disapproval over extravagance and extortion in the form of legislation (Sheel 1999: 168–170). Later, when the ineffectiveness of this legislation became quite clear, and in response to the reports of the 1983 Law Commission and the 1975 Committee on Status of Women in India, the Dowry Prohibition (Amendment) Act was passed in 1984, and a revised Act with further suggestions from women's groups in 1986 (Sheel 1999: 182–183). But the changes, which allow for somewhat stricter legal penalties, a broader definition of gifts, including post-marriage ones, as well as guidelines to register marriages and gifts, have basically no power to curb extravagant marriages or haul in offenders, and are unable to tap into the circuitous routes through which dowry is solicited. In the course of fieldwork on the workings of the Family Courts in Kolkata in 2001, I ran into several examples of such indirect methods, whereby cash payments would be made by the bride's brother or uncle to the groom's aunt or business associate in a seemingly unrelated transaction, such that the groom and his immediate family could not be connected to the taking of dowry.

The issue of putting legislation into practice gets even more complicated. Getting a handle on the extent of dowry and its relation to dowry deaths has been a statistical and legal challenge. Official information is gathered regularly about deaths attributed to dowry in various parts of India: the figures reveal a fourteen-fold increase from 427 in 1983 to 6006 in 1997 (Umar 1998), and a starkly gendered profile as well as a particular risk to women in the 18–30 age group. (See table 1, at end of introduction) But this tabulation in no way documents dowry practices or marriage payments as a broader cultural phenomenon, and captures only those examples that are officially reported in connection with death or domestic violence. Moreover, determining which deaths are attributable to dowry is also problematic. It is often reported (e.g. Gautam and Trivedi 1986: 6) that women constitute only 10 per cent of homicide victims but 41 per cent of suicide cases, and 35 per cent of suicide victims are women; 65 per cent of burn victims, a high proportion of these being young wives, are women. But this figure may say more about the myriad pressures upon and torture of women than dowry per se: closer investigation of 'dowry death' figures has often revealed that dowry may be one of numerous causes for assault, and may be prominent partly because of its overdetermined legal status (Umar 1998, Kumari 1989, Khan 1984). The ubiquity of exorbitant marriage expenses and the fact that both sides are held equally culpable, despite the very different pressures on them, means that there is no incentive to report except after death or as retaliation or in association with other lawsuits (Umar 1998, Gautam and Trivedi 1986). As I described above, people seem well aware of legal guidelines and are constantly defining creative ways to get around them. Marshalling evidence under legal provisions proves difficult as well: police have refused to use dying declarations as grounds to investigate deaths thoroughly; corroborative evidence from neighbours about violence or torture is often discounted; making the connection to direct economic gain is a further obstacle; abetment to suicide seems impossibly difficult to prove; burning is a particularly efficient method of destroying evidence on the body; bribery is rife, and the police are often reluctant to interfere in 'domestic disputes' (Umar 1998, Kumar 1994, Gautam and Trivedi 1986). Jethmalani and Dey's mapping of three prominent cases provides a vivid chronicle of judicial indifference and quibbling over definitions and evidence (alongside the growing awareness of legal lacunae that emerged as a result of feminist agitations): for example, in the Satya Rani Chadha case, the magistrate refused to consider demands made at the birth of the first child as being within the definition of dowry demands (1995: 48), and in the Tripta Sharma case the judge dismissed it despite medical evidence because he found a motive for murder lacking, unconvinced that an employed woman would be killed off if she was being harassed to hand over her salary money (1998: 66). As these examples indicate, academic dissension about the definition and purposes of dowry is mirrored in the legal confusion, exacerbated by the binary logic of law.

Is dowry, then, so ephemeral a legal entity that it is best tackled as a broad-based social movement? The notion that dowry is a 'social evil' that should be tackled through social pressures and incentives is a recurrent theme in numerous venues. Official studies from the Police Department, e.g., Gautam and Trivedi (1986) discuss the shortcomings of legal intervention and suggest the need for social reform. Much of the substance of parliamentary debates on dowry is taken up by lengthy speeches about possible measures: during the 1984 debates, there is mention of legislators being role models by undertaking dowry-less weddings for their own children, 'brainwashing' (sic) children against the idea in school and college, providing job-related incentives such as promotions or priority in housing allotments to those volunteering to have dowry-less weddings (Dowry Prohibition [Amendment] Bill, 1984). The 1975 Report of the Committee on the Status of Women in India has, understandably, a much broader rubric of suggestions: locating the problem as being 'against the goal of a socialistic society' and connecting it to women's economic dependence, the authors suggest measures that, 'though aiming at proximate ends, should take a determined step forward towards an egalitarian society' (1975: 76). To this end,

> Social consciousness needs to be aroused particularly amongst women to enable them to understand that, by encouraging dowry,

they are perpetuating the inequality of the sexes. Reforms in marriage customs to simplify the ceremony, increasing opportunities for employment, condemnation of the ideal of a parasitic existence for women, a reassessment of the value of household work and home-making as socially and economically productive, and the enforcement of the Anti-Dowry Act are some of the measures necessary (1975: 76).

They also suggest setting a cash limit on the amount of gifts to the groom and his family as well as on entertainment costs; prohibiting displays; and re-examining gifts to the bride if they are just an excuse for the transfer of wealth (1975: 115–116). Here, specific anti-dowry measures (all of which were deemed too restrictive to be a part of the eventual law) are placed within a nexus of problems related to gender discrimination, underlining the problematic connection between ideologies of gender and class- and gender-based accumulation of resources.

The CSWI report was produced as an official government product, but it is an integral part of the feminist activist discourse on dowry that was especially visible and influential in the late 1970s and 1980s. Interestingly, as the recent AIDWA report points out, in launching a call for a national campaign against dowry, feminist organizing around dowry seemed to fade away in the 1990s. The feminist social movement around dowry worked on several fronts: legal interventions such as filing public interest lawsuits (Jethmalani 1995) and mobilizing to lobby politicians and publicly shame dowry murderers, were undertaken alongside sustained campaigns to interrogate gender norms. As Radha Kumar describes at length in *The History of Doing* (1993: 117), the Progressive Organization of Women in Hyderabad organized the first protest against dowry in 1975, but Delhi soon became the most prominent site of protests, possibly because it reported the highest number of dowry murders. Stri Sangharsh, Mahila Dakshata Samiti and Nari Raksha Samiti organized demonstrations which gave a great deal of national visibility to the issue of domestic violence and murder connected to dowry, as well as marches which protested the commercialization of weddings (Kumar, 1993). Sometimes, demonstrations exerted pressure by taking place in the victim's workplace and home, as well as the victim's husband's workplace. Street plays such as *Om Swaha* in Delhi and *Meye Dilam Shajiye* in Calcutta became an important and popular means of interrogating the culpability of families in providing dowry and revelling in displays of status, staying silent on domestic violence, and making married dependence the ideal of women's lives. Malini Bhattacharya's 1985 play *Bandornach* (The Monkey Dance), for example, cleverly mimicked the rhythm of a street monkey-dance to underline the contrast between ideologies of romance and the mediation of dowry demands, urging dowry givers to embrace humaneness and stop spinning in an imitative 'monkey dance'. Radha Kumar argues that the anti-dowry movement included people from a range of ideologies, from the 'utopian patriarchialism' of 'men who feel it is their duty as good patriarchs to protect and care for their wives' to the 'anti-capitalist' stance typified by Stri Sangharsh, and to the 'anti-patriarchal' segment which protested against the situation of dowry but did not accord with 'feminist' critiques of the institution of marriage (1993: 125). Perhaps this range in points of identification explains why it has been one of the most prominent aspects of the recent women's movement: it incorporates the domains of economy, marriage and the 'cultural', and violence against women. Indeed, most feminist organizations involved in the anti-dowry movement have highlighted the connection between these domains; they have pointed to the ways in which conspicuous consumption and family dynamics contribute to the problem, but they have firmly located the source of the problem in the political economy of patriarchy. Rajni Palriwala quotes the 1982 memorandum of the Dahej Virodhi Chetana Manch (the anti-dowry consciousness forum) which insisted that dowry not be viewed as an 'isolated phenomenon' but as 'linked with the entire gamut of inferior female condition. Its increasing incidence is symptomatic of the continuing erosion of women's status and devaluation of female life in independent fashion. It is equally related to the worsening socioeconomic crisis—structural inequalities have accentuated, and black money power has grown, fuelling greater human oppression' (1989: 943). Thus, Palriwala contends, 'Dowry and harassment and murder for dowry are the most immediate and inhuman expression of the coalescence of those processes and relationships which are objectifying and degrading women, turning them into commodities and into means for commodities, in the context of a largely patrilineal, patri-virilocal society' (1989: 943).[20]

How culturally unassailable is dowry (and bridewealth, in relevant communities) as an institution? One of the most radical gestures recommended as part of the package to deal with the problem of dowry extortion and violence has been to seek a commitment to 'dowry boycott', to have weddings without gifts and possibly weddings lacking ostentation, as in the slogan *Dahej mut do dahej mut lo* (don't take or give dowry) or the 1980 statement from the Manushi collective entitled 'Beginning with our Own Lives: A Call for Dowry Boycott' (included in this volume). Directed first at activists but also as a broader social message, the strategy called upon people to act as role models and strike at the root of the problem, by saying 'no' first within their own circles, resisting enormous community pressure and possibly ostracism. It was different in nature from the sort of agreements made by caste groups to restrict dowry within their own communities, because it questioned the very salience of marriage payments, called upon women as agents, and highlighted women's need to claim the value of their labour and their inheritance.

I remember being enormously impressed by the radical simplicity and self-evident wisdom of the gesture when I first read about this in my late teens, the breezy power of saying to anyone who seemed worried about the money they had to save for their daughters' weddings, 'Just don't do it'! I do continue to believe that it is a step that is fundamentally important, indeed necessary, for challenging the hegemonic ubiquity of marriage payments. But it has also become evident that the power to challenge community norms in the face of ideologies that believe that marriage is the woman's one route to an economic safety-net, to take the risk that rejecting dowry may mean forgoing marriage, entails very different sorts of pressure on families, depending on jobs, economic circumstances, residence patterns, and also the socioeconomic impact of community approval. I realized with a sinking feeling, watching one after another of my middle/upper class feminist friends getting married with the full array of gifts and ostentation, that in these milieus, displays of class status were being negotiated simultaneously with gifts as signifiers of love and care, childhood fantasies, or impeccable taste, and that conspicuous consumption became entirely guiltless because it seemed to lie outside the domain of coercion or demand. My fieldwork further confirmed that displaying wealth was only one of the parameters, and that I had to acknowledge dowry as a site where women negotiated the meaning of their relationships to their natal families: typical gifts of clothing and jewellery for the bride were largely a marker of status rather than a parallel fund of wealth, but appeared to be accepted enthusiastically by women even though they were fully aware of its symbolic nature and were under no illusion that such presents represented the best or most useful form of financial resources. Their acquiescence and even enjoyment of dowry can be read in terms of what these gifts actually represented: the only substantial expenditure from natal families for female children, the only culturally acceptable female entitlement to the fund of natal wealth (1999: 16).

These questions about the difficulty of countering gender norms and their embeddedness in discourses of class and community connections have been at the centre of a virulent debate launched by Madhu Kishwar's gesture to take back her pledge of dowry boycott. Kishwar contended that women's lacklustre response to the call to boycott dowry got her thinking, and she came to realize that 'under the existing family structure, giving up dowry does not entail any alternative advantage for a woman' (1999: 12). As long as women effectively have no access to other forms of property including inheritance, she argued, dowry offers the potential for a woman to exercise some control over parental resources in the affinal household. As far as brides were concerned, dowry demands were only one ground of harassment in the affinal home, although brides' parents were wont to emphasize the primacy of dowry pressures and to sublimate discussions of harassment and domestic violence, as a whole. Conspicuous consumption in elite weddings, she felt, ought to be classed in a separate category alongside other over-the-top displays such as at birthdays (1999: 13–16). Rather than focus on abolishing dowry, she advocated increasing women's control over their lives, making sure a woman 'is equipped to take care of herself and of what belongs to her', together with a stringent enforcement of women's right to natal property (1999: 17–18).

Kishwar's stance enraged some feminists who had been deeply invested in the anti-dowry movement. In 'Reaffirming the Anti-Dowry Struggle', (included in this volume) Rajni Palriwala took issue with Kishwar's contention that dowry was a culturally widespread practice, not harmful in itself, by pointing out that contemporary dowry practices as addressed by the women's movement marked a coalescence of oppressive practices:

> the intensification of homicidal violence against wives was a consequence of changes in dowry practices due to social and economic changes resulting from the colonial and post-colonial capitalist development in India (1989: 942).

While dowry was linked to class and caste mobility, the 'devaluation of women' was at the heart of the practice, which fed off women's economic dependence and reliance on marriage; dowry was thus part of a nexus of problems, not the one 'root cause of harassment', but it was 'no phoney symbol' (1989:

943). Palriwala (in an essay included in this volume) questioned both whether one could expect people to simply step out of ideological constructs (challenging 'the woman's parents or single-handedly changing socially constructed relationships' [relating to inheritance]), and whether it was feasible for feminism to take ideological constructs at face value (challenging 'accept[ance of] the socially constructed desires of some sections of women as what they 'truly' want as the basis of struggle') (1999: 943). Such an argument seemed to end in a Catch-22 situation on the relationship between ideology and social change. Examples drawn from the umbrella organization Dahej Virodhi Chetana Manch demonstrated that women's organizations focused simultaneously on legal strategies against dowry and for inheritance, as well as on broad-based social changes in attitudes towards daughters; that is, they tried to look beyond women's immediate concerns towards transformative possibilities. C.S. Lakshmi's response to Kishwar took strong aim at the idea that dowry was a voluntary transfer of property by pointing to the widespread hardships (selling off body parts or one's only home) associated with its compulsive force. But she also discussed a more fundamental point about the nature of marriage itself: she alleged that Kishwar was accepting that status within a marital system has nothing to do with individuals, it has to do with goods and property, and challenged the idea that the true path to women's happiness was to bolster their position within the affinal home. Rather, the problem lay in the alienation of women from their natal families through marriage, and the construction of their identity and status solely in terms of their affinal families; the solution lay in repudiating the compulsory nature of marriage. She provided an apt illustration of this principle from Sister Subbalakshmi who, in response to a question about what would happen 'if women can't get married because they refuse to give dowry', said, 'Then women must have the dignity and courage to remain single' (1989: 189). Kishwar's rebuttal of Lakshmi's article reiterated her position that the affinal home becomes women's only place to belong and dowry becomes so significant as a 'crumb given to the slave deprived of choice' *because* women are effectively deprived of inheritance to natal property and rendered entirely dependent (1989: 587). She unerringly pointed to a 'romantic' thread in Lakshmi's article when the latter switched from economic views of marriage to the notion that marriage ought to be about a relationship between two individuals; she also contended that dowry marked not so much a change in consumer attitudes as a longstanding site of male power based on male control of resources. She opposed the abolition of dowry as a strategy, and advocated inheritance rights along with ensuring 'that women are not made mere vehicles for the transfer of property' (1989: 587).

What is most remarkable about the acrimonious exchange in these articles is that they are overwhelmingly in agreement with each other. Kishwar's emphasis on women building up cultural capital in the affinal family and her support for women's decisions to take dowry in the absence of a change in patriarchal relations; and Palriwala and Lakshmi's insistence that dowry lies largely in the realm of coercion and that dowry abolition be at the forefront of feminist efforts, apparently place the two groups in no-compromise, mutually exclusive positions. However, all the authors focus on patriarchal ideologies about women's alienation from the natal family and the devaluation of women's labour as being at the heart of the problem, and they all concur that the solution lies with solid inheritance rights and less dependence on marriage for survival. These are all powerful visions that point to the fundamental workings of patriarchal relations, but they are also all caught in the problem of translating these visions into a wide-ranging change in social practices. Kishwar's position can be critiqued on the grounds that unless reforms in inheritance and dowry are simultaneously enforced, they can each be used exploitatively. I have argued that affinal families can use either resource fund to coerce women's natal families:

If women's structural subordination remains constant, strict legislative attempts to either ban dowry or enforce equal inheritance are likely to increase women's vulnerability and dowry-related violence against them. On the one hand, removing dowry entirely in the absence of guarantees of inheritance (wills, gifts, etc., being common strategies to bypass legal directives against equal inheritance) deprives women of the few natal resources they garner and value. On the other hand, emphasizing inheritance for women without being able to stem the custom of wedding prestations leaves open possibilities for harassing women and their families for years over property, while dowry expenses are not curtailed in any way, and there is no return flow of resources in the form of eldercare or other financial help (Basu 1999: 225–226).

The problem of inspiring women, and men and families to undertake these changes, the question of how agents might be persuaded to act against the grain of a range of ideological structures (not just nay-saying to one isolated practice) is even more difficult than the obstacles encountered in legal change. Kishwar may contend that she is backing women's strategic decisions, but in focusing on inheritance rights rather than dowry abolition, she is shifting the grounds of radical change that she suggests families take on. Similarly, Palriwala and Lakshmi call for a fundamental change in women's economic and cultural subjectivities, and for marriage to be seen outside the realm of status transactions. These essays thus point to the enormity of what feminist social movements seek to undo and the necessity of working at multiple levels, including challenges to the very semiotics of cultural exchanges. The disagreements illustrate the difficulties with engaging communities in these visions, against the tide of material and cultural norms.

Inheritance: norms of disentitlement

Women's property inheritance occupies markedly little space in anthropological discussions on distribution of resources, compared to marriage payments as a form of property associated with women. As Renee Hirschon points out in the introduction to the classic anthology, *Women and Property, Women as Property*, the reticence is particularly striking in view of the importance accorded in feminist theory to Engels' contention that women's subordination can be traced back to the development of private property and monogamous marriage (1984: 1). And yet, according to Hirschon, studying property as an analytical category illuminates critical feminist issues:

> 1) property as the social construction of resources is an integral aspect of both domestic-group organisation and of forces in the wider sphere of social life (economic, political, legal, ideological); 2) the nature of 'property' requires that we consider linking two other features of the social order, conceptually distinguished as the material and the ideological. What is construed as a valued resource, whether personal or productive, is an expression of the material conditions of existence in terms of values and perceptions pertaining at that time (1984: 5).

Hirschon emphasizes the dynamic character of property as a category, and urges attention to historical specificity in defining it (1984: 6).

The relationship between dowry/bridewealth and inheritance seems a particularly apt case study for understanding the relationship between the material and the ideological, between public and private. Why does dowry as a formal institution vanish from many cultures in the late nineteenth/early twentieth centuries? Is it a coincidence that married women's property rights are solidified at about that time, or is the development of the capitalist mode of production the primary reason for the change? Muriel Nazzari's study of *Disappearance of the Dowry* in Brazil concludes that

> The changes experienced by Brazilian society that help explain the decline and disappearance of dowry are many of the same transformations that have been observed in more central regions of the Western world. Through a long process that started in the eighteenth century and continued into the early twentieth century, Brazil changed from a hierarchical, *ancien regime* type of society in which status, family and patron-client relations were

primary, to a more individualistic society in which contract and the market increasingly reigned. A society divided vertically into family clans changed gradually into a society divided horizontally into classes. As the state grew stronger, it took over functions previously performed by the family (1991: 164).[21]

Others have argued, to the contrary, that men's access to wages and entry into capitalist relations have brought about increases in dowry (Kapadia 1993, Moors 1995). The development of property laws for English and American women has also been connected to the need for adjudicating debtor relief and legal definitions of equity (Basch 1986, Shanley 1989). The Indian scenario is one of rising dowries and minimal inheritance for women, alongside the entrenchment and spread of capitalist relations and the erosion of customary usufructuary rights in the family fund, confounding the above categories because of the simultaneity of individual resource accumulation related to capitalism (and women's increasing vulnerability here related to their labour market position) and the pressure exerted by families to enhance the joint fund of resources.

There is little disagreement among Indian feminists about the necessity of strengthening women's position by increasing their access to and control of productive resources and capital funds, property inheritance being one prime route. The difficulties lie with the mechanisms through which this may be achieved, with the gendered meanings assigned to property, and with the problematic status of property as an instrument of equity between women. As the Kishwar/Palriwala/Lakshmi debate revealed, feminists have mostly argued that ownership of property has a broadly positive effect on women's well-being: in addition to its immediate economic benefits, property ownership affects areas such as nutrition, fertility, household decision-making and resistance to violence. Bina Agarwal's comprehensive study of women and land rights in South Asia, *A Field of One's Own*, begins by laying out a rubric of the theoretical advantages of women's property ownership. Agarwal points out that the claim for women's land rights requires a radical reformulation of axioms in economics:

> To argue that women's economic needs require a specific focus, distinct from those of men, is to challenge a long-standing assumption in economic theory and development policy, namely, that the household is a unit of congruent interests, among whose members the benefits of available resources are shared equitably, irrespective of gender ... . To go further and argue that women need independent rights in land—the most critical form of property in agrarian economies—is to challenge the assumption that women's economic needs can be accommodated adequately merely through the employment and other income-generating schemes that typify development planning. It means admitting new contenders for a share in a scarce and highly valuable resource which determines economic well-being and shapes power relations especially in the countryside (1994: 3).

Agarwal identifies three broad categories of advantages for women having independent rights in arable land: a) welfare effects: giving women economic resources independently of men is likely to reduce the poverty and destitution of households, given that women tend to spend proportionately more resources on family sustenance and that women's access to earnings seems to have more positive effects on household nutrition, mortality and morbidity; b) efficiency effects: giving women direct (rather than de facto) ownership can increase their access to credit and technological help, while ensuring better returns because women have tended to be better at paying back loans and at environmental preservation. Plus, subdividing land to include women as owners does not decrease efficiency because productivity is not necessarily lower in smaller plots; c) equality and empowerment criteria: recognizing women as equal heirs has symbolic value, and is likely to affect women's greater participation in political and social arenas as well (1994: 27–42). Property inheritance in other forms, or inheritance of other family assets, may be seen to have similar benefits: the ability to provide for themselves and their children without depending on marriedness itself as an economic resource, and the strength to participate in civil society. This scenario, then, propounds an alternative to marriage payments (dowry or bridewealth) as an economic base.

While Agarwal's framework is meant to apply to women across the board, and is not directed towards women with substantial family property alone, it does assume that the solution lies with transmission of family property and individual property ownership, even among families with minimal land. Interestingly, perhaps pragmatically in a world of dominant capitalist relations, feminist theorists have done little to follow through with recommendations on Engels' contention about the connection between private property and class and gender subordination. Indu Agnihotri's review of Agarwal's work is one of the few pieces that raises this issue by problematizing the question of land and class:

> Land becomes a matter of juridical rights, and has value only as property. The contrast is striking. More so, since the Marxist viewpoint, which Agarwal critiques, emphasises an enquiry into the relations of production to arrive at a more integrated picture of land, caste, class and gender. This would also appear to be crucial if the question of land rights has to be addressed beyond arguing for the rights of women from the standpoint of ownership alone. Can the argument for the rights of dalit and landless women be advanced if the dominant framework remains one of primarily identifying the *patriarchal* underpinnings of control over land and property? (1996: 527).

Agnihotri emphasizes that land itself is a privileged entity: landlessness has arisen from specific colonial and postcolonial processes, and the government claims only 0.56 per cent of arable land as being earmarked for redistribution (1996: 527). Shared property ownership thus affects a select group, and a comprehensive strategy of women's empowerment must include wage reform for agricultural tenants and landless labourers alongside substantive land reform.[22]

While Agnihotri's reminder of the partiality of property ownership as a solution is a critical one, it is also important to remember that such ownership has the potential to improve the quality of life for the poorest of women. Robin Jeffery argues that land reform in Kerala may not have transformed class hierarchies or even lowered poverty substantially, but it has been marked by a rise in living standards, and a much higher sense of security in women who have received even minimal land for housing (1993: 184). In the urban context, women who have something as nebulous as registered 'ownership' of *jhuggis* in squatter colonies are in a better position to protect their homes and livelihoods against husbands' threats or errant sales (Basu 1999: 54–55). Research on widows shows that those who have even minimal property are treated with more care and respect in their families than those without property, whose neglect is widely documented (Chen 1998, Gulati 1993).

Ensuring inheritance rights for Indian women has, if anything, met with more intransigence than calls to abolish or reform dowry. Male entitlement to land has been cast as a fundamental component of Indian custom and culture, with the legal arena reflecting widespread cultural biases. Archana Parashar's detailed study of Hindu law reform in the 1950s demonstrates that gendered rights were one of the critical points of negotiation between groups who sought to establish power in the new nation-state (1992): while 'social progress', including gender equity, was deemed to be significant by proponents of modernization, propositions for equity were compromised at every turn to accommodate groups who sought to retain 'Indian traditions', including, of course, customary privileges of gender and caste. Much is made of the fact that widows have absolute (as opposed to usufructuary) rights to property, but it took eight years to move the Hindu Women's Right to Property Act (1937) through the legislature, with substantial concessions along the way (Sheel 1999: 151–152). Similarly, daughters were included in the category of heirs in cases of intestate succession, but daughters' *shares* of property was a highly fraught issue: in the Constituent Assembly,

> Members expressed their doubts about the ability of Hindu women to manage it; they also added that a daughter in a Hindu household enjoyed preferential treatment because she was the object of worship, so the question of discrimination did not arise. They critisized educated Hindu women clamoring for such reforms as 'social butterflies'. Members also warned that the proposed code would destroy the integrity of the Hindu family through the fragmentation of family assets (Sheel 1999: 152).

Concern was expressed about discrimination against men if women inherited from both natal and affinal families, and about a worsening of the dowry problem (Sheel 1999: 154). Finally, the Mitakshara coparcenary, which includes daughters only as minimal heirs of ancestral property and may be seen as the largest obstacle to Hindu women's equal inheritance rights, was left in place as a sacred 'tradition', and even Ambedkar, the staunchest proponent of family law reform, went along with sentiments that the status quo should not be unduly disturbed, and that legal loopholes for disinheriting daughters through wills and gifts be retained (Parashar 1992: 124–128). Moreover, women's land rights were effectively even more constricted because state laws could override the national law when it came to distribution of agricultural land in some states, and because land under tenancy as well as land ceiling standards did not recognize women as potential heirs (Agarwal 1994: 215–223).

It is important not to see women's legal disenfranchisement from property as a continuation of 'ancient traditions'—rather, the colonial and post-colonial State has whittled down women's customary rights to property in many areas, even as women have been granted expanded rights in others. It may seem from the above debate that it is daughters' rights which are primarily contentious, and that wives' rights are better protected but, in fact, the alleged protection of conjugality has been a ground for depriving women of independent ownership of property. Flavia Agnes argues that the British codification of alleged

Indian traditions further constricted, rather than broadened, the few customary rights to individual property, e.g. *stridhan* or *mehr*, that Hindu and Muslim women had: *stridhan* property was judicially treated in terms of the British concept of a limited estate that was to revert to the husband's heirs (2000: 122–124). Another far-reaching change wrought by the colonial state to further its agenda had the effect of diminishing women's usufructuary rights to maintenance:

> One set of legislations carved out a space for men's individual property rights into a system based on joint-family property and rigid caste affiliations of an agrarian feudal society, and laid the groundwork for the introduction of a capitalist mode of production in an urban setting by making land alienable and transferable ... Unfortunately for Indian women, instead of an enhancement of their right to property, the scope of this was curtailed and became redundant within the changing character of property—which now became alienable and transient (Agnes 2000: 121).

When the Widow Remarriage Act (1856) was instituted, the principle that widows would forfeit husbands' property upon remarriage was homogeneously applied across castes and communities, resulting in widows in many communities losing their existent right to their late husbands' property; Agnes points out that here the courts were setting new precedents detrimental to women's interests rather than following established customary law (2000: 128).

One such example was the institution of *karewa* or levirate marriage in Punjab and Haryana, whereby widows were remarried to one of their late husbands' brothers. *Karewa* is cast as a protective measure towards widows but serves to deprive women of independent control of their portion of widows' property, which remains part of the joint family property—women thus have little recourse against severe neglect, and no choice about remarriage without forfeiting their inheritance altogether. Prem Chowdhry's research (1993) demonstrates that the colonial state gave legal validity to these marriages, and rulings against partition by widows prevailed. Widows were desperate enough to be free of these marriages while retaining access to the property.

> In innumerable court cases, the widows chose openly to deny *karewa* and accept the charge of unchastity and, in British eyes, the notoriety of bearing illegitimate children, rather than forfeit their inheritance by admitting to remarriage (1993: 103).

Brothers-in-law, on the other hand, insisted on the marriage to the extent that

> There are recorded instances of brothers-in-law among Gujars of Sandholi and Jats of Karnal taking over the widows as wives and claiming their illicit children as their own, or instances of pregnant women being married off to brothers-in-law, though pregnancy was openly known to be due not to them (1993: 103).

With the passing of the Hindu Succession Act (1956), widows' absolute rights to property were confirmed and thus property in their name did not lapse back into the common fund, plus they did not need permission from the affinal family to remarry. But allegations of *karewa*, and *karewa* marriages performed by threat or coercion, were used against women to deny them separate portions and also to lay claim to their substantial property entitlements such as pensions for 'war widows' (1993: 110–113).

In a different arena, matrilineal communities where property was always associated with and reverted to the natal line experienced a whittling away of natal inheritance and a strengthening of the conjugal unit. In Kerala, where the Nayar *marumakkathayam* (matrilineal) system of inheritance and the maintenance of joint property within the female-linked *tarawad* unit prevailed alongside a complicated tenancy structure involving various communities, peasant struggles for full and individual ownership of land got tied to the dismantling of the *marumakkathayam* and *tarawad*. K. Saradamoni (included in this volume) points out that the two issues of land redistribution and matrilineality were not necessarily related, and that attitudes towards *marumakkathayam* as a backward custom, whereby men were not responsible for children and women's marital ties were secondary, contributed to the demise. As a result,

> Large scale pauperisation was a common feature of the period, and women were certainly bigger victims ... For many women from the big landowning families, the period under discussion offered many new opportunities for education, employment and even political participation—but life for women in the not so well to do *tarawads*, which were not only losing property by division and alienation, but were also guilt-ridden by litigation and disharmony between members, became suffocating. Naturally they had no option other than accepting the protection and guardianship given to them and their children by the newly emerging husbands. This meant that these women got a right to claim maintenance from husbands as well as a share in the latter's self-acquired wealth. This came along with the dissipation of *tarawad* wealth, and women losing a birthright. But this alternative was not a sure guarantee either for material or emotional security (1984: 8).

Other institutions were dismantled among matrilineal communities in the northeast. The Meghalaya Succession Act (1986) confers on Khasi and Jaintia people the right to dispose of self-acquired property at will: Tiplut Nongbri (1988) contends that the legislation defers to male resentment at having to share wage earnings with mothers and sisters rather than with wives and children, but makes women more economically vulnerable because they are still primarily responsible for the upkeep of the natal family while they can count on no support from men and have a weaker position in the labour market. Bina Agarwal argues that among the Garo, changes in customary practices, including increasing gifts of land to sons and the growing popularity of virilocal residence, and hence women's reduced claims to natal family land, can be attributed to a set of complex factors, such as the change from *jhum* to wet-rice cultivation and the accompanying increase in male agricultural labour; the change from communal to privatized land ownership; the growing influence of Christianity; and State policies of land regulation and appropriation (1994: 101–104).

While the normative assumption in patrilineal communities is that women's economic entitlements are to be secured through marriage, not natal inheritance, widows' and wives' rights continue to be precarious. Contrary to those who protested against Deepa Mehta's film *Water* because it supposedly maligned the customary protection extended to Hindu widows, Martha Chen's anthology *Widows in India* demonstrates widespread economic neglect of widows through statistics and case studies: widowhood is depicted as a prime site of both social and economic deprivation. At the symbolic level, widowhood is cast as social death, and widows are subjected to ostracism and intense scrutiny of sexual behaviour; surveillance of the widowed body in terms of its various appetites is extreme (1998: 25–27). Legally, widows are entitled to full ownership of husbands' share in property and are deemed to have a share even under customary law, but in effect, widows are deemed to have use rights, and have the best chance of securing their claims if they have sons, so that they appear to be holding land on their behalf. Widows are subjected to violence and neglect both from the deceased husband's family, who vehemently oppose their claims, and even from sons especially if the women themselves have no land in their name (1998: 35–38). Chen proposes that public policy in support of widows needs to address all these arenas: 'property rights, social security, employment, and social identity' (1998: 20).

Wives' property rights have become an issue of critical significance as the entitlement of last resort, given women's widespread disinheritance from natal property and the paucity of maintenance available in cases of marital breakdown (even less for Muslim women after the passage of the Muslim Women's Protection of Rights on Divorce Act [1986]). Many organizations have raised claims for joint marital property in recognition of the resources contributed by both spouses to the marriage in terms of labour as well as wages; the model of life-long sustenance from an affinal estate is no longer applicable given that divorce is possible, and usufructuary rights imply a secondary and tenuous access to resources anyway (Jaising 1996: 250–257). In advocating for this in the context of a Maharashtra government proposition to institute joint property rights on marriage, Indira Jaising adds the reminder that the provision should be available across religions, and be transferrable across states, but contends that the demise of the proposition may lie in this very necessity for equitable application (19: 250–257). However, Madhu Kishwar strenuously objects to the Maharashtra government proposition to treat wives as co-owners of husbands' property from marriage and to deem them entitled to half the share of joint matrimonial property at the time of divorce; she cites practical difficulties such as determining individual shares of jointly-held land, but also contends that this measure would further weaken women's chances of securing natal inheritance and would intensify intra-familial conflicts between women, lead to abuse of mothers-in-law, and cause women to file spurious legal charges (1999: 71–77). This is surprising given that Kishwar has often argued for women building strong connections within their affinal families because that is where their economic sustenance lies, but also because natal inheritance and marital property insurance need in no way be visualized as mutually exclusive. Questions of equity—daughters getting an equal share of parental resources and wives getting an equal share of resources from a marriage to which they have contributed labour, and likely, also wages or goods—are not competing claims and are equally valid ones. When Kishwar raises the challenge that the idea '... would make sense only if women brought their share of inheritance at the time of marriage', and asks whether one is willing to allow husbands to be co-owners in the wife's inheritance, she seems to forget her previous argument regarding dowry, that women do indeed bring a share of inheritance with them upon marriage; only, they are unable to hold on to gifts that can provide them with future economic security. The projected outcome is for women not to be disenfranchised either natally or affinally, and ideally, for men to partake of the benefits of women's resources as well, if women do habitually become property owners.

While the issue of property rights has not been as prominent a rallying point for the women's movement as dowry, it has been raised as part of some radical projects for gender equity. A few urban organizations have taken up the issue of married women's property with regard to urban women, such as the Madurai organization, Pennurimai Iyakkam, which focused on women's ownership of house-sites as part of the struggle against the eviction of slum-dwellers (Omvedt 1993: 96). The issue of rural peasant and landless women's property ownership has, however, been most prominent. When the socialist organization, Chhatra Yuva Sangharsh Vahini, worked among dalit landless labourers in Bodhgaya, Bihar in the late 1970s, women pointed out that demands for part of the religious estate's land would result in new plots going by default to men as 'family heads'; the organization's decision that the newly won land be registered in women's names, despite familial and bureaucratic intransigence, was seen as a turning point in the feminist campaign for land rights (Omvedt 1993: 95). Agarwal's analysis of this movement demarcates it as a significant moment with regard to Indian women's participation in social movements, because for the first time 'we begin to see women articulating their gender interests in a group-overt form, in addition to recognizing their common interests with the men in the movement in class terms' (1994: 438). Women were challenged on the grounds that land registration was just a token gesture, that it weakened class solidarity, that the transaction was complicated because women left natal homes after marriage, and that men would not cooperate with ploughing; they countered by pointing to the transformation in gender relations that was needed for their continued solidarity with the movement (Manimala 1983: 15–16). Notably, women turned down the offer for joint titles in this case because they felt it complicated matters by tying them to a particular marriage. Kishwar's study of Ho women in Singbhum (Jharkhand) also argues that legislation for non-alienation of tribal land does not sufficiently address questions of equity unless married women's legal disenfranchisement from property is addressed (1987); similarly, Kelkar records that the Bihar Kisan Samiti proclaimed that only direct ownership could benefit women because they had no right to produce with any forms of indirect family ownership (1993: 134). The Mahila Aghadi or women's wing of the Shetkari Sanghatana, which started out as a farmer's organization, resolved in 1989 to make women's equal property rights an important part of their agenda, and appealed to male members to give a small part of their land to wives, who could control the income from it. The resolution was passed, and shortly thereafter, in Vitner village, 127 women received shares in their husband's property ranging from a half acre to seven acres (Omvedt 1990).

Many of these schemes had to revisit gendered prejudices at great length when it came to executing reform measures. Kelkar reports that in the area she surveyed, women received less than seven per cent of the distributed land, and that women recipients were either widowed or divorced or perceived to be physically handicapped, i.e., that it was hardest for married women to secure property rights because they were presumed to be protected within the family (1993: 135). Jayoti Gupta (included in this volume) focused on women's equal rights in productive resources in West Bengal because the state had taken up land reform measures since 1977, and found immense confusion and misinformation, as well as resistance to issuing joint *pattas* (registration of land titles) despite government memos in 1992 and 1994 specifying and emphasizing the measure as a critical component of land redistribution (2000: 19–21). Her study of two districts revealed that guidelines are loosely followed, gender disaggregated statistics are not maintained, women are kept uninformed about dates and numbers of distribution, widows are the main recipients (as with Kelkar's study), husbands claim joint *pattas* without wives' knowledge or signature (the lack of joint signatures renders the receipt invalid), joint *pattas* have not been extended to already distributed land despite a provision for this, and women are overwhelmingly included only on *pattas* for home-sites rather than agricultural or orchard land (2000: 31–37). Moreover, single men, but not single women, are deemed beneficiaries for single *pattas*, and women who are part of a joint *patta* are expected to leave the land to the husband if there is a divorce (2000: 23, 37). Women's organizing around land reform measures thus demonstrates some radical hands-on measures for transforming women's economic and hence social position, but also reveals the resilience of hegemonic beliefs about women's disentitlement to property among legislators and officials, as well as village adjudicators and male recipients.

As with feminist strategies against dowry that come up against women/brides who appear to be willing collaborators in accepting it, feminist measures relating to inheritance have had to contend with the fact that few women make claims to property, citing complex emotional factors including fear of family discord (Agarwal 1994, Basu 1999). While these non-claims may be read not as compliance, but as strategies through which women negotiate various competing needs (Agarwal 1994: 424–437; Basu 1999: 117–158), there is also ample direct evidence that women are deeply concerned about protecting their own and their children's well-being. Agarwal cites several examples of women's expressed need for independent resources for themselves and their children, where they might hide or secretly gather assets (1994: 425), or see 'their interests as congruent with those of their children, but antagonistic to those of their husbands' (1994: 434). She quotes a landless woman (cited in Mies, 1983) "We want [arable] land, all the rest is humbug," indicating what women consider this the most significant resource (1994: 17). This is also supported by my findings that women attached emotional meanings to jewellery and other *stridhan* items, but consistently said that productive resources such as land or housing or businesses would be most useful for addressing the difficulties they considered most critical (1999: 161–179). In Gupta's study of four villages in West Bengal, peasant women laid out the following demands: equal legal rights in inheritance and matrimonial property and the erasure of women's dependence as a legal category; independent rights to productive resources (with, and often without) joint titles; the ability to rely independently on land as livelihood even when high dowry demands make marriage impossible; limiting freedom of testation so that daughters cannot be disinherited through wills; and equal rights to the parental home so that they can return freely (2000: 2–4). The assumption that the status quo is maintained because women are content to receive jewellery and wedding gifts as their share of parental resources, and that they support the idea that property is a male entitlement, can thus be seen as an ideology that helps propagate the current distribution of resources, a profoundly intransigent one that permeates families, judges, officials and lawmakers.

Conclusion

'The practice of dowry itself is a crime, not just its excesses', a recent AIDWA report declares in its title (2002). This declaration reflects the heart of Indian feminist concerns with dowry in the last three decades: the central problems lie with the symbolic status of dowry (or bridewealth) as transfers of wealth, marking women's status as transacted objects, and the corresponding assumption that marriage itself will provide a woman with all the security she needs. Doing away with dowry in any substantive fashion thus requires confronting this fundamental formulation which is at the core of the patriarchal transmission of resources. Familial and official resistance to dealing with the problem continues to be very strong, but the difficulties are also severely compounded by the fact that women are constituted as subjects and agents in the midst of these very ideologies, as well as ideologies of class and status privilege: dowry and inheritance become heavily loaded as emotional gestures carrying messages of kinship, while they are simultaneously used to signal affluence and to build enhanced positions in communities. Arguing for a radically new gendered distribution of resources (and hence radically new subjectivities), thus requires us to deal with present patterns of resource accumulation (local, national, global) and the institutional structures which hold these in place.

Reforms or appeals that pertain to dowry and inheritance may seem to ask for altruism or sacrifice related to an isolated evil phenomenon, but they are a call for profound semiotic and material changes. I return here to Gayle Rubin's assertion that it almost seems like the feminist critique of marriage payments is that of dismantling 'culture' altogether, unless one remembers that 'culture' is capable of being fluid and inventive (if also immensely resilient). Strategies such as boycotting dowry, avoiding extravagant weddings, extending full inheritance to daughters, or making women co-sharers of marital property are critical gestures that begin the work of transforming 'culture' at the level of intimate practices—the challenge is to take these gestures further into revisualizations of gender and status norms, and to engage women in interrogating and resisting the intersection of gender and class oppression.

I. Dowry Deaths, 1990–1997

Year	1990	1991	1992	1993	1994	1995	1996	1997
Number of deaths	4836	5157	4962	5817	4935	5092	5513	6006

II. Incidence of Female Suicides Cause: Dowry Dispute, 1990–1994

Year	1990	1991	1992	1993	1994
Number of suicides	1298	1310	1370	1486	1613

III. Incidence and Rate of Cognizable Crimes under Special and Local Laws (SLL) by Crime Head, 1989–94

Year	1989	1990	1991	1992	1993	1994
Crime Head: Dowry Prohibition Act	1918	2155	1841	2102	2679	2709

IV. Incidence of Crimes Against Women by Crime Head, 1990–94

Year	1990	1991	1992	1993	1994
Crime Head: Torture	13450	15949	19750	22064	25946

V. Number of Suicides by Sex and Cause, India 1994

	Male					Female				
Age	<18	18–30	30–50	>50	Total	<18	18–30	30–50	>50	Total
Cause of Suicides: Dowry Dispute	10	47	11	6	74	149	1267	194	3	1613

VI. Incidence of Female Suicides by Causes, 1990–1994

Year	1990	1991	1992	1993	1994
Cause of Suicides: Dowry Dispute	1298	1310	1370	1486	1613

Source: Women in India: A Statistical Profile–1997. New Delhi: Department of Women and Child Development, Ministry of Human Resource Development, Government of India, 1997. 478p. Compilation from www.gendwaar.org: Dowry Statistics.

Notes

[1] *Indian Express* June 19, 1993.

[2] '"Something Had to be Done to Teach Him a Lesson": Dutiful Son Finds Himself in Jail on Dowry Charge' *Sunday Observer* April 26–May 2, 1992. This is a rare feel-good story about dowry demands: the bride sought prosecution under the Dowry Prohibition Act when the groom's family stepped up demands after the wedding cards were printed. Her lawyer colleagues refused to represent him as a show of support, and so he languished in jail for a while even to get a bail hearing.

[3] 'Marriage Proves Fatal for Young Bride—Dowry Claims First Koli Victim' *Indian Express* February 27, 1993.

[4] Marriage transactions are often grouped by economic anthropologists into three main categories: dowry, bridewealth and brideservice. Dowry and bridewealth are often visualized as marriage payments travelling in reverse directions (see text for discussion of why they cannot really be treated as mirror images): 'dowry is defined as the transfer of valuables from the family of the bride to the new conjugal estate', and 'bridewealth refers to the transfer of goods, valuables and sometimes cash from the kin group of the groom to that of the bride' (Bossen 1988: 128). 'Brideservice is defined as a period during which a prospective groom provides labour service to the family of the bride in order to marry. It usually involves a period of uxorilocal residence resembling trial marriage', and is often seen as an alternative to bridewealth in less stratified societies (Bossen 1988: 127). Bossen (1988) discusses the androcentric nature of these definitions at length. 'Brideprice' is often used as a synonym for 'bridewealth', although it is notable that the word 'dowry' contains many more dimensions than 'groomprice', which usually refers only to amounts paid for the groom's value.

[5] Patricia Uberoi's Introduction to the anthology *Family, Kinship and Marriage in India* (1993) provides a lucid overview of critical issues in kinship studies and the significant role that anthropological studies of India have played in this area.

[6] The question of whether women's 'status' in a given ethnic group can be unproblematically assigned a unitary high or low value has been a fraught one for feminist anthropologists; a classic sample is provided in Reiter's *Towards an Anthropology of Women* (1984).

[7] In neolocal residence patterns, couples set up their own 'new' households upon marriage.

8   The 2002 AIDWA report provides recent evidence, from a broad spectrum of communities, that dowry is becoming compulsory in many communities which had bridewealth or minimal marriage payments. Among Muslims, *mehr* amounts were very low while dowry-style payments had grown enormously.

9   Sharma 1984, Srinivas 1984, Bleie 1987, Kishwar 1987, Billig 1991, Heyer 1992, Kapadia 1993.

10   See also discussions in Deolikar and Rao (1998: 122–123) about studies by economists who relate the marriage payment amount to the 'utlility' derived by individuals or families from the marriage: that is, those who depend more on marriage will be the ones paying. Dowry, thus, is related to a disproportionately high number of women relative to men of marriageable age in a given group.

11   Deolikar and Rao (1998:138) demonstrate, in a different context, that both 'improved groom traits' and 'enhanced bride attributes' co-exist with rising dowry amounts.

12   There is extensive evidence of the coexistence of payments in both directions: Kangra Rajputs (Parry 1979), urban Christians (Caplan 1984), Karnataki Okkaliga (Srinivas 1984), Lewa Patels of Nandol (Goody and Goody 1990), Purohits in Rajasthan (Unnithan-Kumar 1997).

13   In the recent film *Devdas*, Parvati's family is deemed to be of low status because they are *betibechnewale*, people who sell their daughter; Parvati's mother, seeking parity with Devdas' family, claims that this is is no longer applicable and that they now give their daughters dowry.

14   Umar (1998). Caplan's (1984) research on caste-related dowry among Christians is only one example that ideologies of dowry are not exclusively applied among Hindu high-caste groups.

15   Miller (1981: 152) argues in a comparative study that South Indian weddings among many groups are characterized by a high level of reciprocity, although examples of brides' families paying more are also abundant.

16   Vatuk 1975, Paul 1986, Tambiah 1989, Caplan 1994, Basu 1999.

17   Jhutti (1998) confirms brides' participation in the practices, although he contends that there is considerable pressure exercised by grooms' families.

18   Bhachu 1993, Paul 1993.

19   An example of the ways in which the onus of greed can be placed primarily upon women is provided by the MP Mul Chand Daga during the 1984 Parliamentary debates: *In auraton ne to yah kar rakhaa hai desh me apne ghar aur izzat ki shobha barhane ke liye...raat ko patiyon ke kaan aap log hi bharti hain, chaabi ghumaati hain* (These women have

created this situation in the country for increasing their own status and show....You women are the ones who fill your husbands' ears with this at night, who run the show. [My translation.]) (Dowry Prohibition (Amendment) Bill, 1984, 279)

[20] In contrast, the series of conferences dealing on dowry sponsored by Harvard (e.g. Menski 1998: 18–20) carefully bemoan excesses in dowry and dowry-related deaths, while explicitly confirming the validity of dowry and the patrilocal joint family as important 'Indian' institutions, a position reminiscent of 'culture' based apologia from legislators.

[21] Kaplan (1985) similarly argues that dowry disappeared in Europe as capitalism developed and the significance of family property declined.

[22] Gail Omvedt also documents that farmers' organizations such as Shetkari Sangathana included wage reform for laborers as a central issue (1993: 109), and Kelkar records the need for wage reform for women agricultural laborers to improve living conditions as well their bargaining positions within their families (1993: 133).

Section I

Some Reflections on Dowry

M.N. SRINIVAS

I

Very little is known about inter-caste differences in the matter of dowry. Also, dowry commonly tends to be viewed in isolation from the series of prestations that link the two kin-groups coming together in marriage. To some extent, indignation at the horrors of dowry, and at its spread to ever new castes and sections, have been responsible for the feeling that academic curiosity about the institution is a luxury if not evidence of the reactionary outlook of the social scientist concerned. But calm reflection should convince intelligent laymen that detailed knowledge of the working of dowry among diverse groups is an essential pre-condition to its removal. Further, such knowledge will also enhance our understanding of kinship system, of saving, expenditure and the economic behaviour of the people and of the role of the emulation of the higher castes by the lower in the spread of dowry.

It is essential to distinguish between dowry in India to the north of the Vindhyas—continental India—and dowry in peninsular or south India. The former area is broadly characterized by either hypergamy or a hypergamous ideology and dowry seems integral to hypergamy. This point needs to be highlighted since it has been frequently missed out and especially by those who have put forward an 'economic interpretation' of the institution.

Hypergamy refers to the custom of marrying a man from a superior grade or clan, within the same *jati*. Sometimes, the

3

superior grade or clan may not be specified, but the general notion prevails that a girl should wed a superior male. The basic idea here is that a girl should marry into a higher division and, under no circumstances, into a lower one. Mckim Marriott, who studied in the Fifties a village near Aligarh in U.P., states that the family to which a girl is given, becomes respected and that from which a girl is taken, becomes low. In other words, it is the fact of the girl being given that makes the recipient superior just as the act of giving the girl makes the donor family inferior. He stands, however, alone in this view of hypergamy.[1]

A major consequence of hypergamy is status asymmetry between affinal groups, the boy's kin being higher than the girl's kin. The latter improve their status through marriage while the former secure cash, jewellery, costly clothing, furniture and other goods. To quote Marriott,

> Behind this organization of marriage is the feeling that one's daughter and sister at marriage become the helpless possession of an alien kinship group. To secure her good treatment, lavish hospitality must be offered and gifts made to her husband's family throughout life. The economic effects of this patterning of marriage are considerable. Not only marriage and other expenses are kept high, but quantities of goods follow the women in later years by the same non-rational path. One quarter of all milk animals are obtained as gifts from marital relatives and about one quarter of all debt is incurred to fulfil marriage demands i.e., in Kishan Garhi, his field village in U.P. The persistence and vigour of such a structuring of marriage puts limit on the degree to which a village can manage its economic affairs as a local unit. (Marriott, 'Social Structure and Change in a U.P. Village', in *India's Villages*, edited by M.N. Srinivas, Bombay, 1955, p. 112).

Status asymmetry between the bride's and groom's kin, is, however, absent in the South. (Kerala with matriliny is, however, unique, and I exclude it from my purview). Marriages are basically isogamous in the South and this is further reinforced by the preference for cross cousin, and cross uncle and niece, marriages. Finally, the custom of bride-price, which was universal among south Indian castes, resulted in, if anything, a tilt in favour of the bride's kin as far as relations between the affines were concerned. In fact, even as recently as 1948, I was present at the wedding negotiations of two Okkaliga kin-groups in Rampura in Karnataka, where I found the bride's kin listing their demands about the saris and jewellery which the groom's kin had to provide at marriage. Such demands were the rule though that did not mean that prestations moved only from the groom's kin to the bride's. Indeed since weddings were invariably performed in the bride's house, the burden of hospitality was generally heavier on the bride's kin than on the groom's. Thus, the bride's kin had to give at least two big dinners, one of which was non-vegetarian, in addition to providing hospitality and refreshments for the groom's kin and other guests, while the groom's kin had to give only one dinner, a non-vegetarian one, on their return to their home from the wedding.

Weddings, then, are occasions when the two affinal kin-groups exchange gifts. But such exchanges are rarely symmetrical, a tilt towards one group or the other being more common. Further, weddings also initiate such exchanges between affinal kin, and these continue for a long time. For instance, in great parts of India a woman had traditionally the right to have her first few confinements in her natal home, and her parents had to bear the expenses of the confinements and give gifts to the new-born infant and its mother. Among hypergamous groups, the woman had to carry along with the infant, gifts of food, grain and flour to her in-laws. The Patidars of Gujarat joke that a woman was likely to be sent back if the provisions she brought with her were deficient in quality or weight. Among Anavil Brahmins of south Gujarat, the woman had to carry, among other things, sweets to all the Anavil households in the affinal village.

While in the North, and in particular, among the hypergamous castes, modern dowry is in line with the unidirectional flow of cash, goods and service from the bride's kin to the groom's, in the isogamous South, modern dowry is really a totally new development. Traditionally, weddings were much less asymmetrical in the South, but nowadays there is complete asymmetry among the dowry-paying castes. That is, dowry has introduced a new status asymmetry in the South, and to that extent it has become more like the North.

Modern dowry presupposes a high degree of monetization in the community, increased agricultural and general prosperity, and access to the 'organized sector'. Until a few decades ago marriage was the only 'career' for a woman except among the landless labourers and other poor where women had to hire themselves out for daily wages. Young men who had salaried jobs, or careers in the profession, were sought after as bridegrooms. They were 'scarce commodities', and their scarcity was exacerbated by the rule of *jati* endogamy and the need to marry a girl before she came of age. The parents of the lucky youths demanded cash and such goods as cycles, woollen suits, etc., as part of the wedding agreement. The monster of modern dowry has grown from such humble beginnings.

In the dowry of today large sums of cash—frequently amounting to a few lakhs of rupees—are transferred along with furniture, gadgetry, costly clothing and jewellery, from the bride's kin to the groom's kin. In addition, the bride's kin have to meet all the expenses of the wedding including the travel expenses of the groom's party. An element of unpredictability may be regarded as integral to modern dowry: the bridegroom's kin may demand that the male members of the *barat* (procession of groom and his kinsmen to the bride's house) be given real Scotch and not be fobbed off with Indian whiskey. In the days when pre-pubertal weddings were the rule additional demands were frequently made at the time of the consummation of the wedding, or when the ritual of *simanta* was performed for the pregnant woman, and the threat held out that otherwise the ceremony would not take place, amounted almost to a repudiation of the marriage itself.

In south Indian upper caste weddings, the groom's kin assume that it is the duty of the bride's kin to keep them pleased, and they appear keen to find fault with the arrangements made and the gifts given, and they are also known to make sudden demands. The bride's kin have to take all this in their stride for they are the inferior party. And they know it.

The 'dowry' that obtains in higher caste weddings in India today is a totally new phenomenon, and ought not to be mixed up with traditional ideas such as *kanyadan* and *stridhan*, though such confusion is widespread. A gift or *dan* has to be accompanied by a subsidiary cash gift (*dakshina*), and in *kanyadan* the bride is given as a gift to the groom. On this analogy, the dowry becomes the *dakshina*. *Stridhan* usually refers to the gifts given to a woman by her natal kin or by her husband at or after the wedding.

But modern dowry is not *dakshina* or *stridhan*. As already stated the amount of money given as dowry is substantial if not huge among the higher castes and its payment is demanded, directly or indirectly by the groom's kin.

It is absurd to regard it as a sub-gift incidental to the main gift. (A cynic might say that the reverse is true). In addition to paying the dowry, the bride's kin give gifts of jewellery and costly saris to her, and it is difficult to state with confidence that the bride will have control over the jewellery. Traditionally, however, it was hers to dispose of, at least in south India, and she passed on as much of it as she could to her daughters. If the husband sold a piece of jewellery belonging to her to meet a crisis, he was expected to make good when his circumstances were better.

Among the Anavil Brahmins of Gujarat dowry marriages are regarded as the proper ones in sharp contrast to marriages by exchange and marriages by paying bride price. They are so prestigious that one way of identifying a Desai—i.e., the higher subdivision of the Anavil Brahmins—is to find out whether his relations had all married paying dowry. Further, dowry marriages are equated with *kanyadan* marriages, and Klaas van der

Veen, in 'I Give Thee My Daughter—A Study of Marriage and Hierarchy among the Anavil Brahmans of south Gujarat', has rather uncritically accepted such an equation.[2]

The Pedivala Desais, the highest division among the Desais, got their girls married in the *kanyadan* form and paid dowry to the bridegroom's kin, even though the latter were, except very rarely, their inferiors. According to van der Veen there were ideological reasons for this: 'The Pedivala are the superior group still strongly cherishing the ideal of dowry marriage, in which any thought of financial profit should be avoided. In such unions the character of the hypergamy was quite different from that in the marriage of status unequals arranged from financial need by the two Desai families...'[3] The Pedivala dowry was, according to Pedivala thinking, the *dakshina* accompanying the 'gift' of the girl to the groom. They gave this even though the groom was status-wise, inferior.' They regarded dowry as part of the ritual of *kanyadan*. This is very different, however, from modern dowry.

As stated earlier, modern dowry is entirely the product of the forces let loose by British rule such as monetization, education and the introduction of the 'organized sector'. The attempt to equate the huge sums of cash, jewellery, clothing, furniture and gadgetry *demanded* of the bride's kin by the groom's, to *dakshina* is only an attempt to legitimize a modern monstrosity by linking it up with an ancient and respected custom, a common enough and hoary Indian device. What is surprising is that the imposture has had so much success.

II

Pre-British dowry needs to be distinguished from 'modern dowry', the former being integral to hypergamy, as I have stated already, while in the non-hypergamous areas, the payment of bride-price seems to have been the rule. Thus far I have only referred, and that too only very generally and superficially, to hypergamy in Gujarat. Bengal was the other classic area of hypergamy, the institution being extremely popular among the

Kulin Brahmins many of whom also practised polygamy at least during the first half of the nineteenth century. At the prompting of the reformer, Ishwar Chandra Vidyasagar, the Government of Bengal appointed, in 1866, a committee to inquire into and report on Kulin polygamy. A brief and readable report was produced by the Committee within six months. According to H.T. Prinsep, one of the members of the Committee, Kulin polygamy was widespread in Bengal and ... 'there were instances of Brahmins having nearly 100 wives, many of whom they had never seen since their marriage with them as girls' (H.H. Risley, *The People of India*, Calcutta, 198, p. cxl). Prinsep added further:

> ... The father of a girl is obliged by Hindu law and the custom of the country to marry her before she attains puberty; she must marry in her own caste; and he has to bring a suitable husband for her. Kulin polygamy... appeals to Brahmins of the mendicant and priestly classes of small means. Education may have done much to reduce its sphere; but education has not reached such classes, and obviously they will be the last to come within its influence (Risley, p. clx-xi).

Immediately after expressing his belief in the ability of education to liquidate dowry, Prinsep seems to have had second thoughts on the matter:

> ... I would point out [that] though education may have done something to mitigate its [dowry's] evils, it cannot claim to have done much to reduce the rates payable in the marriage market. The usual rate demanded by one who has taken the degree of Bachelor of Laws in the Calcutta University is, I have credibly informed not many years ago, Rs.10,000 or nearly £ 700 ... (Risley, pp. clx-clxi).

The passages quoted above have been taken from a letter which Prinsep wrote to the editor of *The Times*, London, on 27 September 1907. A few India hands including Sir Henry Cotton were discussing the subject of Kulin polygamy in the prestigious but, from the Indian point of view, rather remote columns of *The Times* of London. In his letter Prinsep first stated that the

Kulins who were practising polygamy were uneducated Brahmins of the mendicant and priestly classes. And like a true product of the Victorian era, he declared his faith in education as a solvent of social evils. But immediaely after his declaration of faith, he seems to have been overtaken by a sense of reality. Bengalis who had a BL from Calcutta University were, even in those days, collecting Rs. 10,000 as dowry. The point that I wish to emphasize in this connection is that Prinsep is here confusing two different types of dowry, one traditional, and the other, modern. The candidates for the former were poor, mendicant and priestly Brahmins while for the latter, they were the Western-educated sons of the elite.

While the richer and higher strata of hypergamous castes paid huge sums by way of dowry to obtain desirable grooms, the poorer members of the lower strata were often required to pay bride price, or have recourse to marriage by exchange, either direct or indirect. Direct exchange was when two men married each other's sisters, and indirect, when other parties were also involved to complete the exchange. Thus the rich, land-owning Patidars of central Gujarat paid dowry, while poor Patidars paid bride price. Again the rich land-owning Desais (upper layer of Anavil Brahmins) paid dowry while the Bhatela, the poorer division of the Anavils, practised marriage by exchange, both direct and indirect.[4] In the extreme south of Gujarat lived the Pardi Desais (also called Kay Desais) who were also Anavils but who were very poor until recently and had the custom of marrying by exchange. But during the last twenty years many of them became prosperous through the cultivation of new and profitable crops, and dowry has come to stay amongst them.[5] There is a 'cargo cult' aspect to dowry marriages—the groom's kin regard his wedding as an occasion for securing, without paying a paisa, the many and much-desired products of modern technology. Among Tamil Brahmins, for instance, a video cassette record of the wedding is the latest demand made by the groom's kin.

It is necessary to ponder on the implications of the fact that parents of girls born in the lower grades pay dowry to get them married to men of the higher grades while men in the lower grades pay bride price, or resort to exchange, to be able to marry girls in their own grades. Bride price and marriage by exchange are then integral to the dowry system of the hypergamous castes. It is not only that there is a drift of all girls towards the men of the highest grades, but some men of the top grades indulge in polygamy (synchronous or serial) while some others marry after becoming widowers or divorcees. All this results in making brides scarce for the poor bachelors in the lower groups. Sometimes this is compounded by the incidence of female infanticide in the higher grades, and as mentioned earlier, both the Patidar and Rajput practised female infanticide till it was stopped by the British in the nineteenth century. Indeed, female infanticide seems to have been practised among several groups in the western and north-western regions, and also near about Banaras.

In studying dowry the continous desire of the bride's kin to improve their family standing or status needs to be kept in mind, particularly in hypergamous areas. Secondly, dowry and bride-price have also to be studied in the context of changing male-female sex ratios wherever the data are available. In this connection, it may be mentioned that demographic history is woefully neglected in India and there is not even awareness of the fact that it is neglected.

III

... The tendency of the lower castes to emulate the customs and rituals of the higher castes is part of the dynamics of the caste system. In the context of dowry and bride-price, it means that lower castes tend to give up bride-price and replace it with dowry even when their womenfolk are engaged in productive work outside the home.

But a caste, in particular, a non-dominant caste, was traditionally *not* allowed to emulate the customs of a high caste of its choice. The dominant caste of the region normally prevented it from doing so. For instance, the Anavil Brahmin

Desais, who were the dominant caste in the Surat region, did not permit the inferior Bhatela to switch over to dowry from bride-price though impoverished Desais took dowry from rich parents of Bhatela girls. But the parents of Bhatela grooms were denied the privilege.

However, the dominant castes themselves had greater freedom to emulate the customs of ritually higher castes. As an example, I may mention the efforts of the dominant caste of Okkaligas in the Mysore-Mandya region, since the 1930s, to switch over from bride-price to dowry. At this time, education was spreading among Okkaligas, and better prices for agricultural produce during the War years, resulted in increased prosperity. Educated Okkaliga youth thought that bride-price amounted to sale of the bride, and *muyyi* (gifts of small cash made to bride or groom by kindred and friends), demeaning. In the late Thirties wedding invitations of the richer and educated Okkaligas stated explicitly that bride-price and *muyyi* would not be taken. By the 1950s the more prosperous and educated Okkaligas in this region had given up these institutions. Today, dowry is the rule among the educated. As Epstein's Beregowda put it, 'What is good enough for Brahmins is good enough for me!'

IV

Indian weddings are occasions for conspicuous spending and this is related to the maintenance of what is believed to be the status of the family. Maintaining, or giving expression to, family status, involves in turn the articulation of networks, networks of kin and caste, and nowadays, of professional colleagues, friends and acquaintances, members of one's club, etc. Care is taken to invite as many important acquaintances as one can, and these become indicators of one's status just like the number of cars parked outside the wedding hall. It must be made clear that both the kin groups coming together in the wedding are sensitive to considerations of family status or honour, though the bride's kin are usually a little more eager to impress everyone, especially the groom's kin.

Apart from the cost of clothing, jewellery, the cash given to the groom or his parents, the bride's kin have to meet the cost of two if not three lavish dinners given to the groom's kin and other guests, of the beverages and snacks supplied to the guests during the wedding, the shamiana, lights, band, music, processions, and sometimes, fireworks.

The hospitality must be on the lavish side, and the guests, especially the groom's kin, are only too eager to find fault. Their praise is keenly sought. Nowadays, among several high and educated castes, the groom's kin may stipulate that all the expenses of the wedding be met by the bride's kin, including the cost of their travel to the bride's city or town. Sometimes the groom's party may express its desire for having a 'grand' wedding, and the girl's kin have to agree.

It is essential to mention that resources are consumed on a large scale at a wedding. The dowry money is far from being 'a rotating capital fund' as some imagine it to be. There is nothing to prevent the parents of the groom from putting the dowry money to any use they like, and it is not always that they have an unmarried daughter to whose spouse the money is given as dowry. What it leads to is certainly the impoverishment of the girl's parents, and it does not always buy security for the girl. There is no guarantee that it will prevent the groom's parents from making new demands on the bride's.

While bride-price was always a fixed amount within an endogamous *jati*, and the various prestations that needed to be made were also specified, dowry is characterized by asymmetry, uncertainty and unpredictability. All the expenditure might be on the bride's side only, and there are no norms as to what the groom's kin may ask. That is not all. Months after the wedding, when the girl is pregnant or on some other occasion, the groom's kin may demand from her kin, that a particular item of costly jewellery be presented to her. If the parents of the girl do not produce the jewellery the girl might be harassed, and in extreme cases, even set aside.

I have said above that great expenditure is frequently incurred on weddings due to the bride's family's desire to vindicate their status, and less frequently, to the demand of the groom's kin that the wedding be performed 'grandly'. There is also a third and perhaps much deeper source of lavish expenditure at weddings (and funerals). Briefly stated, the argument may be summed up in the following manner: Rural society is divided into conflicting, multi-caste factions, each faction being led by a single patron or combination of a few friendly patrons. There is competition among the rival patrons for winning over the allegiance of clients, many of whom shift their loyalty from patron to patron. The huge dinners which are given at weddings, and the procession with fireworks, etc., are means to retain the allegiance of clients. Villagers talk of the great dinners given at the wedding of so-and-so. They mention the number of sheep slaughtered, the number of people fed, the wonderful dances of nautch girls, etc. Since the techniques of preserving grain were primitive until recently, and it went bad if kept for a long time, feeding clients was a good way of putting such grain to use.

These deep-rooted tendencies have been carried on to modern times and they have gained strength by getting linked to the status of the family celebrating the wedding, its desire to articulate its networks, consumerism, etc. ...

Notes

1 See his 'Social Structure and Change in a U.P. Village', in *India's Villages*, ed. by M.N. Srinivas, Bombay, 1955, p. 112.
2 Van Gorcum & Co., N.V. Assen, 1972, pp. 25, 32 and 47.
3 Ibid., p. 191.
4 Van der Veen makes the point that while poor Patidars had no objection to paying bride-price, the Anavils were allergic to it as such marriage had been classified by the law-givers as *asura*, and therefore forbidden for Brahmins.
5 Van der Veen, pp. 262–3.

J.P. Naik Memorial Lecture, 1983. Published for the Centre for Women's Development Studies, New Delhi, by the Oxford University Press, New Delhi: 1984.

Dowry in North India:
Its Consequences for Women

URSULA SHARMA

Dowry divides women

Traditionally, dowry in India was regarded as a burden for the bride's parents but an honour for the bride. Feminists in India now argue that this institution brings no honour to women; indeed the pressure put upon young brides to persuade their parents to give more dowry may lead to their humiliation, ill treatment or even death. If this is the case, how has the dowry system survived for so long and why are attempts to challenge it not more successful? In order to answer such questions, it is necessary to look at dowry not only as part of the symbolic order of Hindu society (as 'saying something' about marriage and the relations between affines) but as a concrete form of property in which the members of the household, both men and women, have different kinds of interest and over which they have different kinds of control. In north India dowry consists of movable property made over to the husband's family, or to the newly married pair at or soon after the wedding.

According to the conventional ideology in north Indian society, property accrues to the household as a corporate group rather than to individual persons. Of course, land and houses will be officially registered in the name of a single individual (usually the senior male) but the property is administered by the senior members of the household on behalf of all its members. Modern legislation assumes a more individualistic notion of property. Where land is concerned, the corporate responsibility of the wider kin group (where it existed) was

15

eroded long ago during the British period. Recent legislation, especially that concerning the inheritance rights of women, shows an increased tendency to accentuate legal individualism. There is often a tension between the legal and economic individualism demanded by modern capitalism and the traditional more corporate attitude to property which still operates informally within the domestic unit. To give an example, a young woman who earns an individual wage— whether as a stenographer or a farm hand—may be expected to hand over her wages to her parents-in-law who will pool them with those of other members of the family and make decisions about how this income should be spent or saved. Obviously the prior rights of individuals over goods of certain kinds will be recognized in practice (over items of clothing, for instance) and the particular circumstances of the household as well as the personalities of its members will affect the precise way in which day to day decisions are made.

But two main principles underlie the structure of authority in most households, those of seniority and of gender. Juniors of either sex are expected to defer to elders and women are expected to defer to men. Where these relations of authority correspond to relations of dependence, this deference is easily exacted, but discrepancies do arise, as we should expect in a period of rapid economic change, and each household has its internal complexities. Broadly speaking, what all this means in relation to dowry and the position of women, is that as brides women have little control over the way in which dowry is given and received. As they become older they participate in the dowry system more actively as givers of dowry (mothers of brides) or as receivers and redistributors of dowry (mothers of sons). We cannot understand the consequences of dowry for women unless we look at the processes of decision-making and also at the relations of dependence within the household, especially since it is changes in this latter area which have, in my view, intensified the importance of dowry as an element in the marriage system.

... Dowry distribution and control

Parents begin to collect items for a daughter's dowry well in advance of her wedding, even years in advance, depending on how many daughters they have to provide for and on their circumstances at the time. It is usual for the girl herself to prepare some of the items, e.g. embroidered bed-covers, cushions, etc., and nowadays wage-earning daughters may buy some items from their wages, although strictly speaking the ideology of *kanya dan* marriage does not countenance this. However most parents, whatever their financial status, will reckon on receiving some help from other relatives.

The bride herself will have very little say in what happens to her dowry once it leaves her parents' home. As a new bride she is in any case expected to behave in a modest and self-effacing manner and if she wishes to win her new family's favour she will not risk her future happiness by asserting her wishes until she has established a firm footing in her new household. If, as is common, the newly-married couple are to spend some time living together under the husband's parents' roof then the household dowry items will be merged with the common stock of household goods for the time being, on the understanding that most of them will be made available to the young couple if and when they eventually move out and set up house on their own. However, this separation of goods is not always easy once other members of the household have become used to enjoying the use of the refrigerator, television or whatever the new bride brought with her. S.L. Hooja, in a perceptive discussion of the way in which dowry goods are redistributed, notes that there may well be conflict between the couple and the husband's parents on this issue. Such conflict arises from the contradiction between the traditional idea that since children are effectively the property of their parents, then the property of the children may be controlled by the parents, and the more modern notion that if a young man has the means to set up his own household independently of that of his parents he is entitled to complete autonomy so far as the organization of this new household is concerned. It is not just the bride therefore who has only limited control over the dowry goods; even her husband may find it difficult to assert his rights in them (especially if he is very young) owing to the close relationship between seniority and authority in the family (see Hooja 1969: 9–11).

Where household goods and items of clothing are concerned, it is likely to be the bride's mother-in-law who has the greatest say in how these items are distributed. This is partly by virtue of her position of seniority, but also relates to her position as senior woman. It is largely women, and especially senior women, who control the flow and pace of gift-giving both within the household and with other households. This is not the place for an extensive discussion of systems of ritual gift-exchange among women in South Asia (see Vatuk 1972, and Eglar 1960 for accounts) but suffice it to say that the proper regulation of gift-making at all important ritual occasions (life-cycle rites, seasonal festivals, etc.) is an important function of the women of the household, and where these gifts consist of goods (sweets, clothing, household items) as opposed to cash, it is the senior woman of the household who has the prime responsibility for seeing that obligations are met and proper relationships maintained. So one can see the control which the mother-in-law has over the goods which nominally are the property of the newly-wed couple partly in terms of the general authority which senior members of the household have over juniors, but also in terms of the senior women's responsibility to maintain correct relations of reciprocity within and outside the household. So when the mother-in-law appropriates items of clothing from the dowry and distributes them among her own married daughters or to other daughters-in-law, she may not just be exercising her prerogative over valuables entering the household, but will see herself as meeting obligations to make regular gifts to her daughters in their married homes, and to provide good things for the other junior women who are part of her household by virtue of having married into it.

What say do men have in this redistribution? The mother-in-law may well consult her husband when she hands out the clothing and other personal items as described above. But if any sums of cash are involved (and in middle class urban families this is more and more the case) they are likely to be under the immediate control of the father-in-law. It is up to him whether some portion of these funds are earmarked for the future use of the young couple or whether they are merged with the general funds of the household, although if the bridegroom is already living separately from his parents, as may be the case with urban employed men, it is more likely that he will have a measure of control over such important resources. The pattern of control in the process of redistribution therefore is in keeping with the informal principle that women (especially senior women) have immediate control over things in the household, and men (especially senior men) have immediate control over any large reserves of cash.

The ideology of the jointness of interest of the members of one household makes it very difficult to identify the kind of control over resources and property which individual members may exercise in empirical cases. Even when they do make unilateral decisions about the disposal of property they do not always recognize themselves as doing so. They will see themselves as members of the group on behalf of other members and will find it difficult to explicitly countenance any division of interest among the members. This problem besets the study of household decision-making generally in this kind of society. But even a scrutiny of the norms regarding relationships within the household (the ideology of seniority, of male competence, of the distinction between daughters and daughters-in-law) ought to suggest that the dowry property will not be under the control of the woman in whose name it is given, although that does not mean that it will not be controlled by other women. The Hindu bride's dowry may bring her self-respect and prestige in the household (and indeed in the community) if her parents have been particularly generous, but it will not of itself bring her economic power.[1]

... Dowry and inheritance

Hindus themselves say that the bride is given movable property for her dowry as her share of her parents' estate. It is regarded as a form of pre mortem inheritance which women receive when they leave the parental home at marriage. Sons remain members of the natal family and they receive the immovable property after the death of their father, divided equally between them either then or at some subsequent point. Daughters traditionally did not inherit land unless they had no brothers and although the law now allows them to do so, very few exercise this new right. In the course of my fieldwork I found that many women considered that a sister who claimed her share of land would seem greedy and might risk forfeiting her brothers' goodwill. Had she not already received her share of the family property at marriage?

Some anthropologists, such as Goody and Tambiah (1973) have also represented dowry as a form of inheritance. Goody treats dowry in India as one instance of a form of inheritance common in Eurasian societies. In 'diverging devolution' children of both sexes inherit, but women often receive their portion at marriage in the form of dowry property. Dowry also helps to ensure that women secure partners of at least equal and at best superior position, in short it contributes to class formation and maintenance, whereas in Africa bridewealth contributes to the maintenance of a fundamentally egalitarian distribution of goods and wealth among groups (Goody 1976: 9ff).

But if Hindus themselves represent dowry as a form of inheritance, are we obliged to view it in this way too? In some societies this is clearly a legitimate way of looking at dowry. Friedl notes that Greek brides are allocated land and/or house sites at marriage strictly equivalent to the share which their brothers receive later when their father dies, and that daughters thus endowed retain control over this property (Friedl 1962: 49). Goody would be correct in treating the dowry system here as part of a total system of inheritance which disperses property among sons and daughters. But in my opinion it would be stretching the term inheritance well beyond its conventional limits if we were to apply it to Hindu dowry, for reasons which I have demonstrated already.

Firstly the dowry does not represent a fixed share of a particular divisible estate; the amount is fixed with reference to the state of the marriage market (what prospective bridegrooms will accept) and the bride's family's circumstances (what they can afford) at the time of marriage. Secondly, as I have reiterated, the dowry is not paid to the bride herself but to her husband's family. If it is a form of inheritance, is it not really a form of inheritance by the son-in-law since he will have more control over it than the daughter herself? Better still, ought it not to be seen as the lateral transference of property between households but within the same generation since, as I have shown, it may well be the parents-in-law of the bride who have the greatest say initially as to how the dowry property should be used or distributed? If any proportion of the goods is designated as the bride's personal property this part of the dowry is usually small in relation to the whole (Van der Veen 1972: 44). Contrary to the dominant ideology and the terminology of traditional Hindu law, dowry property is not women's wealth, but wealth that goes with women. Women are the vehicles by which it is transmitted rather than its owners.

The inflation of marriage expenses: dowry as a social problem

The inflation of dowries which has taken place in most sections of Indian society is out of proportion to the general inflation (in prices in the Indian economy). So providing a dowry for a daughter nowadays constitutes a relatively greater strain on family resources than it might have, say fifty years ago. In Punjab, and probably most areas of north India, the composition of the dowry used to be more or less conventionally determined and many of the items could be made in whole or in part by members of the bride's family themselves (e.g. rugs, clothing, bedding). As there was little change in the style of consumer goods or household furnishings, many items could be accumulated well in advance of the marriage, slowly and as household circumstances permitted; there was no pressure to provide the very latest style of bed or the most up-to-date type of cooking pans. I would argue that the quantitative increase in the amount of dowry given has led to a qualitative change in its significance for women. More than it ever used to be, the dowry is one of the major determinants of whom a woman may expect to marry and of how she will be treated by her in-laws after marriage. What a bride is worth is measured more and more by the amount of material goods and cash her family can provide rather than by the reputation and prestige with which they can endow her, the skills they have ensured she has acquired. In consequence, the provision of a dowry involves a great strain on the household and this encourages daughters to see themselves as burdens rather than blessings.

I do not think that this can be dismissed as an ethnocentric assessment of the situation because dowry has during the present century come to be regarded as a social evil by Hindus themselves, but somehow as an evil which no-one knows how to stop. Parents who bewail the need to accumulate dowry for a batch of daughters are unlikely to bring themselves to refuse it when the time comes for their son to marry. To a large extent the goods which enter a household when a son marries are actually substitutes for the goods which must leave it on the marriage of a daughter.

British administrators during the first decades of this century cast a disapproving eye on the practice of dowry as evidence of the extravagant customs which encouraged the honest hardworking peasant to waste his substance and prolong his dependence upon the money lender (although disapproval on these grounds had a lot to do with the fact that the honest hardworking peasant was regarded as a more useful and reliable prop to the Raj than were the commercial classes). However, Indian social reformers took a broadly similar view and, after independence, laws were passed officially restricting marriage expenditure. But like so much other well-intentioned legislation, these laws have not been enforced. Indeed many rural Hindus are not aware that they exist (Murickan 1975: 85). Reports in the press, especially the Indian feminist journal *Manushi*, suggest that those who suffer most from the inflation of dowries must help themselves rather than look to the law. In recent years there have been numerous cases of 'dowry deaths' in which young wives in urban families have either been driven to suicide by their in-laws' excessive demands, or in which brides have actually been murdered by families disappointed in the first dowry and hoping to reap a second from the re-marriage of their son, trading on the qualifications of a young man with a secure job or good prospects. Manini Das describes one case which attracted a good deal of publicity, the case of a Delhi woman, Tarvinder Kaur. This young woman was, it seems, burnt to death by her mother-in-law when her parents failed to meet the constant demands for more gifts. Her relatives were able to mobilize a large number of people to demonstrate outside the in-laws' house, petition Parliament and give the case maximum publicity.

This case was followed by several similar ones, in which feminists and reformers joined with the families of women who had suffered in this way. Apart from public meetings, the main techniques of protest used were attempts to shame grasping in-laws through public exposure. Manini Das notes, however, that there is really very little hope of the police and judicial machinery providing a solution (*Manushi* 1: 16). Police are unwilling to register or investigate cases of murder of women within the family.... In addition to this, if the in-laws are influential and wealthy people they will be able to see to it that the police will either change the case from one of murder to one of suicide, or that they drop the investigation altogether.

Remember that, given the tendency in India for women to be married to status equals or superiors, few brides are likely to have parents who are more powerful and influential than their parents-in-law. Manini Das concludes that it will be difficult to do anything unless women cease to be divided amongst themselves. So long as they identify themselves in some situations as mothers (dowry-givers) but in others as mothers-in-law (dowry-takers) their interests appear forever divided and they cannot realize common cause as women.

The interpretation of dowry inflation in terms of the cash economy is supported by the evidence provided by elderly informants in the course of my fieldwork which suggests that in the early part of this century dowries in Himachal Pradesh (a much more backward area than Gujarat) were limited to a conventional number of sets of clothing, household items and jewellery, with very little variation. Only with the large scale injection of cash into isolated hill areas after the First World War did dowry rates begin to rise. But another possible factor is the relaxation of ritual and social barriers to marriage; in those areas where hypergamous marriage is usual, dowry property already provided a qualification for women to marry upwards into high status families. The erosion of some caste restrictions which we find in certain urban classes has really had the effect of introducing hypergamous competition among women in groups where it did not exist before, only this is a hypergamy based more on socio-economic factors than ritual aristocracy. Where caste is less of a barrier, any girl with some education from a moderately respectable family can compete in the scramble to get a husband who is an Indian Administrative Service officer, an Air India pilot, son of a large scale entrepreneur, etc. With this loosening up of conventional restrictions on marriage, dowry becomes more and more (not less and less) the criterion by which one respectable girl with an MA in History or Home Science is deemed more desirable than another.

These factors help to explain, I think, why dowry deaths (a) have become more common in the past ten or twenty years, and (b) why they appear to be confined to the urban middle classes and are not found among rural groups or the urban poor, groups who still observe more strictly the traditional barriers to marriage based on caste, language and religion.

Dowry favours and is favoured by a cultural ethos in which brides can be viewed as objects to be passed from one social group to another, both as a means for the procreation of children and as vehicles for aspirations to social prestige. Although there is no space here to deal with the extensive literature on bridewealth, it is likely that exactly the same can be said of bridewealth, at least as it exists under modern conditions. In 'developing countries' the effects of capitalist relations of production are penetrating the household and transforming the relations between men and women in the household. Usually these effects are most immediately experienced in terms of the consequences of wage-labour, migration and a market economy in which cash is the medium of exchange. Usually this transformation involves a devaluation of the domestic sphere and the activities of women within it and an increased dependence of women upon men within the domestic group. There is considerable evidence from Africa, where bridewealth has always been more common than dowry, that these changes have brought about a similar inflation of marriage payments to that which we find in India. And this inflation has had rather similar consequences for women, in that their marital destinies are open to more (not less) manipulation by others as the types and amounts of property transferred at marriage become relatively more important considerations in marriage negotiations ... .

Looking at the matter from a feminist point of view, therefore, the opposition which anthropologists have traditionally drawn between dowry and bridewealth may not be so important as other distinctions made on the basis of the degree and kind of control which brides can exert over their own marital fortunes and over the property which is transferred at the time of marriage. It would seem that in India the rapid inflation of dowries in modern times has led to a situation in which brides are more controlled by, than controllers of, property. Feminists have grasped this very clearly and are active in their protest. However, if the institution of dowry diminishes the social power of brides and even endangers their lives, it strengthens the hand of the mother-in-law. Even the mother of the bride may derive a deep moral satisfaction from a public and honourable display of generosity. Feminists are hampered in their efforts by the fact that in this sphere, as in so many others, property divides women among themselves.

Notes

[1] In this respect it is interesting to compare the dowry system in north India with that obtaining in parts of rural Greece. In many respects they are similar, but in Greece land gifted as part of the dowry remains under the bride's control to the extent that it cannot be alienated without her formal consent. Potentially at least, the dowry property gives her a source of power in the household which the Hindu wife does not have (Friedl 1962: 59).

Excerpted from *Family, Kinship & Marriage in India*, Patricia Uberoi (ed.) 1994: Oxford University Press, New Delhi.

Girasia Brideprice and the Politics of Marriage Payments

MAYA UNNITHAN-KUMAR

As a feature of Girasia society, brideprice immediately, if superficially, distinguishes it from dowry paying, upper-caste Hindu culture. In the present chapter I suggest that Girasia brideprice transactions are similar in function and meaning, if not in form, to the dowry payments in the region.[1] While a number of studies have been made on the Indian dowry system and its relationship with concerns of prestige and hierarchy,[2] there has been little research on brideprice and bridewealth transactions, although many lower-caste and 'tribal' groups are known to practise them. While popular caste opinion in the region considers a brideprice payment as a reflection of a group's morals, gender theorists have in contrast championed the cause of brideprice as it supposedly acknowledges the work 'value' of women.[3] The positive valuation of women embodied in the concept of brideprice is, on the face of it, a contrast to the popular image of the 'economic liability' of wives in dowry-practising communities. In this chapter I question this view to show that Taivar brideprice payments do not improve upon the structural gender inequalities found in dowry-paying communities. The ideology of Taivar brideprice constructs women as economic liabilities although objectively they are not so.

In this chapter I first consider some of the important issues raised in studies on marriage payments generally but more specifically in relation to caste status and hierarchy in India. I then describe the notion and practice of brideprice payments among the Taivar Girasia with specific reference to the economic transactions involving property, adoption, divorce and the death of a spouse. The third part of the chapter compares the structural inequalities of women in brideprice and dowry-paying communities. The similar processes at work in both societies which devalue women's labour contributions allows me to question the use of brideprice to describe some communities, especially 'tribal' communities, and dowry to describe others. In the final part of the chapter I outline the impact of a rising inflation in the market economy on the levels of Girasia brideprice payments. Contrary to popular academic opinion which states that dowry is replacing brideprice as an institution,[4] I suggest that brideprice is firmly established within the Girasia community and is manifested in continuously rising amounts. Apart from an economic rationale to brideprice payments, there is also the important component of identity maintenance in Girasia marriage transactions, which promotes a lineage identity at one level and a sublineage identity at another. I argue that the continuation of brideprice as a Girasia institution is related to the fact that it satisfies both lineage and gender hierarchies, the economic needs of the community, and the symbolic requirements of the Taivars to distinguish themselves from other caste communities.

Girasia brideprice

... The Girasia marriage payment is called *dapa* (literally, *da* meaning to give, and *pa*, to get) and denotes an amount in cash given to the father of the bride by the father of the groom. The *dapa* or brideprice is transacted only in the form of money, as far back as the oldest women could remember. The only variation over time has been in the actual amount. The payments made for the eldest to the newly married Taivar women ranged from Rs. 80 through Rs. 100, 500, 1000, to between Rs. 3,000 and Rs. 4,000 at the time of my fieldwork. The brideprice money could be paid all at once or delayed, depending on the process or type of marriage (i.e., sooner at *hagai* than at *khichna*. Usually an initial payment is made and the remaining brideprice amounts transferred over the span of a year, frequently in three instalments, approximately every four months. The Girasia brideprice transaction is not a simple transfer of the brideprice received for a daughter to another (wife-giving) group for a daughter-in-law. Brideprice money is put together by pawning an item of jewellery and in a small part was obtained by borrowing money from relatives. The whole or part conversion of the brideprice payment received to silver, and vice versa, in differing amounts, is usually substantially supplemented by the wage-labour income of all the household members. Other contributions, from the geneologically closer sublineage members, are only in denominations of tens rather than in hundreds.[5]

In 1986–87, brideprice rates were between Rs. 3,000 to 4,000 for young women who were brides for the first time. There were, however, a range of brideprice rates for 'better' or 'worse' wives. More brideprice was paid for younger as opposed to older women and, within the same generation, for those who were more physically fit and reproductive.[6] Women with physical handicaps had low brideprice rates attached to them. For example, Hoja Mada paid Rs. 500 as brideprice for Velki, which he himself considered to be quite a low amount. This was possible, he explained, because Velki was deaf and dumb. Hoja Mada's wife had died several years previously. At the time of my fieldwork he was in his late forties. Hoja decided to bring a wife to look after his household, more so because his 'adopted' (younger brother's) son had brought a wife and was setting up his own household. It was not because Hoja could not afford to pay higher rates, but more because he was seen as someone who was older and had a weak social status that he could not expect to get a 'better' woman as a wife. Although brideprice reflects the importance of the labour of women, this direct connection is not made by the Taivar Girasia. When I asked Teja why he accepted a brideprice for his daughter, he said, "I have not fed and clothed her so that she may work on another's field". The Taivar Girasia view brideprice not so much as recognition of a woman's contribution to the household nor as a payment for the loss of a productive member, but as a compensation to the father and his agnatic group for the past expenditure on her maintenance, particularly consumption of food.

In most of the conversations I had with the Taivars on *dapa*, I got the impression that it was regarded as a major Girasia institution. The Girasia take pride in their custom of brideprice, especially the high rates they pay. They are aware of dowry payments, but feel their system is proper because it does not require them to 'buy a man'. In contrast, the inhabitants of the surrounding villages who pay dowry look down upon brideprice because it amounts to 'buying a woman'. I suggest that Girasia brideprice is an institution which is enhanced as a symbol of their identity because it places them in a distinct opposition to outsiders.[7] Apart from the sense of Girasianess evoked by their practice of brideprice payments, the *dapa* also legitimises the husband's control on his wife's labour and procreation, as the following sections reveal.

Brideprice and economic transactions
Labour

As among other lower castes and classes in the region, Girasia women work at home as well as in the fields and forests and make trips to the market. Some of the early to mid-morning chores of the women are filling earthen water pots, sweeping, collecting dung, grinding grain, making food and feeding livestock, in that order of priority. The day usually ends with filling water pots, making food and feeding the livestock. Other domestic assignments include a weekly to fortnightly washing of clothes and the monthly repasting of the floor with a mixture of cowdung and water (*leepna*). During the agricultural season, women sow the seeds, weed, water and cut the cobs and stalks of the maize. Women are also carriers of grain to and from the market. In the lean season they carry head loads of wood and grass (*vanda, bhara, gaitha*) and berries for sale. The chores of the household are shared by women of all generations but the burden is heaviest on the new bride. Girasia men are more usually involved in activities which require a certain level of specialisation, such as carpentry, baskctry and the construction and repair of the house and well. In agriculture, the specific male task is to plough the field and channel the water in cases of irrigation. Usually the agriculturally specified male activities are those concerned with the cooperation of the lineage brothers .... Otherwise, in the household, men substitute women wherever extra labour is required. Men seem more like stop-gap workers and were mobile between jobs. (Children also functioned in this manner although they undertook lighter tasks than men).

As in other castes, the main difference between Girasia men and women lies in the control over each other's labour. Girasia husbands control the labour of their wives and children. The power to control a woman's work and her procreative capacity lies in the hands of her father and brothers and becomes most clear at times of brideprice negotiation. There are, moreover, monetary incentives involved in the allocation of women's work, as Teja's example below reveals. Teja was annoyed because the village council (*panchayat*) had not resolved the dispute regarding the brideprice payment of his daughter. He said it all began when his wife was sick and admitted to the hospital and he had needed Rs. 500 for her treatment A Girasia of Siyawa (an affinal village of the Taivars, approximately twelve kilometres from Abu Road) had agreed to loan him the money, provided Teja gave him his daughter. Teja agreed and the girl went to Siyawa. According to Teja, after a short while had elapsed the man bought himself another wife. Teja first heard that his daughter and her co-wife (*mahi*) quarrelled, through a villager of Dhamaspur (also in Abu Road *tehsil*). The Dhamaspur villager said he would take Teja's daughter provided Teja gave him the money to repay the debt and money for the brideprice *dapa*, which totalled Rs. 1,100. Teja told me he had agreed to this man's offer but initially kept it secret as he had organised a *panchayati* (meeting of the village council) to ask for the return of his daughter from her first husband as a result of her ill-treatment at his house. Teja essentially wanted a *kayda* (compensation) payment of Rs. 100, which he claimed was justified as his daughter had worked on the fields of the Siyawa villager. In sum, Teja said he would return Rs. 400 rather than the initial sum of Rs. 500 which he had borrowed. As the above example emphasises, women become wives as a consequence of the monetary transactions between men. A brideprice in cash greatly enhanced a gendered access to material benefits.

Property

Marriage marks the division of Taivar property which passes exclusively to male heirs. This division takes place in the lifetime of the father, unlike the property division among north Indian middle and upper castes. In the latter case, the division often only takes place after the death of the father as in the Indian *dayabhaga* system (Tambiah 1973, Parry 1979). The Girasia are, however, copartners in the joint family property at birth, as in the Indian *mitakshara* system (see Tambiah, 1973, for a discussion of these two major schools of property transmission stated in the classical texts). Girasia women, whether at marriage or otherwise, inherit neither the movable nor immovable property of their natal lineage. Often the only item the bride brings to her husband's house and village are a metal plate (*vadku*), a small metal drinking pot (*lota*), the clothes she wears, and the few pieces of cheap jewellery acquired as gifts or purchased over the years. Sometimes the bride may be 'gifted' her favourite goat or calf, if she belongs to a richer family. At her husband's house the Taivar wife is given silver jewellery which she can wear but which remains the property of the husband and his sons by her. While the jewellery she wears displays the status of her husband, the pot and plate are symbols of the wife's 'outsider' status. Girasia women do not have any rights in their children. Where the husband dies or when she becomes a wife to another man, a Girasia woman is separated from her children. This is essentially because children are regarded as their father's property (born of his 'water' ...). When a Girasia man dies, his children are brought up by his father's brother's wife and the mother is encouraged to leave (in practice this depends on whether the woman is in her reproductive age span or not, see subsection on death, below).

Like other caste women, Girasia women cannot have a share in the immovable property of their father. In most upper- and middle-caste households, in the absence of a brother, the daughter may inherit the father's land. In the Girasia case, however, and unlike other castes, in the absence of sons the father's land passes to his male collateral relatives (in the FB category). Thus Girasia property transmission is determined by gender apart from descent. For example, in the hypogamous-type of *ghar-jamai* (resident son-in-law) marriage, after the death of the father-in-law the land reverts to the father's brothers, and does not pass to either the daughter or the son-in-law, who must return to the latter's village. Tambiah (1973) has pointed out that in the Hindu-Indic model of inheritance, lineal relatives are preferred over collateral relatives for the purposes of inheritance. In other words, daughters may be preferred as heirs to father's brothers or their children. On the other hand, the West African, non-Islamic, bridewealth societies stress male survivorship and the reversion of property to male collaterals, women being excluded as heirs (Goody, 1973). As in the Hindu model, Girasia inheritance is lineal and stresses partition and adoption. However, as in the West African case, Girasia women are rigorously excluded as heirs and are displaced by the father's collateral relatives.

The difference between Girasia and other caste women in terms of their actual control over property might not be different in practice, in that the relationships between brothers and sisters in both cases are similar. Ideally, relations between middle- and upper-caste Hindu sisters and brothers are non-conflictual because there is no competition for the irreplaceable economic resources such as land and water shares. The dowry is considered to be the daughter's share of her father's wealth (although a movable and replaceable part). The relations between a sister and her brothers are tense only if the sister claims a share in the immovable property on the death of her father. In order to avoid displeasing their brothers, most middle- and upper-caste women give up even their marginal claims to a share of their father's property. It is such a common practice for a sister to forgo her share in her father's property and thereby ensure her brothers' 'protection', that most families do not expect otherwise. There are very few exceptions to this practice, because women look to their natal households (i.e., their brothers) to provide a means of security, especially in times of disagreement arising in the husband's household. Not surprisingly this expectation is greatest in the initial period in which the wife stays in her affinal household. The protective role of the natal household weakens over time and simultaneously the wife gains a footing in her husband's household. Relations between Girasia brothers and sisters are ideally 'good' as there is no uncertainty about land ownership. There are also expectations of 'protection' from the brother ... . The absence of conflict among cross-siblings over parental property and the brideprice money, as well as the affinal contacts generated by the sister, keeps the relations between Girasia brothers and sisters harmonious.[8] Both in the Girasia and other castes, we see not only a minimal control of women over material resources, but that women trade even the partial control they may assert, for a greater security.

Similarly, in both the Girasia brideprice and regional dowry cases, the movement of wives not only facilitates inheritance in the form of a flow of money or goods, but also redistributes rights between the natal and affinal male-headed households. Women in other castes strengthen their husband's household by bringing in dowry. They strengthen their brother's household by forgoing their claim on the immovable property in favour of their brothers. Girasia women strengthen their husband's household with their labour, children and food. They strengthen their brother's household by providing brideprice and transferring their consumption needs.

Adoption

The gendered control of property is also reflected in the pattern of Girasia child adoption. I observed that there are different rules for the adoption of male and female children, because of the lineal and gendered transmission of property. Boys are adopted within the village by a father's brother while girls are adopted in an affinal village by a father's sister. For Girasia boys, it is usually a permanent adoption whereby the boy is most likely to inherit land from his *kaka* or *baba* (in this case also his adoptive father). Gopa, who lived with his *haga kaka* (father's true younger brother) Duda, said he would inherit Duda's land. Gopa would not get a share of his father's property, nor would he share his adoptive father's inheritance with his brothers. The adoption of girls is a more temporary arrangement compared to the adoption of boys. Girls usually stay only until their marriage. Then they either return to their natal village to be wed or, as was usually the case, would form a marital alliance in the village of their adoptive mother (aunt). In both cases, the brideprice goes to the girl's father and not to her adoptive mother's husband. An adopted boy's brideprice, however, was paid by his adoptive father and not his natural father. In other words, the adoptive father has a greater control over a boy's labour and the related brideprice money than an adoptive mother has over a girl's labour and brideprice.

In the ideal pattern of inheritance among the upper and middle Hindu castes, the preferable order for inheritance is the son, his grandson, his great-grandson, the daughter's son, the brother's son and, lastly, the adopted, 'outsider' son (usually a distant relative's son). The Girasia preference, on the other hand, is in the order of son, father's brother, father's elder brother's son, father's younger brother's son; father's father's brother's son and so on. The major difference between the

Girasia and the upper Hindu is that the Girasia adopted son is treated as the son, and the daughter's son does not inherit property.

Divorce

Like adoption, divorce also reflects the preoccupation of Girasia men with transacting money and labour, and is determined by brideprice concerns and negotiations. Descriptions of divorce are, however, made by men and women in terms of a woman's assertion of independence. The Taivar term for divorce is *pairi-melo* (which translated as 'send back').[9] 'If a woman is unhappy, she simply runs away.' This is how a Taivar man described a woman's attitude to marriage. The spontaneity of a woman's action is meant to convey her disregard for the authority the brideprice transaction has given her husband and is therefore couched in terms of her lack of responsibility for the work at her husband's household. To a casual observer, a Girasia woman's decision to go away might seem freely determined but usually the decision to 'run away' is dependent on men of other affinal, or potentially affinal lineages. Often the difficulties faced by a woman at her affinal home are conveyed to her father or brothers through the unofficial channel of 'relatives' and 'friends'. Frequently the news reaches a wider circle of persons than those of the natal and affinal villages. Interested suitors might approach the woman's brother, who might even encourage them to take her away. It is then that she 'runs away' with her second husband. A woman's ability to leave her husband is determined primarily by how suitable a wife she was considered by men of other lineages.

While a woman may run away and thereby initiate a divorce, a man resorts to a separate set of procedures to break the marriage. According to Phoola (who spoke to me in Hindi), a man will want to divorce his wife when she causes him displeasure, particularly in two ways: either she does not prepare *roti* for him when he is hungry (*samai pe roti nahi dena*); or she answers back, especially to any reprimands her husband might give her (*moonh pe bolna*). The frequent general complaint was that wives are lazy and shirk their work to wander around (*bina kam kare ghoomna*. ... According to Phoola, if the wife continues in her displeasing behaviour, the husband first beats his wife. If she continues in spite of this then the husband and his family members, with the counsel of the other lineage members, explain to her what is expected of her and the deviance her behaviour constitutes. If the woman remains adamant in her behaviour, a complaint is sent to her parents to return the brideprice. The parents often try to convince their daughter to remain and to prepare food when the husband demands it. Despite all these measures if the situation remains unchanged, the wife's brother is summoned and she is handed over to him (*sompna*), and it is expected that the brideprice will be returned. On the other hand, if the wife is willing to work in her husband's household but it is her husband who wants her to leave, then there will be no return of the brideprice.

The main concern of the husband following a divorce is the loss and replacement of labour for the household. The father or brothers of the woman, on the other hand, are concerned with organising the return of the brideprice. The acceptance of Girasia divorce, in contrast to the difficulty of divorce in upper- and middle-caste marriages, is enhanced by the easily repayable brideprice sums (in cash) and the wife's identification with her father's lineage rather than her husband's kin group.[10] There are, however, considerable negotiations between the wife-exchanging families before the brideprice is returned. The girl's father is interested in as much money as he can get and usually claims a *kayda* (compensation fee) from the husband for transgressing the social norm ... . If, for example, the brideprice was Rs. 2,000, then a Rs. 200 compensation fee may be deducted and Rs. 1,800 would be returned by the girl's family to her husband. The amount of compensation is a marginal sum which depends upon the negotiation strengths of the parties, which in turn also depended on the level of guilt assigned to each party by the panchayat of the wife-exchanging lineages.

There are different kinds of compensation involved in the dissolution of marriage ties. For example, if a woman leaves her husband for another husband, the second husband pays a *dava* (literally, challenge; also close to the Hindi word *dhava*, attack) to the first husband. *Dava* is distinct from *dapa* (brideprice) both in amount and in meaning, Although mainly to compensate the first husband for the brideprice he has paid, it also includes a sum in compensation to him by the second husband for 'cheating' another Girasia. Therefore the *dava* amount is more than the *dapa* by at least one-and-a-half times. The term *dava*, like *khichna* (marriage by 'capture'), implies force. But here the force used is not so much on the girl but rather against her husband's control of her, for which he had paid a brideprice. The second husband usually informs or connives with the girl's brother in a mutually beneficial arrangement. In other words, the girl's brother need not return his sister's brideprice if the second husband takes her and pays the *dava* amount. When the woman fails to return home, the first husband with his closest male lineage members go in search of her to demand either her return or an exorbitant *dava*. Both parties negotiate the compensation fee. Sometimes the fee is settled by intermediaries, usually the girl's brothers and the *patels* (headmen) of the villages to which the parties involved belong. In Girasia divorce, as in *hagai* (the engagement ceremony), the major concern centres on the settlement of the amount and the return of the brideprice respectively. Consequently, a considerable time is spent in negotiating money-related agreements between men of affinally related lineages.

The compensation aspect attached to brideprice payments is not unique to the Girasia. In Awan, in eastern Rajasthan, Gupta (1974) notes that a *jhagara* (in Hindi, literally 'fight') marriage payment is made for the *nata*, or second, non-ceremonial and less prestigious marriages held among castes other than the twice-born. According to Gupta, *jhagara* consists of the initial brideprice payment and an initial sum for minor expenses incurred by the first husband and paid by the second (ibid.: 146). Even though it is commonly believed that lower castes are able to practice easier divorce because there is a lesser concern with property, the Girasia material suggests the opposite may be true. The Girasia institution of divorce is used as a means of negotiating rights to money and labour and the more movable and consumable aspects of property, precisely because there is a concern with property.

Death

Money matters arising from death are seen to link widowhood with brideprice. On the death of either the husband or wife, there is no return of the brideprice. According to Palvi, *mitgyo, phir kun dopa aale?* (finished or wiped out, then who will give brideprice?). Ideally, after the death of the husband, the connection of his wife with his lineage becomes tenuous. This is particularly the case if the widow is young. During my stay, Jabli's husband Gona was murdered. Jabli was young, and it was believed that she was infertile. Palvi told me that soon after her husband's death, Jabli had begun to stay with Daga (her HFBS). Palvi predicted that Daga would discard her later, and; 'Her own brothers will not keep her because she does not listen to them, otherwise she would have gone back to them. In the end she will have to beg for *roti*'. Usually when a woman is widowed young, and whether or not she has children, she returns to her brother's household while her children remain with her late husband's brothers. Other men are interested in young widows, primarily because they will have to give a smaller brideprice to her father or brothers.

It is common for older widows to stay with their sons who have already established a separate household. No brideprice amount is returned for older widows, and they frequently do not go back to their brothers. Older widows are less welcome in their natal households as they have weaker ties with their brother's sons and their wives. However, the duty of the husband's lineage towards a widow is symbolically terminated on the twelfth day of the *nyath* (funeral). So the older widow who continues to stay in the household of her son is dependent on the attitude of his father's brothers towards her as well as her continued contributions to the domestic chores in the household. All older widows whom I met were continually busy with small but time-consuming jobs. Nathi Bai, who died in the year following my fieldwork, said, 'if I do not watch the field which is at some distance from our house, and which often involves sleeping out in the open, they will throw me out'. Nathi was in a particularly vulnerable social position as her son had died soon after her husband. Although she lived with her grandsons, they lived next to her husband's brothers who were averse to her presence.

Girasia widowhood is in contrast to the ideal-type Hindu case, where the widow remains attached to the husband's kin who are duty bound to look after her. The widow in turn has a duty to her husband's kin. She must bring up her husband's children and manage the property for them until they are adults (Tambiah, 1973). In practice, the upper- and middle-caste. Hindu widows are subject to social restrictions such as wearing white, shaving the head and a prohibition on remarriage. It has been argued that because Hindu widows remain attached to the husband's agnatic group and remain the caretakers of his children's property, it becomes necessary to impose restrictions on widows as a means of containing property within the husband's lineage (Tambiah 1973, Parry 1979). In contrast Girasia widows who have no links with the property of the husband's lineage are less socially restricted but more economically vulnerable.

Notes

[1]   In the text I use the word 'brideprice' to describe Girasia marriage transactions, because, firstly, only cash is transacted between the wife-

exchanging groups, and secondly, the payment is not made to the bride but to her father, or in some cases to her brothers.

2   Khare 1972, Van der Veen 1972, Goody and Tambiah 1973, Vatuk 1975, Sharma 1976, Parry 1979, Fruzzetti 1982, Kishwar 1987, Goody 1990, for example.

3   For example, Kishwar 1987.

4   Shah 1982, Kishwar 1987, for example.

5   The Girasia strove to keep all debts to a minimum, not just vis-à-vis the Hindu money lender or affines, but also within the lineage.

6   As the amount of money transacted varied according to the 'type' of bride, I use the term brideprice rather than bridewealth to describe Taivar marriage transactions.

7   Berreman (1972), studying categories and interaction in an urban town in Uttar Pradesh (north India) suggests that the social or economic arrangements of a community often act as indicators of identity, and are the 'focus of self-esteem' (ibid.: 575). The Pahari Hindu community he studied were proud of their brideprice marriages in contrast to the dowry marriages of the plains Hindus. ... not all brideprice paying communities necessarily have the same pride in their marriage transactions.

8   If the brothers have tensions amongst themselves, the sisters usually take sides as well.

9   Other terms with the same meaning were *naasotka* and *haathsawera*.

10 According to Ortner (1981), difficulties in divorce in dowry societies are a result of the weakened relationship which the woman has, after marriage, with her natal group. Goody however asserts, 'one cannot interpret the rule against divorce as indicating a complete detachment from the natal family' (1990: 173).

Excerpted from Maya Unnithan-Kumar, *Identity, Gender and Poverty; Perspectives on Caste and Tribe in Rajasthan*, Berghahn Books, Providence: Oxford, 1997.

Economics of Brideprice and Dowry

INDIRA RAJARAMAN

A major socio-economic development of the last few decades is the switch that seems to have taken place, all over the country, among entire endogamous groups from a brideprice to a dowry system. The phenomenon calls for an explanation and causes concern, because of the common association of dowry with exploitation and indebtedness—an association that does not extend to brideprice to anywhere near the same extent.

The source of bafflement here lies in the conversion of *whole* communities, not merely that segment of each that impinges on the organised-sector. For dowry as an organised-sector phenomenon is very easily explained. Employment in the organised-sector, and access to such employment through acquisition of appropriate skills, is largely restricted to males. Such males as do gain entry receive, relative to their unorganised-sector counterparts, a remuneration that is generally higher and less variable. It is inevitable, therefore, that marriage to such males would be highly desired, and that the resulting competition could result in a dowry where none existed before. For example, in an endogamous group consisting of weavers, say, eking out an uncertain livelihood and among whom the payment of a brideprice upon marriage is customary, the lone male who has achieved employment in, say, a government office may be able to command a spouse at a zero brideprice. His desirability might be such that he can even get one at a negative brideprice. At that point, a dowry comes into being. The transition from a positive to a negative brideprice may not be confined to this male alone. Other males in the family may achieve a similar desirability by association and so may be able to cross over as well. But there the process must clearly stop. The initial male cannot carry with him his more distant kin, let alone all the males in the community. It goes without saying that, in those endogamous groups in which the incidence of organised-sector participation is above some threshold level, all the males could cross over through the organised-sector connection.

But it is the evidence on communities which impinge little or not at all on the organised sector that compels attention. There appears to have been, over the last 30 to 50 years, a widespread transition among such communities from a brideprice to a dowry system.

The question that immediately arises, of course, is whether the evidence can be believed. What we have to go by consists chiefly of the findings of the National Committee on the Status of Women,[1] whose first-hand collection of information, to complement specially commissioned studies, were conducted all over the country during 1971–74. Casual evidence also supports their findings, though casual evidence is not enough in matters such as this. The only type of study that can establish conclusively whether, and what extent, the transition has occurred in different endogamous groups is the anthropological field-study with a sufficiently long time span of observation. Such studies are time-consuming and consequently scarce.

One prominent example of a study which does have a long enough time span to assess such trends is that by Epstein.[2] It is a study of two villages in Mandya district of Karnataka state spanning 1954/56 to 1970. Epstein observed that in 1970 a transition to dowry was complete among the "peasant" community in one village, and it was in process in the other. In Epstein's observed community, however, the transition appears to have been initiated by males who gained foothold in the organised sector. Thus Epstein does not really provide evidence of a wholly or largely unorganised-sector transition.

The findings of the Status of Women Committee will need to be corroborated or qualified for different endogamous groups by studies of the kind done by Epstein. Meanwhile, the findings of the Committee are sufficiently persuasive to compel a search—first, for an explanation, and second, for an answer to the question of whether, and in what circumstances, a system of dowry payment has a more widely punitive incidence than a system of brideprice payment.

First, what factors explain the widespread transition from brideprice to dowry payments? The Status of Women Committee ends the search for an explanation with the well-known evidence from the decennial population Census on the declining participation of women in the labour force, starting with the Census of 1911 (the decline persists even after adjustment for changes in definitions, which have over the years been increasingly restrictive with respect to participation in the labour force). The only other source of information on long-run trends in labour force participation is the National Sample Survey, which has conducted a series of sample surveys to assess labour force participation starting with the 9th round (1955). However, when surveys that are conceptually or otherwise non-uniform are excluded, there are very few points of comparison left on the basis of which a confident statement can be made on long-run trends.[3] Aside from issues of internal comparability, the problem with both the Census and the NSS as sources of data on labour force participation is that neither provides information at the level of specificity required—i.e. by endogamous groups. Aggregate figures conceal a great deal of variation from one group to the next. Indeed, there is casual evidence to suggest that female labour force participation may have gone up in certain groups in response to new opportunities.

But let us suppose that a decline in the female participation rate does occur within an endogamous group. By-passing, for the moment, the all-important question of why such a decline in female participation occurred in the first place, will this be a sufficient condition for a transition from bride-price to dowry? And is it a necessary condition? The answers depend on the variation of the constituent elements of the initial brideprice payment.

Any positive brideprice can be characterised generally as a compensatory payment to the family of the female for the production loss they suffer on her departure. But there can be wide variations in the relative importance accorded to the different constituent elements that go towards its specification. There are essentially three such elements. Two elements make for a positive compensation, arising first on account of the female's economic contribution and second on account of her contribution to child-rearing and other household work.[4] The third element is a factor making for a negative compensation arising out of the cost of maintaining her. Clearly, if the brideprice is positive, the sum of the first two outweighs the third.

However, what is crucial from our point of view is the relative valuation of the second and third components. Suppose these two together were to sum up to zero—i.e., the discounted present value of the time stream of her contribution by way of household work was considered equivalent to the discounted present value of the time stream of clothing and feeding her—then the brideprice would be equivalent to the present value of the time stream of her gross economic contribution alone, and a stoppage of female labour-force participation would simply reduce the brideprice to zero. If the second component outweighs the third, a stoppage of female labour-force participation would not even reduce the brideprice to zero; it would remain positive. In either of these cases, there is no question of a dowry coming into existence.

The key variable, therefore, is the valuation placed upon household work performed by the woman. If this component is valued *less* than the cost of clothing and feeding her, then and then alone will the brideprice become actually negative with a stoppage of female labour-force participation. It is clear that, in this circumstance, it is not even necessary that women should actually leave the labour force. As long as the cost of feeding a female net of her domestic contribution is valued positive, all that is necessary is that female earnings should decline to a smaller number in order for the transition to take place. In the limiting case, a zero valuation may be placed upon her domestic contribution. In that case, the dowry which comes into existence will measure in full the present value of the cost of supporting a woman over her lifetime if female earnings drop to zero, and something less if female earnings drop below the cost of subsistence but not all the way to zero.

Two conditions thus need to be satisfied for an unorganised sector transition from a brideprice to a dowry system. First and most important, in the specification of the brideprice, the domestic contribution of the woman must be valued at less than the cost of her subsistence. Secondly, the female contribution to family income must fall below a threshold value given by the net excess of subsistence cost over value of domestic contribution. It is not necessary that the female contribution should drop to zero— i.e., it is not necessary that women should withdraw altogether from the labour force in order for dowry to emerge as an unorganised-sector phenomenon.

Why might there be a decline in the female contribution to family income? There are two possibilities.

First, that the decline is exogenously imposed by a decline in demand for the goods produced or services rendered by the women in the group in particular, or by both women and men in the group taken together. In either case female labour-force participation might either fall in response, or be maintained at old levels but at greatly reduced productivity. It is important to reiterate that a dowry system could come into existence in the second case as well—provided the cost of subsistence of a woman net of her domestic contribution is valued to be positive and provided the value of her gainful contribution falls below that.

The second possibility is that a decline in female labour-force participation might have been endogenously generated in some of the land-owning communities, by the rise in recent years in the productivity of irrigated land and by the prosperity consequent upon it. The decline in female participation in gainful work—i.e., the increase in female leisure may then simply be something that is purchased by the community with its increased prosperity. These communities however, will also be those that have a higher incidence of organised-sector participation, and the transition from brideprice to dowry could come about through the mutual interaction of these two forces. Epstein's seems to be a classic instance of this.

Let us now suppose that the two conditions which together are sufficient for a transition exist and that a dowry system results. Such a dowry payment, like the brideprice preceding it, will have a purely compensatory character. It will compensate in part or in full for the lifetime subsistence cost of a woman. The important point is that, since the amount of this compensation will be essentially determined by the valuation placed by the community as a whole on the subsistence cost of a woman net of her domestic contribution, the compensation sum will be basically uniform. It may not be *perfectly* uniform of course; there may be factors that will mitigate or augment the dowry in particular cases. Nevertheless, where the dowry system comes into existence on account of a decline in the female contribution to family income alone, there is enough underlying uniformity in the valuation of a woman that these factors will not alter the essential uniformity of the resulting payment.

The next issue is of how extensive the punitive impact of such a dowry system will be, relative to the brideprice system that is replaced.

It must be emphasised that what is being examined is the impact of the dowry system itself, as distinct from the impact of the underlying decline in female earnings. It is obvious that the latter leads to a very real worsening in the fortunes of all families in the community with daughters. (This will be so even when a decline in female labour-force participation is generated endogenously by the rising prosperity of the community. The social purchase of increased female leisure with higher income is essentially imposed on all families with daughters). Prior to the decline, a family with a female child would have reaped a surplus over her subsistence directly until her marriage, and as a present value-equivalent in the form of a brideprice when she married. After the decline a female child does not yield as great a surplus over her subsistence. Indeed, as we have seen, dowry comes into existence only if this surplus is valued to be negative.

The question then is: to what extent does dowry as a system impose an *additional* hardship by requiring a family with a female child to pay the capitalised present value of this drain at the time of her marriage? We must assume, in what follows, that marriage of all female children is an unavoidable imperative imposed exogenously on all families.

It is clear that, as long as dowry retains its character as a purely compensatory payment, where the compensation is determined by factors not specific to individuals, it amounts essentially to a rotating capital fund. Families with an equal number of sons and daughters would break even (assuming monogamous marriage).[5] There will be leaks *out* of the rotating fund into those families that have a greater number of sons than daughters and who would be the net gainers in the system. There would have to be a corresponding contribution into the fund from families with more daughters than sons, who would be the net losers in the system.

It is this last group of families alone on whom dowry as a system imposes an additional punishment, and who will have to get indebted to a greater or lesser degree so as to cope with its demands. What is important is that, as long as dowry remains a purely compensatory payment, its punitive impact extends not to all families with daughters but only to those with daughters unmatched by an equal number of sons. This will be so no matter how large the absolute value of the dowry payable—although, of course, the greater the amount payable the greater the hardship for families with an excess of daughters over sons. For this reason, we are not greatly concerned here with secular trends in variables such as age at marriage and female life expectancy which will make for a change over time in the absolute amount of the payment.

All this is necessarily highly abstracted. With a positive interest rate, the sequence of daughters and sons will also clearly matter. In that case, families with an equal number of sons and daughters will still lose if a dowry has to be paid for the daughters much before the sons can yield. Also as mentioned earlier, the compensation payable may in a few specific cases be altered from the norm. None of these considerations significantly affects the essentially circulating nature of the payment.

Such a dowry system then will be no more extensively punitive than the brideprice system from which it has evolved. There, too, a family with a greater number of sons than daughters would have had to resort to borrowing in order to be able to pay the capitalised present worth of brides for all excess sons. Families with an equal number of sons and daughters would have broken even, and those with more daughters than sons would have gained. Thus, in either system, some families lose[6] and others gain from a lack of the right balance, with the remainder emerging more or less even.

There is one important lack of symmetry however. A brideprice fetches a bride; any loan contracted to pay the brideprice can in principle be repaid from the productive contribution over time of the woman.[7] A dowry, on the other hand, fetches nothing equivalent. Thus a dowry cannot be termed a 'groom-price' for it does not fetch a groom in the same sense in which a brideprice fetches a bride.

The essential point thus is that, if a dowry system results solely from a decline in the female labour force participation rate, with no other parallel developments, its punitive impact will be restricted to those who are forced to contribute to the circulating compensation fund. For each such contribution there will be a corresponding leak out of the fund to the benefit of someone else. The remainder will be neither punished nor rewarded.

On the subject of leaks it must be noted that it is obviously perfectly possible for an imprudent family to eat into a dowry received, and thus to have to borrow when a dowry becomes payable. This kind of debt, however, is clearly incurred by a conscious choice and is not imposed by the system itself.

A brief digression on organised-sector dowries is in order here. Do these also have a uniform character? The answer is quite obviously no, since the organised-sector dowry is the result of a bidding process whereby potential grooms in the organised sector are bid for by aspirant families. Each aspirant family will derive utility from both the monetary and the non-monetary prestige attributes of prospective grooms. The choice of male, then, becomes another case of the standard constrained utility maximisation problem. The family budget constraint in turn will be a sum of both money offered by the family and its prestige, translated into money terms in some trade-off. There is thus no uniformity whatever in the dowry payment. A family already within the organised sector, for example, can, by virtue of the higher prestige-by-association which it offers, achieve the same groom as a family still in the unorganised sector with a far smaller monetary dowry.

Going back to the unorganised sector, there must thus, in the transition from a bride-price to a dowry system be something more than a simple decline in the female contribution to family income if dowry is to have the more extensively punitive aspects associated with it. There must develop more leaks from the circulating fund so that every family is forced to contribute to it, regardless of balance. In the limiting case there might be no circulating fund whatever, the dowry payment at every marriage leaking out of the fund entirely and immediately. Whether or not it has reached this extreme, the system now begins to punish all families with any female children at all, not merely those with more daughters than sons, and thus to resemble more the system as it is perceived with all the associated hardship and indebtedness.

The question that immediately arises is: do we know anything about the incidence of indebtedness on account of dowry? The answer here, as in so much else, is that we really know very little in any hard sense although casual evidence abounds. In the All-India Debt and Investment Survey of 1971–72, conducted in the course of the 26th round of the NSS, no effort was made to capture the indebtedness arising on account of dowry—or, for that matter, on account of brideprice in the few remaining pockets where brideprice still prevails. The survey tabulation of indebtedness by purpose allows for six categories, viz, farm, non-farm, litigation, financial investment, repayment of previously incurred debt, and lastly a comprehensive 'household expenditure' category that includes consumption loans and much else, besides dowry.[8] Household expenditure accounts in rural areas for 52 per cent of total indebtedness, aggregated across regions and occupation groups. By occupation group, the figure ranges from a low of 49 per cent for cultivators to a high of 80 per cent for agricultural labourers, with artisans falling somewhere in between at 64 per cent. Distress borrowing is clearly a major cause of all loans incurred. But this does not tell us very much about how much dowry accounts for.

Let us assume, however, that casual evidence on the extensive distress caused by dowry is indeed correct, and that the system does indeed punish all families with female children. What might be the nature of the developments, that should make such a situation possible? Before answering this question, a more comprehensive definition of dowry is called for than what has hitherto been used. Dowry has been defined, so far, as what evolves out of a brideprice system as a purely compensatory payment. Now that precipitating factors other than a simple decline in female contribution to family income are to be considered, dowry must accordingly be defined to include all outlays required at marriage as a necessary condition of the contract, regardless of the disposition of the outlay.

There are no hard data on the breakdown of dowry by disposition category. Further, because of the variation in such practices from one endogamous group to the next, it is impossible to extrapolate from one to the other. It is particularly important not to extrapolate from organised sector practices, with which members of the organised-sector are likely to be casually familiar.

In the absence of any information on the quantitative importance of the different disposition categories, they can merely be listed. Broadly there are essentially two: expenditure on the ceremony itself, and gifts in cash and kind. The first can be broken down further into food and non-food expenditures, and the second into gifts going to the bride and those to the groom and his family.

Expenditure on the ceremony clearly constitutes a total and immediate leak out of the rotating fund. To the extent that this category gains in importance, therefore, the punitive incidence of the dowry widens. (However, it must be remembered that in respect of the food component, and to a lesser extent of the non-food component as well, some benefits of a real nature could be considered to flow to the community as a result. In effect, a nutritional supplement is introduced into the diet of the community, by taxing, at every marriage, the parenthood of a female child.)

The major non-ceremonial component of a dowry viz, gifts in cash and kind, could on the other hand, potentially at any rate, go entirely into a rotating fund. To the extent, however, that there is an appropriation of the cash or non-cash gifts by the recipients a leak could develop here as well. If all gifts in cash and kind are totally appropriated by the recipients, the capital fund altogether ceases to exist (or exists for a notional instant before leaking out totally to the various beneficiaries).

The important question is: to what extent have these further developments accompanied the transition from brideprice to dowry? If the feeding of kin and other ceremonial expenditures, and the giving of non-rotating individualised gifts, were as important a component in percentage terms of the brideprice, the dowry system will once again be no more a cause of hardship than the brideprice system it replaces: the only difference will be that the incidence of the tax shifts from parents of sons to parents of daughters. That certainly does not accord with popular perceptions of the two systems. What is more probable is that ceremonial expenditures and individual gifts might have existed previously to some extent, but untied to the brideprice— i.e., not as components of it. Instead, such expenditures might have been allotted in accordance with some formula whereby the burden might have been more equally shared. Again, along with the brideprice system there might have been a practice of providing ornaments to the bride from her family—but as an expression of her share in the family property rather than as a contractual element in the marital transaction itself.

Thus, to the extent dowry has assumed a more widely punitive character than the brideprice system, there has to have been, as a necessary condition, a change in the composition of the payment. The non-rotating component, consisting of the sum of expenditures on festivities and the provision of non-rotating individual gifts, has to have assumed a far larger percentage significance in the contractual payment than it had in the previous system, if any.

To conclude, the replacement of a brideprice by a dowry system, to the extent it has occurred as an unorganised sector phenomenon, can be a consequence (though not a necessary one) of declining female contribution to family income (with or without a decline in female labour force participation). The particular cause for this underlying decline will vary from one endogamous group to the other. What is important is that it need not be the result of developments exogenous to the community. Whatever the cause precipitating the transition, it is clear that the resulting system of dowry payment will have no more extensive a punitive impact than the brideprice system it replaces, as long as it retains a purely compensatory rotating character.

The dowry system will assume a more widely punitive aspect only if expenditures of a non-rotating character, i.e., on ceremonial or on individualised gifts, form a larger fraction of the payment than in the system replaced. Without such a paralled development, dowry as a system can be no more widely punitive than brideprice as a system. That there has been such a parallel development is supported by casual evidence, and is clearly a response to the demonstration effect of organised-sector dowries.

The policy implications of the foregoing are as clear as they are probably impossible to implement. With a reduction of expenditure on ceremonies and gifts in kind, the dowry payment will more nearly approximate the system it has replaced, even if the cash equivalent of these stifled expenditures is absorbed into an augmented cash payment. The cash payment itself will disappear, of course, only with a rise in female contribution to family income to some threshold value, where the required threshold may vary fairly widely between endogamous groups.

Notes

[The author is grateful to Clive Bell for useful comments.]

[1] Because the full report of the committee is not easily available all references hereafter are to a synopsis of the report published by the Indian Council of Social Science Research, *Status of Women in India* (New Delhi: Allied, 1975). See pp. 20–27.

[2] T. Scarlett Epstein, *South India Yesterday, Today and Tomorrow—Mysore Villages Revisited* (London: Macmillan, 1973). See pp. 194–200.

[3] Indira Rajaram, "On the Socio-Economic Condition of Women: The National Sample Survey and Labour Ministry Surveys" (*mimeo*: 1977).

[4] The dividing line between contribution to gainful activity and household work may be thin or non-existent.

[5] The incidence of polygamous marriage, as discovered by a Census study in 1961, is low and has declined over the decades. Even among those tribal groups where polygamy has increased over the years, it had an incidence of as little as 15 per cent in 1961.

[6] In *Status of Women*, op. cit. p. 24, it is noted that, among some Scheduled castes and tribes of Uttar Pradesh, debts incurred for brideprice

payment were reported to be sometimes cleared by sending wives for prostitution. It would be interesting to know in these cases what was the particular reason for the leak from the circulating fund.

[7] Provided the brideprice system has not survived a decline in labour force participation, which as we have seen, it can. Among the groups mentioned in the preceding footnote, recourse to prostitution does not mean that there are no other means of earning for the wife in question, but only that the debt is more quickly cleared this way.

[8] National Sample Survey, *All-India Debt and Investment Survey 1971–72.*

First published in *The Economic and Political Weekly*, 1983, 13, pp. 275–80.

Sociology of Brideprice and Dowry

SHALINI RANDERIA & LEELA VISARIA

This article is provoked by Indira Rajaraman's article on the 'Economics of Bride-Price and Dowry', which appeared in these columns, and by the discussion which followed it (February 19, April 9, June 4, September 3–10 and November 19, 1983). Neither Rajaraman, who seeks to build an economic model of the presumed switch of "entire endogamous groups from a bride-price to a dowry *system*" (our italics), nor her critics provide any empirical data in support of their generalisations. On the basis of our data from north Gujarat, we have serious doubts about Rajaraman's premise that entire sub-castes had a brideprice system in the past, and have given it up in favour of a dowry system now. Our interpretation of the census and the NSS data seems to invalidate her other premise that there has been a significant decline in female participation in the labour force. We also fail to see the casual relationship between these two premises as is sought to be established in Rajaraman's model.

First, we attempt to understand the terms 'brideprice' and 'dowry' which have been left undefined by all contributors to the discussion so far. We then turn to our own field work data on the scheduled castes of North Gujarat. (We feel free to do so, because Rajaraman's model is neither region nor caste-specific.) Finally we look at the labour force data from the censuses as well as the National Sample Surveys and try to assess whether there has been any significant change in female participation in the labour force. In our view, the observed decline is an artifact to the definitional changes in the concept of work, which make the 1961, 1971 and 1981 census data non-comparable.

Terms and their connotation

Both brideprice and dowry involve the transmission of property between the two families linked by marriage. The first exchange of gifts (clothes, ornaments, cash, household goods) takes place at the time of engagement, continues upto the time of marriage (which is the occasion for some of the most spectacular and elaborate gift-giving) and well beyond it at all important life-cycle rituals. The exchange continues for a span of two generations at least (e.g., gifts from the mother's brother to his sister's son or daughter on the occasion of the latter's wedding) and decreases in amount and number only in the third generation. The chain of prestations between affines may begin with the formal engagement well before marriage, and continues for many years after the death of the woman whose marriage originally brought the relationship into being. Whatever the symbolic nature of some of these exchanges, they also have their economic functions as ways of transferring property.

Brideprice and dowry can be seen as contrary to one another only insofar as the direction of the gift giving is concerned. Brideprice is a transmission of goods from the kin of the groom to the kin of the bride on return for which certain rights in the bride are transferred. In the classic African case, where women and goods can be seen to travel in opposite directions, brideprice forms a part of the community's circulating pool of resources. In such cases, brideprice may be seen as an economic compensation to the bride's family for the loss of her labour and the bride-wealth received by the father or brothers of the girl is used to get wives for her brothers. As we shall show, brideprice among the lower castes and the scheduled castes of Gujarat has no such connotations.

Dowry, however, is not the minor-opposite of brideprice which would technically be groomprice. Strictly speaking, dowry is property given to the bride by her kin, to take with her to her husband's family (and a broader definition may include gifts from her family, to members of her husband's family as well). Theoretically at least, dowry is *stridhan*, property which belongs to the woman, and which may be controlled jointly by her husband, who does not have the right to dispose it off. At the time of the partition of the joint household, the woman takes with her into her new nuclear household each and every one of the household goods brought with her as dowry. Parents often argue that they accept a dowry for their son, because they have to give one for their daughter. But this does not mean that a man has the right to use his wife's dowry to marry off his own sisters. Though this may happen, it is done clandestinely. Such pilferage of the wife/daughter-in-law's dowry or *stridhan* is considered shameful and would not be publicly acknowledged. In this sense, dowry does not form part of a rotating capital fund in India as Rajaraman postulates. It is true that with the spread of urbanisation and education, especially when coupled with a hypergamous situation, dowry has come to acquire a coercive character. But that is an issue we leave aside, as we are primarily concerned with the postulated switch from brideprice to dowry. We also do not consider the question whether dowry should be seen as pre-mortem inheritance (Goody and Tambiah, 1973, p. 1. Kaur and Sharma 1983, p. 12).

Ancient Hindu literature is cognisant of both dowry and brideprice, but ranks the latter as lower. The code of Manu unequivocally states: "No father who knows (the law) must take even the smallest gratuity for his daughter; for a man who through avarice takes a gratuity, is a seller of his offspring" (Manu III, 51). The recommended act was *Kanyadan*, or the gift of the virgin daughter, whereas brideprice was seen as the sale of a daughter for profit, and regarded as shameful. Marriage with dowry was considered more prestigious and was recommended for the higher castes.

Gujarat data

In order to examine Rajaraman's hypothesis about "A major socio-economic development in recent times—viz. the switch ... all over the country ... from a brideprice to a dowry system", we must look at data from the lower castes who were forbidden by Manu to practise the superior type of dowry marriage, and who are widely reported to practise brideprice marriage (Towards Equality 1974, p. 69).

There are a few instances of brideprice being paid among the upper caste in Gujarat, as elsewhere in India, in cases where the groom is a widower of advanced age or has a large number of children from a previous marriage, or has a physical or mental handicap, and is unable to get a bride from within his own marriage circle. But such marriages among Brahmins and Banias are exceptions which prove the rule.

The payment at the time of marriage among the upper castes in Gujarat, which is in the same direction as brideprice, i.e., from the family of the groom, is known as *pallu*. It is distinguished from the former, however, in that the recipient of the *pallu* is the bride herself, and not her father or family as in the case of brideprice. The *pallu* was usually kept in custody by the girl's father, until such time as her position in her husband's family was secure (i.e. she was the mother of a couple of children, preferably a son). In north Gujarat, if the girl were to die childless, the *pallus* would have to be returned to the husband's family among the Brahmins and Banias, unlike the brideprice among the scheduled castes, which is non-returnable. Only the direction of payment of *pallu* makes it appear similar to a brideprice. Goody has termed it 'indirect dowry' and Tambiah calls it an "analogue of brideprice which is redirected and transformed into a gift of jewellery to the bride, which she takes to her new home" (Goody and Tambiah. 1973, pp. 20 and 92). Among the Brahmins and Banias of Saburkantha district (north Gujarat), the *pallu* is usually paid in gold and interestingly over the years there has been a decline in the stipulated amount (from 51 tolas 50 years ago to 5–7 tolas today among the Banias).

In north Gujarat, a payment akin to 'brideprice' (known as *dapu*) is customarily made among the lower castes like tailors, oil-pressers, leather-workers, barbers, among ex-nomadic groups like Rabaris, Vanjaras, Bharvads, among tribals like the Bhils, as also among all the scheduled castes like Vankars (weavers), Chamars (tanners), Bhangis (scavangers), Tirgars (bow and arrow makers), Garos (Brahmins of the 'untouchables') and Turis (musicians and geneologists of the 'untouchables'). Among all these groups, brideprice is paid in cash, the first transaction taking place immediately after the marriage ceremony, and the second one a few years later, when a couple of kinsmen of the groom go to fetch the bride to come and reside at her in-law's home for the first time (an occasion known as the first *anu* which is the equivalent of the north India gauna).

The question then arises as to whether this brideprice can be seen as "a compensatory payment to the family of the female, for the production loss they suffer on her departure". For brideprice to constitute such a payment its amount should be fairly high, given the relatively high labour force participation by scheduled caste women. Yet, among the different scheduled castes in north Gujarat the amount of brideprice paid varies from Rs 351 to Rs 901 (if one combines the sum paid at the marriages as well as the *anu* as many of the castes themselves do now in view of the higher age at marriage). This can hardly be an adequate compensation for the woman's life time of domestic and other labour which her natal family loses. Another indicator of the brideprice not being an economic compensation is the fact that the brideprice for a divorced woman is significantly lower than for the never-married and that for a divorced woman with a child is still lower, even though the woman does not take the child with her to her husband's home. The people themselves see brideprice as partly a contribution by the groom's family to the wedding expenses borne by the bride's family. For example among the Mehasana scheduled caste of sadhus, it was recently decided that the marriage party (Jan) should be served three meals instead of the usual two, and the brideprice was correspondingly increased by Rs 100.

Traditionally, no brideprice was paid in those castes, or in those particular marriage circles of a caste, where a direct exchange of women, know as Satu, was the rule, e.g. among the weavers in Bhiloda taluka (Sabarkantha district) who belong to the Pranami sect, brideprice has to be paid only if the groom's family cannot furnish a girl in exchange.

It is also important to point out that although a payment similar to brideprice is made among many of these lower castes, it does not mean that they have a brideprice system. As Tambiah has argued "... every marriage involves multiple transactions and payments, some unilateral, and others reciprocal, so that it would be said that the modalities of bride-wealth and dowry

Table 1: Labour Force Participation Rates by Sex According to the Censuses of 1911–1981

Census	Males	Females	Persons
	All Areas		
1911	62.0	33.9	48.2
1921	60.6	32.1	47.0
1931	57.9	28.4	43.6
1951	54.3	23.3	39.2
1961	57.2	27.9	43.0
1971*	52.5	13.2	33.5
1981*	52.6	19.8	36.8
	Rural Areas		
1961	58.3	31.4	45.1
1971*	53.8	15.9	35.3
1981*	53.8	23.2	38.9
	Urban Areas		
1961	52.4	11.2	35.5
1971*	48.9	7.2	29.6
1981*	49.1	8.3	30.0

*Including 'secondarily working' in 1971 and 'marginally working' in 1981.
Sources: Various Census Reports.

co-exist in the same series with one or the other type of transaction gaining dominance in specific situation" (Goody and
Tambiah, 1973 p. 71). If it is at all possible to characterise the
complex array of gift exchange between two families over a
period of 2–3 generations either as a 'brideprice system' or a
'dowry system', then the system of marriage-related payments
among the lower castes and scheduled castes must be termed
as a 'dowry system', despite the existence of brideprice like
payment on two occasions. In order to characterise the system

Table 2: Labour Force Participation Rates by Sex in Rural Areas According to the
Various National Sample Surveys

NSS Rounds	Reference Year	References Period	Males	Females	Persons
9	May–Nov 55	Usual status/one year	59.7	26.6	43.5
11 & 12	Aug 56–Aug 57	One day	55.1	23.3	39.4
14	July 58–June 59	One week	56.9	26.7	41.8
15	July 59–June 60	One week	58.7	23.6	41.2
16	July 60–June 61	One week	55.7	27.7	41.9
17	Sept 61–July 62	One week	52.2	22.1	37.5
19	July 64–June 65	One week	53.0	26.8	40.1
21	July 66–June 67	One week	54.0	28.5	41.4
27	Oct 72–Sept 73	Usual status	55.1	32.0	43.7
32	July 77–June 78	Usual status/One year	56.0	33.8	45.1

Source: Planning Commission, Report of the Committee of Experts on Unemployment Estimates, New Delhi, 1970, p. 54; and Pravin Visaria, 'Level and Structure
of Employment, Unemployment and Labour Force in India, 1961–81' (mimeo),
1982.

as a whole, we must look at the totality of gift exchanges, their direction and size, as well as the recipients. It then becomes clear that both among the upper castes and lower castes, a girl receives gifts of cash, jewellery and household goods (usually only utensils) from her parents and other family members at the time of her marriage. In addition, the girl's family makes certain gifts to the groom's near relatives. The total cost of all that the girl receives from her parents at her wedding easily exceeds the amount of bride-price which her father receives from the groom's father. And the marriage only inaugurates the gift-giving. On every subsequent occasion (pregnancy ceremony, child birth, especially birth of the first male child, the wedding of her children, the death of her father-in-law or mother-in-law or her husband, etc.) the girl's family has to give gifts to the girl as well as to her husband's near relatives. An analysis of the totality of these payments shows that they do not differ in content, form or direction from those of the upper castes (only the amounts given are smaller). Although there is a two-way flow of gifts, over a period of time, it is the girl's family which gives much more than it receives. The two bride-price payments seem to be only episodic reversals of the usual pattern of the flow of gifts from 'wife-givers' to 'wife-takers'. Thus the initial brideprice is more than off-set by the subsequent gifts and payments in the opposite direction, so that both in ideology and practice it is the bride-giver who is the gift-giver among the lower castes as well.

In view of our data on the nature and amount of gift-giving between affines among the lower and scheduled castes, we would seriously doubt the claim that these castes have (or have had at least in the recent past) a 'brideprice system'. In the absence of such a system, how could there be a switch over to a 'dowry system'? Not only has the dowry component of their prestation system increased in value over the last ten years (silver jewellery being replaced by gold wherever possible, rough cotton saries by polyester ones, and brass utensils by stainless steel ones), the brideprice component has also been increasing steadily. (Among tribal groups also, brideprice has increased manifold over time. [Towards Equality, 1974, pp. 69–70.]) Of course the dowry component being of much greater value, it is the girl's family which bears the financial brunt of these changes. Among all the scheduled castes, strict rules govern the amount of gift-exchange between affines, and all violations are punishable by fines. The sub-caste *panch* meets every few years to review these rules, and revise them if necessary, and each marriage circle has its own printed booklet which contains this information. A look at some of these 'caste constitutions' for the scheduled castes of north Gujarat shows that 'brideprice' has been steadily increasing from Rs 30–50 about 50 years ago, to Rs 351–901 today. Of course, the amounts written in these 'constitutions' may not be strictly adhered to in every case, but they certainly lay down the lower limits.

What is also significant is that among the scheduled castes especially, entry into the organised sector has been possible only in the last few decades (with the provision of educational and job reservations). This has coincided with an increase in the amount of brideprice, rather than a change over to dowry, as Rajaraman would anticipate. To take her own example of an endogamous group of weavers among whom the payment of brideprice is customary, "the one male who has achieved employment in say, a government office, may be able to command a spouse at zero brideprice or at a negative brideprice". Our data, from precisely such a group of weavers in Sabarkantha district, prove this not to be the case at all. The few weaver men who are in government service are certainly sought after by the parents of prospective brides, but the men's choice of a spouse is limited by their demand for educated brides, who are an equally scarce commodity in the caste. The girl may not be allowed to work after her marriage but the fact of her being 'SSC pass' confers status on her husband's family which is therefore willing to pay a higher brideprice, demanded by the family of an educated bride. Incidentally, among the Vankars, the amount of brideprice is at present subject to a great deal of bargaining so that the money paid in addition to the amount laid down in the caste constitution is known as inflation adjustment (*monghwari*) and some members of the caste compare it to the dearness allowance increases over the basic pay!

Entry into the organised sector by some members of a sub-caste thus does not lead to a reversal in the direction of customary marriage payment. Sub-caste rules of marriage prestations do not differentiate among their members, although Rajaraman is baffled by "the conversion of whole communities, not merely that segment of each that impinges on the organised sector". For Rajaraman, "dowry as an organised sector phenomenon is very easily explained". This implies that it would be less baffling if the men belonging to the organised sector within a sub-caste got dowries, and other things being equal, men in the unorganised sector continued to pay brideprice. Unfortunately such differentiation does not take place in reality.

Moreover, like an exceptional brideprice marriage among the upper castes, an exceptional 'pure gift' marriage also takes place among the lower castes. The latter is known among many of the scheduled castes of North Gujarat as *kanku-kayna*, i.e. a marriage where the bride has been given as a gift without her family accepting any money in exchange. Only families of very high standing with a scheduled caste could give away a daughter in this fashion, for such a marriage entailed more lavish expenditure as well as more than the usual dowry gifts to the daughter. It was an indication of wealth as well as social status for a family to refuse to accept brideprice for their daughters. Curiously enough, such marriages, instead of being on the increase, are actually decreasing and have been altogether abolished among some of the scheduled castes.

Thus in Gujarat, castes like the Rajputs, Leuva Patidars of Kheda and Anavils of south Gujarat have high dowry linked with hypergamy; castes like Brahmins and Banias have 'indirect dowry' in addition to dowry proper; and lower castes and scheduled castes have brideprice in addition to dowry. In such a situation, it is difficult to discern and delineate any "conversion from brideprice to the dowry systems".

Women's participation in labour force

We turn to the second premise of Rajaraman's model, i.e., the decline in women's participation in labour force over time. The major sources of data, especially time trend data, are the decennial censuses and the various rounds of the National Sample Survey. The female as well as the male labour force participation rates from these sources are given in Tables 1 and 2. As we see it, these data have been handled and analysed in three distinct ways by the economists and other social scientists.

One group of researchers accepts the census data as indicative of a marked decline in the female participation in the labour force over time. As the concept of work, its definitions and the changes introduced in it from time to time are understood in a much better way, this view now has fewer adherents. Yet, the conclusion that women are increasingly withdrawing from the labour force remains firmly established in the minds of these social scientists (Towards Equalitly, 1974, p. 152).

A second group strongly feels that the definitional changes, especially since the 1961 census, affect the quantum of female workers to a much greater extent than they affect the male workers. Since men generally have a "stable attachment to economic activity, alternative approaches to measure the extent of their labour force participation would give more or less similar results" (Report of the Committee of Experts on Unemployment Estimates, 1970, p. 47). This is not the case with female workers at all. Scholars who believe that sharp fluctuations in female work participation rates essentially reflect conceptual and procedural changes, either concentrate on an analysis restricted to male workers only (see for example, Lal, 1976 and Jose, 1978) or deal with the employment of women at one point in time but across regions or sub-groups (Gulati, 1975 and Dholakia and Dholakia, 1978).

A third group of researchers adjusts the data, wherever possible, by taking into account the problems of reference period, grouping sub-categories into broader categories to remove intercategory transfer problems, and by looking at other sources of data for comparison. These scholars then try to delineate time trends in the participation in work by men and women.

Data for the country as a whole, as Rajaraman admits, conceal a great deal of variation from one group to the other. Accepting that as a very important limitation of the data, we first try to understand whether there has been any significant decline in the female participation in labour force or not.

The census data on labour force participation rates (percentage of workers in the total population) from 1911 onwards, if accepted at face value, do indeed suggest a dramatic decline in the female participation, especially between 1961 and 1971 and a rise between 1971 and 1981. The 1981 level of female participation, however, is significantly below the 1961 level. These data do imply a trend towards withdrawal of women from the labour force. Is the trend real or is it an artifact of the conceptually different data which are, strictly speaking, not comparable?

Rajaraman prefers to skip the conceptual problems and states that the decline in the female participation persists even after adjustment for changes in the definitions. In fact her economic model rests on the presumed decline in female participation. We examine the concepts used in the censuses and the NSS at some length.

The 1961 census aimed at obtaining a good inventory of the country's working force and recorded as worker everyone who had worked "for at least one hour a day throughout the greater part" of the normal "working season". However, in the 1971 census, at the suggestion of the Planning Commission, persons for whom work was their main activity were distinguished from others for whom work was secondary activity, secondary to some other activity such as house work or studies. Interestingly, the 1971 census enumerators enumerated only

0.1 per cent of males and 2.0 per cent of females who were 'secondarily working'. So that even after adding these secondarily working individuals to the "main" workers, the worker-population ratios based on the 1971 census data are unduly (and artificially) low. The rates for females are affected to a much greater extent because they are involved in house work regardless of their work for wages away from home or their contribution to the family farm or enterprise. Many of these women would not consider work to be their main activity (or not reported as working by other, typically male, respondents of the family) (Jabwala, 1984, pp. 2–3). Also the enumerators have admittedly failed to record the economic activities of those who did not report 'work' as their main activity. In fact, the two sets of data (i.e., 1961 and 1971) are conceptually non-comparable and offer no possibilities of 'adjustment'.

The 1981 census also has attempted to distinguish the mainly working persons from others who are termed "marginal" workers. The main workers are supposed to have worked for a "major part of last year" (i.e. six months or more), whereas the marginal workers would be those who had worked for some time during the previous year but not for a major part of the year. The 1981 census data (based on 5 per cent sample) indicate that the marginal workers formed about 1.8 per cent of male and 29.2 per cent of female workers (or 1.0 per cent of male population and 5.8 per cent of female population). The labour force participation rates for 1981 for females, including these marginal workers, turn out to be significantly higher than that reported by the 1971 census (where also secondarily working are added to the main workers), but lower than that estimated by the 1961 census.

These rates are compared or can be compared to those estimated from the various rounds of the NSS shown in Table 2. The survey period, and more importantly, the references period have not remained the same in these inquiries, both of which would affect the data of female workers to a much greater extent than they affect the male workers. And yet, there is considerable stability in the rural female participation rates over time—the range is from 22.1 to 29.4 per cent which is nowhere near the 1971 estimate of 15.9 per cent (inclusive of secondarily working) for rural India.

If we confine ourselves only to those rounds of the NSS where the reference period is 'one year' or the question on work status refers to the usual activity (a category similar to that used in the 1961 census), we have three observations from the 9th round (1955), 27th round (1972–73) and 32nd round (1977–78). Admittedly, even these are not strictly comparable. In the 9th round the term 'usual status' referred to the usual activities of a person without reference to any specific point or period of time. But it was understood that it referred to activities that the individual was engaged in over a long period, generally a year.

In the 27th round also there was some vagueness about the reference period. In the 32nd round, the previous year was clearly stated as the relevant reference period. Further, in the 32nd round, two distinct categories were delineated i.e., (1) those who attended to "domestic duties only" and (2) those who attended to domestic duties in addition to undertaking "free collection of goods" and other (unpaid) work involving economic gain for the household. The information on the usual activity supplemented by the data on the second of the above two categories would provide a more realistic estimate of female participation in labour force.

It is our reckoning that the NSS data for 1955, 1972–73 and 1977–78, on labour force participation which encompass more or less all, regardless of their contribution being of secondary or marginal nature, are more or less comparable to the 1961 census data. Looking at Table 2, we see very little change in the female participation in labour force in the decades of the 1960s and 1970s, when the influence of the organised sector should be more evident than at other times. In fact, with minor fluctuations, the situation has virtually remained unchanged in the last half a century!

Evidently, there has not been any decline in the participation of women in the labour force. Has there been any significant decline in the earnings (or the female contribution to family income), or the level of productivity of women as postulated by Rajaraman in her thesis of a switch from brideprice to dowry? Earning or income is an extremely elusive category and most researchers confess that it is difficult to fully capture and measure earnings. What is available for agricultural labour households is the agricultural wage rates. But these, as is well known, give only a very partial view of the earnings. Data on the quantum of employment available per some unit of time, say a year, are equally important. Employment of women tends to be more seasonal than that of men. Also, unemployment affects female agricultural labourers more than it affects men.

As far as the cultivator households are concerned (regardless of the size of the land) we again have to take into account several components to be able to measure income or earnings. It has been shown that the contribution of woman has often been in the form of unpaid family labour, and that their help obviates the need for hiring helpers. However, among the large land owning class, women's leisure may be bought by replacing them either with modern technology and mechanisation and/or with hired labour. But we are not at all sure that this is happening on the subsistence plots as well. The earnings of women, now belonging to the large farms may have dropped, but their number and proportion in the total would be so small that it would not make any significant difference to the total picture.

As far as the organised sector is concerned, the wages and earnings have generally been moving upward, although women are paid less than men for the same quantum of work. Women's contribution to family income might be declining (partly because the contribution of men might be rising at a higher rate) although their earnings over time (even real earnings) may not have declined at all. However, in the absence of any hard data on earnings, much less on time-trend in earnings, one is left in the realm of conjectures only. Yet, we are unable to see any causal link between the presumed switch from brideprice to dowry and women's earnings.

Conclusion

The presumed switch from brideprice to dowry and a decline in female participation in the labour force have caused so much concern because both are assumed to be closely linked to a lowering of the status of women. We would argue that employment of women *per se* is unlikely to lead to an improvement in their status in the absence of control over their own earnings as well as lack of authority in decision making within the family (See Horowitz and Kishwar, 1982, p. 15). Ironically, the women themselves tend to devalue their own economic contributions as well. The process of socialisation and the internalisation of norms which view women as dependent, begins very early and is all-pervasive.

It is true that the increasing coercive character of dowry has led to a decline in the status of women in addition to it being a threat to their very existence. But it must be pointed out that contrary to popular wisdom, women do not have a higher status in those castes and communities where brideprice is paid for them (Gupta, 1983, pp. 5–6 and Shrivastava, 1983, p. 10). Both brideprice and dowry are paid in a patrilineal system of descent and a patrilocal system of residence. With the change of residence after marriage, a woman comes under the control of her husband's family and has no rights of inheritance to property in either her natal or conjugal family despite the laws. Irrespective of brideprice or dowry, a woman is seen as only a receiver of periodic gifts and one from whom no gift may be accepted. The relatively stronger position of lower and scheduled caste women compared to that of upper caste women may be attributed to their better bargaining position due to the traditional practice of divorce and remarriage. In the final analysis, neither work participation nor brideprice can be indicative of a high status of women in an institutional and ideological framework which devalues and discriminates against women.

References

Dholakia, Bakul H. and Dholakia, Ravindra H. 1978, 'Interstate Variation in Female Labour Force Participation Rates in India', *The Indian Journal of Labour Economics*, Vol. 20, No. 4.

Goody Jack and Tambiah S.J., 1973. *Bride Wealth and Dowry*, Cambridge University Press, Cambridge.

Gulati, Leela, 1975, 'Female Work Participation: A Study of Inter-State Differences', *EPW*, Vol. 10, Nos 1 and 2, January 11, 1975.

Gupta, Jyoti, 1983, 'Bride-Price and Polyandry in Jaunsar Bawar', *HOW* Vol. 6, No. 3, pp. 5-6.

Government of India, Ministry of Education and Social Welfare, 1974. *Towards Equality*, Report of the Committee on the Status of Women in India, New Delhi.

Government of India, Planning Commission, 1970, *Report of the Committee of Experts on Unemployment Estimates*, New Delhi.

Horowitz B. and Kishwar Madhu, 1982, 'Family Life—The Unequal Deal', *Manushi*, No. 11, pp. 2-18.

Jabwalar, Renana, 'Nardam Vastavikta' (in Gujarati), 1984, *Naya Marg*, Vol. 6, No. 24, p. 2-3.

Jose A.V. 1978, 'Real Wages, Employment and Income of Agricultural Labourers', *EPW*, Vol. 13, No. 12.

Kaur, Malkit and Sharma M.L. 1983, 'Dowry in Haryana', *HOW*, Vol. 6, No. 3, pp. 11-14.

Lal, Deepak, 1976, 'Agricultural Growth Real Wages and the Rural Poor in India', *EPW*, Vol. 11, No. 26, June 26, 1976.

Shrivastava, Ginny, 'Dowry and Dappa—Sides of the Same Coin', 1983, *HOW*, Vol. 6, No. 3, p. 10.

Visaria, Pravin, 1982. 'Level and Structure of Employment, Unemployment and Labour Force in India, 1961-81' (mimeo).

First published in *The Economic and Political Weekly*, April 14, 1984.

Legal Reform in Dowry Laws

D.N. SANDANSHIV & JOLLY MATHEW

Introduction

Prior to 1983, every form of violence committed within the family, either in the natal or the spousal home, was not considered an offence. Indian law lacked specificity which could bring such an offender to public trial, largely because domestic violence was considered a private affair not open to public scrutiny and state action. The doctrine of 'space' was used to argue that domestic affairs should be confined to the private space of the family. This doctrine stated that there should be a dividing line between both private and public affairs, and all matters within the family should be kept out of the interference of law.

Implicit in a number of judgments is the notion of cultural relativism which suggests that Indian women are accustomed to a certain amount of violence, and therefore, violence against them is not considered a serious infringement on women's right. Section 498-A of the Indian Penal Code (IPC) was constructed to rectify this notion by criminalizing both physical and mental "cruelty". Despite S. 498-A's cruelty definition, the interpretation of the law is so broad that procuring physical evidence of such subtle forms of cruelty is an almost impossible task. Firstly, it is important to take into account the immediate facts and circumstances leading to such cruelty in order to determine the culpability of the accused. Secondly, this provision covers cruelty in relation to the demand of dowry, which was empirically discovered to be uncommonly high. Nevertheless, with the employment of S. 498-A, Indian women subjected to spousal violence can find some form of relief.

The consumerism debate

In an era where India is witnessing unprecedented economic reform, there has also been a commensurate increase in the rate of dowry deaths and bride burning. In 1987, there were 1912 reported cases of dowry death. The number increased to 5157 in 1991. Thus there was a 169.7 per cent increase in the span of four years in the cases of dowry death. The Indian Statistics Institute announced that there has been a 40 per cent increase in reported cases of domestic violence.

Historically, dowry was given to provide economic security for the daughter who was not entitled to any inheritance. Dowry has now become an insidious practice whereby the in-laws family augment their material possessions by pressurizing the newlywed bride to feed their lust for consumer goods. The economic boom and the overall impact of the consumer-driven society has reconstructed the ancient practice of dowry into a lever for extorting money and goods from the bride's family. Failure to comply would mean torture that often led to murder. Compliance with a dowry demand is done in the hope that the amount demanded is not too high a price to pay for a daughter's life.

Origins of the term "dowry death"

The term "dowry death" and "dowry murder" first began to be used around 1977–78 when investigations revealed that deaths of married women, which for years had been camouflaged by the police as accidents or suicides, were actually murders or abetted suicides, preceded by prolonged physical and mental torture by the husband and in-laws in connection with dowry demands. Instead of describing them as "wife murders" or "abetted suicides" women's organizations began calling them "dowry deaths".

Three years later, Parliament introduced the matador criminal provision, S. 304-B which penalizes perpetrators of dowry deaths.

It has become increasingly apparent that social change cannot depend on law alone. Both law and society must develop a comprehensive and concurrent approach to eradicating the role of dowry in marriage, and more importantly, the role of violence in dowry. The purpose of this article is to demonstrate the development in substantive and procedural criminal law and the judicial sensitivity reflected upon the social reality of dowry deaths. Additionally, it will evaluate society's role in assisting law and the legal infrastructure in permanently eradicating the dowry system.

Laws pertaining to dowry

The Dowry Prohibition (Amendment) Act, 1986 introduced S.304-B in the Indian Penal Code, (IPC) which defines dowry death. It states that "where the death of a woman is caused by burns or bodily injury, or occurs otherwise than under normal circumstances within seven years of her marriage and it is shown that soon before her death she was subjected to cruelty or harassment by her husband or any relative of her husband for, or in connection with, any demand for dowry, such a death shall be called 'dowry death', and such husband or relative shall be deemed to have caused such death."

The main ingredients of S.304-B are:

- the occurrence of an unnatural death,
- death within a period of seven years from the date of marriage,
- cruelty "soon" before death and
- death "for" or "in connection" with any demand of dowry.

If all of the above conditions are present, then there is a presumption that the accused has committed the crime of dowry death. This presumption is created by Section 113-B of the Evidence Act inserted by Act 43 of 1986. The operative part of this section says: "the court shall presume that such person had caused the dowry death." Its explanation runs: "For the purpose of this section 'dowry death' shall have the same meaning as in Section 304-B of the IPC. For the purpose of Section 304-B dowry shall have the same meaning as in Section 2 of the Dowry Prohibition Act, 1961. Section 2 has defined 'dowry' as any property or valuable security given or agreed to be given either directly or indirectly: (a) by any party to a marriage to the other party to the marriage, or (b) by the parents of either party to a marriage or by other person to either party to the marriage, or to any other person at or before or *any time*[1] after the marriage *in connection with*[2] the marriage of the said parties but it does not include dower or mehr in the case of persons to whom the Muslim personal law (Shariat) applies."

The third and fourth ingredients of S.304-B require further explanation. The word "soon" is used in the Penal Code only twice. It was earlier used in S.114 Illustration (a) of the Evidence Act, where in cases of theft there is a presumption that a man is guilty of the offence of theft if the stolen article is recovered from his possession "soon after" the offence of theft. The Supreme Court had in this case, where a person was convicted of theft based on the evidence that the stolen articles were recovered from his residence around eight months after the theft, concluded that a term of 8–9 months may be included within the term "soon". This was later applied in the case of "dowry death" where the term "soon" was used again. This was in response to the defence argument, that cruelty should have occurred right before death to attract the offence under Section 304-B.

The fourth ingredient provides for both a direct and an indirect form of demand. The term "for or in connection with" signifies a direct demand and "in connection with" takes care of all indirect demands. A manifestation of an indirect demand would imply harassment towards the non-fulfilment of a specified demand. Examples of direct demand would be a car, television etc.

Section 174(3) of the Criminal Procedure Code, 1973 as amended in 1983 makes a "post-mortem" mandatory in a number of cases of suicide when:

(a) the case involves the suicide by a woman within seven years of her marriage; or

(b) the case relates to the death of a woman within seven years of her marriage in any circumstances raising a reasonable suspicion that some other person has committed an offence in relation to such woman; or

(c) the case relates to the death of a woman within seven years of her marriage and any relation of the woman has requested for it; or

(d) there is a doubt regarding the cause of death; or

(e) the police officer for any other reason considers it expedient to do so.

Section 176 of the Criminal Procedure Code as amended in 1983 makes inquiry by a Magistrate mandatory if the cause of death falls under (a) or (b) of Sub-section 3 of Section 174 of the Code.

The evidentiary aspect

The 1983 Amendment Act also inserted Section 113-A in the Indian Evidence Act which raises presumption as to abetment of suicide by a married woman. It lays down that when the question is whether commission of suicide by a woman had been abetted by her husband or any relative of her husband, and it is shown that she had committed suicide within a period of seven years of marriage from the date of her marriage, that her husband or such relative of her husband had subjected her to cruelty, the court may presume, having regard to all other circumstances of the case, that such suicide had been abetted by her husband or by such relative of her husband.

Further, Section 113-B was inserted into the Indian Evidence Act, which makes the presumption of dowry death mandatory once it is shown that the accused had subjected the deceased woman to cruelty or harassment for or in connection with any demand for dowry. This Section is perhaps the most important aspect of S. 304-B of the IPC because it concludes murder if and when the conditions of cruelty against the woman have been sufficiently proven. Another corresponding amendment in the Criminal Procedure Code in the first Schedule made the offence under Section 304-B cognizable and non-bailable.

The judicial response

The attitude of the judiciary at the apex level has been in favour of women, the crux of which can be condensed to Justice Mohan's judgment in Panniben vs. State of Maharashtra:[3] "Every time a case relating to dowry death comes up it causes ripples in the pool of conscience of this court. Nothing can be more barbarous, nothing could be more heinous than this sort of a crime...".

Differentiating S. 304-B and S. 498-A

The Supreme Court in Shanti v/s. State of Haryana,[4] points out the differences between sections 304-B and 498-A of the IPC and that though they may contain offences that have cruelty as the root-cause, they are essentially separate and distinct, and charges have to be filed under both. In this case, the deceased was alleged to have committed suicide though the conduct of the in-laws after the death of the daughter-in-law was extremely suspicious. They hastily cremated her even without informing her parents, and in the absence of material which could indicate a case of natural death, the High Court convicted the accused under section 304-B and dismissed the charge of Section 498-A. The accused came to the Supreme Court to contend that the very fact that the High Court acquitted them under Sec. 498-A, meant that there was no proof of cruelty.

The Supreme Court held that "cruelty" is a common condition in both the sections and it had to be proved. In Section 498-A cruelty is explained but no such explanation is given in Section 304-B. Given the common background of these offences, the meaning of cruelty and harassment under S.304-B falls under the same interpretation as S.498-A, under which cruelty, by itself, is punishable. The difference between the two Sections, the Supreme Court said, was that in Section 304-B, the incidence of death is punishable when it occurs within seven years of marriage. No such period is mentioned in Section 498-A and the husband and the in-laws are liable any time after the marriage. This meant that the person charged and acquitted under Section 304-B can be convicted under Section 498-A. To avoid procedural defects, it is necessary in such cases to frame charges under both Section 498-A in view of the substantive sentence imposed, and under Section 304-B.

Suicide is also dowry death

The Supreme Court has effectively laid to rest the many doubts that were raised continuously about the nature of death for which S.304-B would be applied. A landmark decision was given in Public Prosecutor, Andhra Pradesh High Court v. T. Punniah[5], where suicide, though committed by the victim herself, was considered to fall under "dowry death" as envisaged under Section 304-B.

The court once again reiterated in the same case that irrespective of the mode of death, if the death occurs within seven years and the death is unnatural—homicidal or suicidal—this Section would apply. The Court rejected the contention of the counsel of the accused who argued that the medical evidence showed that the death was due to asphyxia on account of hanging, and that Section 304-B does not apply to cases of suicide. The court held that Section 304-B applies where the death of a woman is caused by burns or bodily injury or occurs otherwise than under normal circumstances, provided other conditions are satisfied. Since the death of the deceased was on account of hanging, it was still death otherwise than under normal circumstances, and even if she had committed suicide by hanging, the death would still fall under Section 304-B as long as it can be shown that she was subjected to cruelty or harassment by the in-laws in connection with any demand for dowry.

The view that S.304-B can also be applied to suicide was reiterated by the Supreme Court[6]. The court stated "in the result (that) the death was unnatural, either homicidal or suicidal, and even assuming that it was a case of suicide, even then it would be death which had occurred in unnatural circumstances." In such a case, Section 304-B is applied and this position is not disputed.

Importance of circumstantial evidence in a dowry death

Several observations have been made by the Supreme Court on the appreciation of evidence and the judicial attitude that should be adopted towards dowry death, given the circumstances that surround the commission of the crime. In Prakash v/s State of Punjab,[7] the court noted that it was its duty, in cases of death because of torture and demand for dowry, to examine the circumstances of each case and evidence produced by both parties, for the purpose of investigating how the death took place. While judging the evidence and the circumstances of the case, the court has to be conscious of the fact that a death connected with dowry takes place inside the house where the husband's family are the only witnesses present. Therefore, the finding of guilt on the charge of murder has to be recorded on the basis of circumstances of each case and the evidence produced before the court.

The Supreme Court also observed that the legislative intent behind the incorporation of Section 113-A in the Evidence Act and Section 304-B in the IPC were to strengthen prosecution for a crime in which witnesses are not generally available because the crime is committed within the privacy of the home. Section 113-A raises presumption as to abetment of suicide by a married woman.

Inherent in Section 113-B is a powerful presumption, whereby the court presumes the accused to have committed the offence of dowry death if the prosecution can successfully show the existence of all the conditions required under Section 304-B. Accordingly in Hemchand v/s State of Haryana,[8] the judge observed that a reading of Section 304-B would show that when a question arises whether a person has committed the offence of dowry death what is necessary to be shown is that 'soon before her unnatural death, which took place within 7 years of marriage the deceased had been subjected to cruelty and/or harassment for or in connection with demand for dowry. At this stage the presumption under Section 113-B is applied. Therefore irrespective of the fact whether the accused has any direct connection with the death or not, he shall be presumed to have committed the dowry death. In the above case, the prosecution proved unnatural death without direct evidence connecting the accused with the actual death. Nevertheless, the court convicted him but decided that the absence of direct evidence was a mitigating factor in his favour and thereby ordered a reduced sentence.

Retrospective application of Section 113-A
The Supreme court delivered a landmark decision in Gurbachan Singh v/s Satpal Singh[9] which made the application of Section 113-B retrospective. It surmises that the provisions of this Section do not create an offence and since no new offence is created, it is merely a matter of procedure of evidence and hence it may be made retrospective.

Dying declaration in dowry death cases
A dying declaration or a statement is made by a person who after making the statement dies. Such a statement is an exception to the general rule that hearsay evidence is not admissible

evidence, unless such evidence is tested by cross-examination. Under Section 32 of the Evidence Act, when a statement is made by a person as to the cause of his death or as to any of the circumstances of the transaction which resulted in his death, in case wherein the cause of the death of that person comes into question, such a statement, oral or in writing, made by the deceased to the witness is a relevant fact and is admissible in evidence. Such a statement made by the deceased person is called the 'dying declaration', and falls in that category provided it has been made by the deceased while in a fit mental condition. A dying declaration, made by the person on the verge of death has a special sanctity to it, as at that moment a person is considered most unlikely to make an untrue statement. Therefore, a dying declaration has a sacrosanct status, as it is verbal testimony given by the deceased victim.

Tests to verify a dying declaration

Once the statement of the deceased victim and the evidence of the witnesses testifying to the same passes the test of careful scrutiny of the courts, it becomes an important piece of evidence and if the court is satisfied that the dying declaration is true and free from any embellishment, such a dying declaration, by itself, can be the basis for recording a conviction even without looking for corroboration. If there are more than one dying declarations then the court must scrutinize all of them to find out if each one of them passes the test of being trustworthy. They must be consistent on the material particulars before the court can accept and rely upon the same.

Reiterating the same view, the court in Kamla v/s State of Punjab,[10] pointed out that in the case of differing dying declarations, the irresistible conclusion is that the court cannot pick out any one of the dying declarations and base a conviction on the one the court prefers. The general principle[11] behind basing a conviction for a dowry death is that the court must establish that the dying declaration is reliable and that it does not contain inconsistencies. If there are inconsistencies, the court must re-examine the case history and attempt to identify corroborating evidence that supports the prosecution case to sustain the crime of dowry death would render the dowry death acceptable.

Non-verbal dying declaration

In addition to the admission of dying declarations as a form of corroborative evidence, the Supreme Court went a step further in Meesla Rama Krishna v/s State of Andhra Pradesh,[12] where it said that a dowry death recorded on the basis of nods and gestures is not only admissible but also possesses evidentiary value to the extent that the recorder can ensure that the victim can clearly understand the questions.

Oral versus written dying declarations

In State (Delhi Administration) v/s Laxman Kumar[13] the court while rejecting the written dying declaration held that it did not attach full credence to the oral dying declarations. There have been instances where conviction has been based solely upon a written dying declaration when it has been found to be totally acceptable. We are not prepared to attach that type of importance to the oral dying declarations in this case. However, the court held that the oral dying declarations would be available for use as corroborative material in this case. The court emphatically pointed out that though it would not have been prepared to base the conviction on the oral dying declarations alone, such dying declarations were not to be totally rejected and the same can be used as corroborative material.

Stumbling blocks in the prosecution case

In State v/s Rajrani and others, the deceased Meena Kumari burnt herself alive to escape the daily torture she endured at the hands of her in-laws, viz. her mother-in-law, sisters-in-law and her husband. Charges under Sections 304-B and 498-A were framed. The trial court acquitted all the accused even from the charge of Section 498-A though there was ample evidence to find a conviction on the basis of the evidence led in at the time of the trial of the sister-in-law. Non application of mind and improper appreciation of evidence led to the acquittal of the accused persons. There was cruelty and the deceased was driven to commit suicide and therefore, there should at least have been a conviction of the sister-in-law under Section 498-A of the IPC.

Implementational break-downs

The offenders in dowry related cases do not see themselves as guilty people, nor do the public perceive their conduct as criminal like in other offences. Dowry death cases are not treated with the seriousness that is required of the state and its enforcement agencies.

In one of WARLAW cases, which is currently sub judice, the Sessions Court took eight years just to frame a charge against the accused persons. Over three judges were transferred in the course of the hearing, thus prolonging the pendency of the case. In the particular case, it was quite evident that the investigating authorities were not impartial in their investigation. The charge has however, been framed against all the three accused, viz. the mother-in-law, father-in-law and husband under Sections 304-B and 498-A of the IPC.

The law enforcement agency's callous attitude can be best illustrated in Lichhammadevi v/s State of Rajasthan[14]. The deceased had strained relations with her in-laws on account of unsatisfied dowry demands. The appellant mother-in-law was charged with having poured kerosene on her daughter-in-law and setting her aflame. During investigation she stated that her son, husband of the deceased, might have burnt the daughter-in-law. He was also seen running down the staircase by the neighbours. Yet, the police chose not to prosecute him. The husband of the deceased, who was a passive spectator, did not bother to arrange for blood for his dying wife, and was not charge-sheeted for abetment for murder. The trial court acquitted the mother-in-law. The High Court reversed the verdict to one of death penalty. The Supreme Court, while deprecating the indifferent attitude of the investigating agency in not prosecuting the husband and the brother-in-law of the deceased, reduced the High Court's sentence to that of life imprisonment cautioning that judicial decisions should not be swayed by anger or emotions. Police, judiciary and public responses are not always conducive in delivering justice to the victim.

Role of bail

Another stumbling block in this whole process is the role of bail. The Sessions Court and the High Courts continually grant bail in cases of domestic violence and dowry deaths despite the Supreme Court's repeated pleas of caution. In Samundar Singh v/s State of Rajasthan[15], the Supreme Court held that the High Court should not have exercised its jurisdiction to release the accused on anticipatory bail in the matter concerning the death of the daughter-in-law in the matrimonial home.

In Amarnath Gupta v/s State of Madhya Pradesh,[16] the High Court's order granting bail to the accused was reversed by the Supreme Court. The High Court granted bail on the ground that the victim's diary contained a letter written by her stating the nobody was to be blamed for her suicide; and further, the High Court felt that since the father-in-law was an advocate there was nothing on record to show that they would misuse the liberty granted to them. The Supreme Court, while reversing the High Court's decision, observed that "sentimentalism has no place in judicial process and yet sensitivity to a social problem and commitment to a constitutional mission is a virtue it has sustained so far".

In the recent macabre Naina Sahni murder case that took place in the central part of Delhi on the night of 2nd July, 1995, the accused, Sushil Sharma, the husband of the deceased Naina, was granted anticipatory bail in a far away southern state by the Principal Sessions Judge in Madras. The High Court cancelled the anticipatory bail *suo moto* and severely criticized the callous and casual response of the Principal Sessions Judge in having granted anticipatory bail without application of mind.

Concluding remarks

An attempt has been made not only to review the entire ambit relating to dowry laws and the judicial attitudes surrounding it, but also to determine the social realities faced in the handling of these cases.

In the final analysis, the most crucial element of a dowry death case is a woman's inability to effectively resist her in-laws' demands and, if necessary, to leave a marriage which causes her humiliation. In Indian society, there is a culture of silence that reinforces an oppressive pressure to keep the marriage going at all costs. This effectively keeps women in abusive homes. Hence, dowry and the increasing demands related to it, are not the sole exterminators of women in this country. Instead, it is the unjust social pressure placed on women to stay in abusive, unwelcome homes when their lives are clearly in danger.

Another disturbing trend is the urgency with which the husband gets married to another woman, after the unnatural death of his first wife. Almost invariably, this happens while the husband is on bail. In the famous Sudha Goel case,[17] the husband, while out on bail, married again and even had two children before he went into jail to complete a term for life. The mother-in-law, when asked whether the second wife had got any dowry with her, said that she was satisfied with the dowry. What is terrifying in this scenario is the calm acceptance by the second family of a man who is charged with the murder of his first wife, and the willingness with which the bride's parents marry her off to him.

Keeping in mind the social realities, it is only pragmatic to assume that the dowry system will be with us for quite some time to come; people will continue to give and take dowry regardless of statutes purporting to prohibit such transactions. But by strengthening the provisions prohibiting the demand for dowry, particularly those made after the marriage, and by concentrating on the property that passes at the time of these transactions, it should be possible to ensure that the property goes to the woman and unequivocally remains with her. Increasing the economic independence and the power of women by putting her in control of the property that passes in dowry transactions will improve the bride's bargaining power and status in her matrimonial home.

It is imperative that the right interpretations be given to the provisions of criminal laws relating to violence against women in the context of specific facts and circumstances. Male oriented interpretations which lack feminist insights and perceptions can lead to increase in dowry deaths. A recent Bombay High Court judgment stated that it is not every harassment or every type of cruelty that could attract Section 498-A and that it must be established that the beating or harassment was with a view to force the wife to commit suicide or to fulfil the illegal demands of the husband or the in-laws. In another case, the same High Court held that occasional cruelty and harassment cannot be construed as cruelty under Section 498-A. In this case the deceased was burnt to death when the husband was present in the house. There had been several demands for dowry. When the deceased had given birth to a daughter she was left behind at her parents' house and her in-laws refused to accept the new-born daughter. Despite these facts the Bombay High Court came to the above decision.

Given the limits of criminal law, the future of dowry laws necessarily depends on community action, public legal education and sensitizing all levels of the implementation agencies.

Perhaps the most important aspect of combating violence against women in our society is providing equal education and increasing economic opportunities for them and encouraging women to expose atrocities against them.

Voluntary organisations have a crucial role to play as they have the experience and strategic capacity to provide victimized women with the support services needed to pursue legal action. Furthermore, meaningful programmes of legal services to enforce dowry laws should include Dowry Prohibition Officers to serve as agents in organizing legal action in collaboration with the women's organizations and in further developing the family courts as a judicial system for gender justice.

Notes

1. Substituted by Act 43 of 1986.
2. Substituted by Act 63 of 1984 (w.e.f. 2.10.1985)
3. 1992 (2) SCC 474.
4. 1991 (1) SCC 271.
5. 1989 Crl. L.J. 2330.
6. Shanti vs. State of Haryana, 1981 Crl. L.J. 2330.
7. 1992 SCC 212.
8. 1994 (6) SCC 727.
9. AIR 1990 S.C. 209.
10. 1993 (1) SCC pg. 1.
11. Shakuntala vs. State of Punjab, 1994, SCC 1781.
12. 1994 (4) SCC 182.
13. AIR 1986 S.C. 250.
14. AIR 1988, S.C. 1785.
15. 1989 Crl. L.J. 705.
16. 1990 Crl. L.J. 2163.
17. Infra, see No. 13.

Excerpted from Rani Jethmalani (ed.) *Kali's Yug: Empowerment, Law and Dowry Deaths*, New Delhi: Har-Anand Publications, 1995.

Section II

A Field of One's Own
Gender and Land Rights in South Asia

BINA AGARWAL

The backdrop

Two decades ago, the question: 'Do women need independent rights in land?' was not even admitted in public policy discourse in most parts of South Asia. Today, the question is admissible, but the discussion on it is limited and the answers to it disputed. Indeed gaining acceptance for the *idea* that women need independent rights in land is itself an arena of struggle, an essential first step in the struggle to translate that need into effective rights in practice.[1]

To begin with, to argue that women's economic needs require a specific focus, distinct from those of men, is to challenge a long-standing assumption in economic theory and development policy, namely, that the household is a unit of congruent interests, among whose members the benefits of available resources are shared equitably, irrespective of gender. This assumption has (until recently) been shared widely by governmental and non-governmental groups, institutions, and individuals. To go further and argue that women need independent rights in *land*—the most critical form of property in agrarian economies—is to challenge the assumption that women's economic needs can be accommodated adequately merely through the employment and other income-generating schemes that typify development planning. It means admitting new contenders for a share in a scarce and highly valuable resource which determines economic well-being and shapes power relations, especially in the countryside; and it means extending the conflict over land that has existed largely be-tween men, to men *and* women, thus bringing it into the family's innermost courtyard.

The process by which the assumption of a unitary house-hold, and more generally of the gender-neutrality of develop-ment, has come to be challenged over the past twenty years is a complex one, which will not be detailed here. What is notable is that it has been a process of negotiation and struggle involv-ing multiple actors—academics and researchers, women's ac-tivist groups, government policy makers and bureaucrats, and international agencies. It was set in motion by at least three interrelated factors: the building up of gender-specific empiri-cal evidence and analysis, especially since the mid-1970s, which exposed a systematic gender gap in how the benefits and bur-dens of development were being distributed; the mushroom-ing of women's organizations loosely constituting a women's movement, since the late 1970s; and changes in the interna-tional context. This last included, in particular, the declara-tion of 1975–85 as the United Nations (UN) Decade for Women, with associated fall-outs in terms of research funding and dissemination, media coverage, and pressure on countries to generate gender-specific data and status of women reports.[2] Indirectly, feminist scholarship and activism in the West were also facilitating factors in promoting the issue internationally.

Today, as a result, the idea that development is not gender-neutral has gained fairly wide acceptance in development en-quiry and policy, even though there is no consensus on the causes of the gender gap or on how it could be bridged. At the level of policy, this recognition of gender disadvantage has been reflected particularly in three types of developments:
- the establishment of separate cells, departments or ministries in government bureaucracies to monitor and coordinate women's concerns in the development process;
- the incorporation of policy directives on women and development in the planning process, as in the Indian

Sixth Five Year Plan, 1980–85 (for the first time in the history of planning in India), with subsequent plans following suit; and
— the initiation of special programmes targeted at women, especially income-generating and literacy schemes.

However, the approach underlying these directives and programmes treats gender as an *additive* category, to be added onto existing ones, with women as a special focus or target group, rather than seeing gender as a lens through which the approach to development should itself be re-examined. The programmes are essentially couched in welfare terms, under the umbrella of the 'basic needs' approach that gained currency in development thinking in the mid-1970s. This approach emphasizes the provision of 'basic' goods and services (such as food, health care, education) to the economically disadvantaged, but usually without seriously questioning the existing distribution of productive resources and political power, or the social (gender/class/caste) division of labour. Most governments typically deliver such programmes in a top-down manner, involving little dialogue with the people (especially women) themselves on the definition of their needs or the best means of meeting those needs.

In this scenario, the issue of women's land rights has, until recently, received little attention in policy formulation. In India, the numerous committees and working groups on the status of women that met between 1975 and 1979, focused almost exclusively on three elements: employment, education and health.[3] It is only in the Sixth Five Year Plan (1980-85) that we see the first limited recognition of women's need for land (and then only in the context of poverty). Several factors appear to have contributed to this recognition. In 1979, at a women's conference in Calcutta, a group of elected women *gram panchayat* (village council) representatives from West Bengal put forward a demand for joint titles (with their husbands) on behalf of destitute Muslim women in their constituencies. They argued that many Muslim women had been evicted by their husbands; women therefore needed the economic security that land provides. This is said to be among the earliest such public grassroots demands. A similar plea was made by landless women in 1980 to a sympathetic Land Reform Commissioner at a camp in West Bengal's Bankura district.[4] Such demands were subsequently included in the recommendations (placed before the Planning Commission) of a pre-Plan symposium organized by eight women's groups in Delhi in 1980.[5] Additional pressure came from the 1979 FAO Report of the World Conference on Agrarian Reform and Rural Development (WCARRD) held in Rome, which recommended that gender discriminatory laws in respect to 'rights in inheritance, ownership and control of property' be repealed and measures be adopted to ensure that women get equitable access to land and other productive resources (FAO 1979). These recommendations were incorporated (albeit in very diluted form) in the country review follow-up to WCARRD undertaken by the Indian Ministry of Agriculture and Rural Development (CWDS 1985: 89–94). The result of all this was a policy statement which, as finally incorporated in the Sixth Plan (in a separate chapter on women and development), said that the government would 'endeavour' to give joint titles to spouses in programmes involving the distribution of land and home sites.

However, even this limited formulation, which stops short of granting women independent titles, remained only a promise on paper. In practice, government land-redistribution programmes continued to reflect the old assumption of a unitary male-headed household, and titles were granted principally to men. In India's Seventh Plan (1985–90), although a separate chapter on women and development was retained, the directive on joint titles was not restated, despite strong recommendations for entitling women by a governmental working group on women and development, during the plan-formulation stage.[6] Meanwhile, the *National Perspective Plan For Women: 1988–2000*, drawn up at the initiative of the Indian Ministry of Human Resource Development, made a number of substantive recommendations for closing the gender gap in access to land, amongst other gender issues needing attention (GOI 1988a). And the report of a National Seminar on Land Reform called by the Planning Commission in 1989, in which I had presented the case for women's land rights, incorporated most of my recommendations on this count (GOI 1989a).[7]

Reports, however, have a tendency to gather dust, their contents forgotten. It is in this context that the passing of the National Commission for Women Act, 1990, is an important step forward. The result of many years of sustained efforts by women's organizations and gender-progressive individuals, this Act has created a Commission with a wide mandate to investigate and monitor 'all matters relating to the safeguards provided for women under the constitution and other laws' (GOI 1990a: 4). In particular, it is mandatory on the government to place any recommendations made by the Commission before both houses of Parliament (or, where relevant, before the state legislatures), along with a memorandum of actions taken or proposed to be taken by the government, and to give reasons in cases of non-acceptance of such recommendations.[8] Of course, it remains to be seen what issues the Commission will focus on, and how much weight will be given by the government to its recommendations.

Certainly, the recently formulated Eighth Five Year Plan (1992–97) for India has left much of the responsibility for monitoring gender-related issues (including keeping tabs on the enforcement of social legislation), on the National Commission for Women, and on women's groups; the appointment of a National Commissioner of Women's Rights is also proposed (GOI 1992a-b). This Plan document (unlike the Sixth and Seventh Plans) does not have a separate chapter on women and development, but subsumes women's concerns largely under the chapter on social welfare (which also deals with children, the disabled, the elderly, and the destitute), and these concerns are couched essentially in the language of women as victims, rather than women also as agents of change and contributors to development.[9] The Plan makes two specific points in relation to women and agricultural land: one, it recognizes that 'one of the basic requirements for improving the status of women' is to change inheritance laws so that women get an equal share in parental property, inherited or self-acquired (GOI 1992b: 392). However, it does not lay down any specific directives to ensure that this is followed through.[10] Two, and this is the only concrete policy directive, state governments have been asked to allot 40 per cent of surplus land (i.e. land acquired by the government from households owning land more than the specified ceilings) to women alone, and to allot the rest jointly in the names of the husband and wife (GOI 1992b: 34). This sounds good until one recognizes how little land is involved: only 1.04 million hectares (mha) remain to be distributed (GOI 1992b: 34). This constitutes just 0.56 per cent of the country's arable land.[11]

In other words, the process of incorporating the issue of women and land into public policy in India has been extremely slow, involving negotiations between the government, women's groups, individual women academics, and international agencies, as well as between different elements within the government. And today, despite the noted progress, it remains an issue of marginal, not central, concern.

The situation in other South Asian countries is even more discouraging. Nepal's Eighth Five Year Plan (1992–97) Summary highlights women's employment and the need to encourage their participation in various activities, but contains no reference to women's need for land.[12] In Bangladesh, the latest Fourth Five Year Plan (1990–95) contains two special chapters on women and development, and some others incorporate women's concerns (Government of Bangladesh [GOB] 1990). But the emphasis throughout is on issues such as female employment, literacy, health, nutrition and credit; there is no mention of land for women, not even in terms of government allocations for poor women.[13] Similarly, although Pakistan's *Report of the Working Group on Women's Development Program for the Sixth Plan* (1983–88) recommended that all land distributed under the land reform programme should be registered jointly in the names of both spouses, this recommendation was not incorporated into the formal plan document. And Pakistan's Eighth Five Year Plan (1993–98) Approach Paper, in its chapter on 'Affirmative Action for Women and other Disadvantaged Groups' promises women preferential treatment in education and employment, but does not mention implementing their property rights. It also casts gender relations in traditional terms, with the State explicitly undertaking to 'protect the marriage, the family, the mother and the child' and to forego any approaches 'which (could) antagonise male members of the community ...' (Government of Pakistan 1991a: 22, 24).

What is especially striking is the disjunction between public policy formulation and the rights encased in personal law. The idea of women having independent property rights (including rights in land) was accepted by most South Asian countries in laws governing the inheritance of personal property in the 1950s (and even earlier in traditionally bilateral and matrilineal communities).[14] But such acceptance remained confined to inheritance laws that affect private land; in development policy governing the distribution of public land, the issue of women's land rights was not discussed (as we've noted) till the 1980s. Hence the redistributive land reform programmes of the 1950s and 1960s in India, Pakistan, and Sri Lanka, and of the 1970s in Bangladesh, continued to be modelled on the notion of a unitary male-headed household, with titles being granted only to men, except in households without adult men where women (typically widows) were clearly the heads. This bias was replicated again in resettlement schemes, even in Sri Lanka where customary inheritance systems have been bilateral or matrilineal.

Underlying this disjunction between government policy in relation to public land distribution and the rights in private land granted to women under inheritance laws are likely to be a complex set of factors. These would include the continued assumption in most public policies of gender congruence in interests within the family; the dominant view that men are the breadwinners and women the dependents; strong male vested interests in all land, including public land; gaps between the central government's policy directives and the shape these are given at the state/province level;[15] and the belief that land distribution to women will further decrease farm size and fragment cultivated holdings, in turn reducing agricultural productivity. The farm size and fragmentation arguments have also been used in many Indian states to undercut post-independence, gender-progressive personal laws,[16] by retaining age-old customary laws that disadvantage women in relation to agricultural land. The weaknesses in these arguments will be discussed later in this chapter. Here it suffices to reiterate the limited progress made in public policy towards entitling women with land and the ambiguities that continue to surround even the idea of doing so.

A similar ambiguity toward this issue is found among groups which have otherwise been strong advocates of redistributive land reform, namely Marxist political parties and left-wing non-party organizations, most of whom still see class issues as primary and gender concerns as divisive and distracting.[17] At the same time, most women's organizations (whatever their political persuasion), with some recent exceptions, have been preoccupied with employment and non-land-related income-generating schemes as *the* means of improving women's economic status and welfare, paying little attention to the issue of property rights.[18] Several years ago, when I began research on this subject and raised the question of women's land rights with a number of left-wing women's groups across South Asia, the responses of most were either that 'we haven't really thought about it', or that advocating individual property rights went against their vision of a socialist society. Yet, to my knowledge, this latter argument has not been used in South Asia against redistributive land reform or peasant struggles through which (typically male) heads of landless households gain rights in land.[19]

This neglect of women's land-related concerns by both governmental and non-governmental institutions mirrors a parallel gap within academic scholarship, where the relationship between women and property has remained virtually unattended and little theorized. For instance, the social science literature on rural South Asia of relevance to this discussion falls broadly into three categories. First, a vast body of economic development and political science studies document a strong interdependence between the rural household's possession of agricultural land and its relative economic, political and social position. Characteristically, these studies focus on the household as the unit of analysis, neglecting the intrahousehold gender dimension.

Household property and women's property

... The links between gender subordination and property need to be sought in not only the distribution of property between households but also in its distribution between men and women, in not only who owns the property but also who controls it, and in relation not only to private property but also to communal property. Further, gender equality in legal rights to own property does not guarantee gender equality in actual ownership, nor does ownership guarantee control. The distinctions between law and practice and between ownership and control are especially critical in the context of gender: for most South Asian women there are significant barriers to realizing their legal claims in landed property, as well as to exercising control over any land they do get ...

This formulation departs significantly from standard Marxist analysis, particularly from Engels' still-influential, though much-criticized, *The Origin of the Family, Private Property and the State,* where intra-family gender relations are seen as structured primarily by two overlapping economic factors: the property status of the households to which the women belong, and women's participation in wage labour. Engels argued that in capitalist societies, gender relations would be hierarchical among the property-owning families of the bourgeoisie where women did not go out to work and were economically dependent on men, and egalitarian in propertyless proletarian families where women were in the labour force. The ultimate restoration of women to their rightful status, in his view, required the total abolition of private property (i.e. a move to socialism), the socialization of housework and childcare, and the full participation of women in the labour force. In the context of industrializing Europe, Engels (1972: 137-8) argued: 'the first premise for the emancipation of women is the re-introduction of the entire female sex into public industry'.[20]

In his analysis, therefore, the presumed equality of gender relations in a working class family rested on *both* husband and wife being propertyless and in the labour force, and the inequality in the bourgeois family rested on men being propertied and women being both propertyless and outside the labour force. This underlying emphasis on the *relational* aspect of gender is clearly important. So is the emphasis on women's economic dependency as a critical constituent of the material bases of gender oppression. However, by advocating the abolition of all private property as the solution, Engels by-passed the issue of women's property rights altogether, and left open the question: what would be the impact on gender relations in propertied households if the women too were propertied as individuals? Entry into the labour force is not the only way to reduce economic dependency; independent rights in property would be another, and possibly the more effective way.

Engels' emphasis on women's entry into the labour force as a necessary condition for their emancipation has been enormously influential in shaping the thinking of left-wing political parties and non-party groups, including left-wing women's groups in South Asia.[21] As noted, they too give centrality to women's employment, but the necessary accompaniments emphasized by Engels, namely the abolition of private property in male hands and the socialization of housework and childcare, have largely been neglected, as has the question of women's property rights.

In my argument that independent property rights can play a pivotal role in women's struggle for equality in gender relations, a critical additional point (missed out in Engels' analysis and associated discussions) that needs emphasis is that of property *control*. Property advantage stems not only from ownership, but also from effective control over it. In societies which underwent socialist revolutions, while private property ownership was legally abolished, control over wealth-generating property remained predominantly with men; any positive effects on gender relations that could have stemmed from the change in ownership if accompanied by gender-egalitarian mechanisms of control, thus went unrealized.[22] Indeed in most societies today it is men *as a gender* (even if not all men as individuals) who largely control wealth-generating property, whether or not it is privately owned, including as managers in large corporations. Even property that is under State, community, or clan ownership remains effectively under the managerial control of selected men through their dominance in both traditional and modern institutions: caste or clan councils, village elected bodies, State bureaucracies at all levels,[23] and so on. Also in most countries, men as a gender exercise dominance over the instruments through which their existing advantages of property ownership and control get perpetuated, such as the institutions that enact and implement laws,[24] the mechanisms of recruitment into bodies which exercise control over property (private or public), the institutions which play an important role in shaping gender ideology, and so on.

A second issue which arises in exploring the relationship between gender and property is: how do we define a woman's class? Marxist analysis, for instance, implicitly assumes that women belong to the class of their husbands or fathers. Hence women of propertied 'bourgeois' households are part of the bourgeoisie and women of proletarian households are counted as proletarian, although they may also have a proletarian status by virtue of being workers themselves. However, as is now well-recognized in feminist literature, this characterization is problematic in at least two respects: (a) A woman's class position defined through that of a man—father, husband, etc.—is more open to change than that of a man: a well placed marriage can raise it, divorce or widowhood can lower it. As Millett (1970: 38) notes: 'Economic dependency renders (women's) affiliations with any class a tangential, vicarious, and temporary matter', (b) To the extent that women, even of propertied households, do not own property themselves, it is difficult to characterize their class position;[25] some have even argued that women constitute a class in themselves.[26]

In fact, neither deriving women's class from the property status of men nor deriving it from their own propertyless status appears adequate, although both positions reflect a dimension of reality. Women of large landed households in South Asia do gain from their husbands' class positions in terms of their overall living standards, their typically lower work burdens, the social status and influence they can command in relation to other village women, and so on. Hence property mediates relationships not only between men and women but also between women. At the same time, there are significant commonalities between women which cut across derived class privilege (or deprivation), such as vulnerability to domestic violence; all women's responsibility for housework and childcare (even if not all women are obliged to perform such labour themselves—the more affluent ones can hire helpers); gender inequalities in legal rights; and the risks of marital breakdown due to which even women of rich peasant households can be left destitute and forced to seek wage work, reflecting their propertyless state and economic vulnerability *as women*. In other words there is an ambiguous character to women's class position.

This complexity impinges with critical force on the possibilities of collective action among women, again in a double-edged way. Class differences among women, derived through men, can be and often are divisive in terms of relative economic privilege or deprivation, the associated ability (or lack of ability) to dominate women's groups,[27] perceptions about which aspects of gender relations need challenging, willingness to engage in collective struggle, and so on. At the same time, the noted commonalities between women's situations and the relatively vicarious character of their class privilege make class distinctions between them less sharp and divisive than those among men, and could provide the basis for collective action on several counts.[28]

A third significant aspect of the relationship between gender and property concerns the links between gender *ideology* and property. Several types of interconnections impinge on our discussion, such as those outlined below:

(a) Gender ideologies can obstruct women from getting property rights. For instance, ideological assumptions about women's needs, work roles, capabilities, and so on, impinge on the framing and implementation of public policies and laws relating to property (as noted earlier). Again, ideas about gender underlie practices such as female seclusion, control of women's mobility and sexual freedom, and so on. These ideologies and associated practices restrict women's ability both to exercise their existing property claims and to successfully challenge persisting gender-inequalities in law, policy, and practice in relation to such claims. Hence ideological struggles are integrally linked to women's struggles over property rights.

(b) How property ownership and/or control is socially distributed can significantly affect ideological constructions, including those of gender. Those who own and/or control wealth-generating property can exercise considerable direct or indirect control over the principal institutions that shape ideology, such as educational and religious establishments and the media (defined broadly to include newspapers, TV, radio, film, theatre, as well as literature and the arts). These can be instrumental in shaping views in either gender-progressive or gender ret-rogressive directions. But to the extent that such institu-tions represent a plurality of views, there are possibili-ties of contestation over ideological constructions through them.

(c) The impact of gender ideologies on women can vary according to their households' property status (other sources of ideological variation such as religion, caste, etc., being held constant). This variation could result from two points of difference between propertied and propertyless households: in what ideas about gender are dominant, and in how these ideas are put into practice. For instance, in both propertied and propertyless house-holds the ideology of female seclusion may be espoused, but the former group would be in a better economic position to enforce its practice, and in so doing rein-force its emulation by unpropertied households as a mark of social status. But would there also be differences in the ideologies espoused within propertied and propertyless households? Over the years there has been considerable debate on the degree to which ideological constructions of gender are autonomous of economic circumstances (excellently summarized in Barrett 1980). The view I take ... is that gender ideologies and associ-ated practices are culturally specific, historically variable, and dialectically linked to property ownership and con-trol. The form and practice of gender ideologies can dif-fer among propertied and unpropertied households; at the same time, gender ideologies and associated prac-tices are not derived from property differences alone, nor can they be seen in purely economic-functional terms. Rather they would tend to shift and change *in interaction with* economic shifts.[29]

A fourth issue that arises in relation to women and property is the possible link of women's property rights with control over women's sexuality, marriage practices, and kinship structures. Engels argued, for instance, that in propertied households the need to ensure the legitimacy of heirs would necessitate strict control over women's sexuality within marriage and provide the logic for monogamy, while such control would be unnecessary in propertyless families. That is, he saw the exercise of control over women's sexuality in essentially economic-functional terms. The observed emphasis on monogamy and male supremacy over women even in European working class families and under socialism, that is even when the presumed material necessity for that control was absent, has been widely used to criticize Engels' formulation.[30] But his argument raises another question: would women with independent rights in property (a category of person which, as noted earlier, he did not consider) be subject to greater or lesser familial control than those without them? Goody (1976) argues the former; he proposes that in societies which recognize women's inheritance rights in parental property, in order to keep the property intact and within their purview, families or kin-networks would tend to emphasize and ensure women's pre-marital virginity, and control women's choice of marriage partners and post-marital residence. ... The relationships themselves are, however, significant ones to explore ...

Notes

1. 'Independent' land rights are defined here as rights that are formally untied to male ownership or control, in other words, excluding joint titles with men. By effective rights in land I mean not just rights in law but also their effective realization in practice, as elaborated later in this chapter.

2. Documents (Reports, Action Plans, etc.) from various international and national Conferences, Symposia and Working Groups, that met during 1975–85 to focus on rural women, provide interesting insights into the changing nature of concerns over this period. For a selected compilation of such documents (international, and those relating to

India), see CWDS (1985). The Report, *Towards Equality*, on the status of women in India, was also a significant landmark (Government of India [GOI] 1974). Brought out by a Committee set up by the Indian Ministry of Education and Social Welfare, the Report compiled evidence of gender gaps in virtually every sector and made recommendations on how to bridge them. The issue of women's land rights, however, was not raised in the Report, although it included a discussion on gender inequalities in inheritance laws. On the role of international aid agencies in pushing the gender question, see especially White (1992) for Bangladesh. In India, I understand, international organizations such as the UN Food and Agricultural Organization (FAO) played an important role in pushing the government to set up review committees on rural women, such as the 1979 National Committee to Review and Analyse Participation of Women in Agriculture and Rural Development, set up by the Ministry of Agriculture (personal communication, Vina Mazumdar, 1992).

3 See various Indian documents compiled in CWDS (1985).

4 Both incidents were related to me in 1992 by Vina Mazumdar.

5 The group brought out a memorandum entitled: 'Indian Women in the Eighties: Development Imperatives' (CWDS 1985: 95–8). The gender-sensitive response of some State planners in authoritative positions within the Planning Commission was of critical importance in ensuring that such recommendations were taken seriously.

6 This group, set up by the Department of Social Welfare, Government of India, made four recommendations concerning women and land: that land and other property be registered in revenue records in the joint names of both spouses; that single women be given preference in land distribution by the government; that all property acquired after marriage be in the names of both spouses; and that loopholes in the Hindu Succession Act of 1956 be plugged (GOI 1983a).

7 These recommendations were based on some initial research I had done on the subject in 1985–86, and published in 1988 in a widely circulated paper (Agarwal 1988) which had previously been presented in several academic and other forums, within and outside India.

8 For further details on the Act and on how the National Commission for Women came to be set up, see *Women's Equality* (1992).

9 In contrast, although the Sixth and Seventh Plans also mentioned women's concerns in their chapters on social welfare, it was their separate chapters dealing with women's programmes which outlined the primary thrust of policy in this regard; and these were framed much more in the language of equality and rights, and recognized women's productive contribution to the economy. Of course, in these

documents, as noted, the issue of women's land rights received marginal (Sixth Plan) or no (Seventh Plan) attention.

10 Indeed, as will be seen in chapter 5, Indian women of most communities already have considerable *legal* rights of inheritance (although gender gaps remain on several counts). It is in the implementation of laws that action is especially necessary.

11 Taking the aggregate of net sown area, fallow land (current and other fallows), cultivable wasteland, and land under miscellaneous tree crops and groves, the country's arable land in 1987–88 was 184.73 million hectares (GOI 1992c). This tallies with the Ministry of Agriculture's method of estimating arable land.

12 The full Plan document has yet to be released.

13 In 1991, however, a Task Force set up by the Bangladesh Ministry of Planning to review the country's development strategies made a modest recommendation that female heads of households, with or without adult sons, and women in households with incapacitated male heads, be given priority in the distribution of government land (see *Report of the Task Force on Bangladesh Development Strategies for the 1990s* (1991)). At present, the Report notes, under the conditions laid down by the Bangladesh Land Ministry in 1987 for the distribution of government land to the landless, women can be given priority only if they are widowed or abandoned and have an adult son who is able to work. It remains to be seen whether the Task Force recommendations will be acted on.

14 Bilateral inheritance: ancestral property passes to and through both sons and daughters; matrilineal inheritance: ancestral property passes through the female line; patrilineal inheritance: ancestral property passes through the male line. The specific, complex workings of such inheritance systems in South Asia will be discussed in later chapters. The terms 'matrilineal', 'bilateral', and 'patrilineal' will be used throughout the book (unless otherwise specified) to relate to *inheritance* practices, and not to those of descent. In any case, in all the communities referred to in the book, those following anyone of these inheritance systems also practised the same type of descent system, with the exception of the Nangudi Vellalars who practised matrilineal descent and bilateral inheritance.

15 In India, the term 'state' relates to administrative divisions within the country and is not to be confused with 'State', used throughout the book in the political economy sense of the word. In Pakistan and Sri Lanka these administrative divisions are termed provinces.

16 The term 'gender-progressive', as used here and subsequently, relates to those laws, practices, policies, etc., which reduce or eliminate the

inequities (economic, social, political) that women face in relation to men. Individuals and organizations that work toward this end are also so described. 'Gender-retrogressive' has the opposite meaning.

17 It is noteworthy that in West Bengal when the CPI(M) (Communist Party of India (Marxist)) government carried out 'Operation Barga' (launched in 1978), a major land reform initiative which sought to provide tenants with security of tenure by systematically registering them, primarily men were registered. A similar male bias has characterized the programmes of most left-wing non-party groups, among the notable exceptions being the Bodhgaya (Bihar) peasant movement initiated in 1978 by the Chatra Yuva Sangharsh Vahini, a Gandhian-socialist youth organization which also took up the issue of women's land rights (see chapter 9 for details).

18 Among the exceptions is the Shetkari Sanghatana's Mahila Aghadi, the women's front of the Shetkari Sanghatana—a farmers' organization founded in Maharashtra (west India) in 1980 (see chapter 9 for details). Also noteworthy is the role played by *Manushi* (a women's journal from India) in reporting such initiatives, and by one of the journal's founders, Madhu Kishwar, who in 1982 filed a petition in the Supreme Court of India challenging the denial of land rights to Ho tribal women in Bihar (see Kishwar 1982, 1987).

19 Joshi (1974) who explains the background to the formulation of land reform programmes in post-independence India and Pakistan, makes no mention of any resistance to redistributive reform on these grounds. Rather he notes (1974: 167): 'The fundamental question of land policy was the question of removing (the) discrepancy between ownership of land and its actual cultivation'; ownership being largely concentrated in the hands of a minority of landlords and cultivation being done by peasants with usually limited or no proprietary rights. However, in a personal communication to me in 1992, Joshi added that a minute section of the left did express unease about measures that could strengthen individualistic tendencies among the peasantry, but this was not a widely shared concern: the preoccupation of most was with the need to break the stranglehold of 'feudal' elements.

What *was* discussed widely, though, both by the Planning Commission and various political parties, was the need to encourage (largely voluntary) cooperation among the peasantry in various forms, including joint cultivation, the joint ownership of non-land assets, cooperative marketing and distribution, etc. (On this debate and the limited success of efforts in this direction, also see Frankel 1978.)

20 This is not meant as a summary of Engels' complex thesis, but merely of one part of his argument. Critiques of different aspects of Engels'

analysis abound: see especially, Sacks (1975), Reiter (1977), Aaby (1977), Barrett (1980, 1985), Coward (1983), MacKinnon (1989). Delmar (1976), Molyneux (1981), and various articles in Sayers *et al.* eds. (1987). In particular, Engels' assumption that gender relations within propertyless groups such as the industrial proletariat or under socialism would necessarily be egalitarian has been widely criticized in the literature: see especially, Delmar (1976), Molyneux (1981), and Barrett (1985).

21 Also see Molyneux (1981) who describes how in socialist countries (including whose which were socialist until recently), the influence of Engels' analysis led to a similar preoccupation with women's entry into employment as the major means of eliminating gender oppression. At the time of Molyneux's writing, although such entry had taken place in significant degree in most of these countries, the types of jobs women held were largely at the lower end of the job hierarchy; progress toward the socialization of housework was extremely limited; and the ideological basis of gender oppression (neglected by Engels) had persisted, in greater or lesser degree.

22 Women's representation in the top political and economic decision-making bodies in such countries remained minimal. For instance, in the late 1970s, in the USSR, Czechoslovakia, Poland, and Yugoslavia, of some 557 top government posts only 27 (that is under 5 per cent) were filled by women (Molyneux 1981).

23 See chapter 10 for figures and a further discussion on this.

24 Scandinavian countries have a better record than most others on this count: in Norway and Finland, for instance, women constituted 34 and 32 per cent of all elected and appointed members of national legislative bodies in 1985–87. This contrasts sharply with the analogous figures for India, Bangladesh, and Pakistan which ranged between 8 and 10, as well as with those for the USA and UK which were 5.3 and 6.3 respectively (United Nations 1990).

25 Also, property differences alone do not distinguish classes. Education, life-styles, and so on, count as well (see especially, Bourdieu 1984). Similarly a group of persons wielding power or authority, which may or may not stem from property ownership, may be seen to constitute a class. On the concept of class' within Marxist and non-Marxist literature, also see Wolff and Resnick (1989).

26 While several feminist authors have denied the significance of class divisions between women, they have done so from different standpoints. Millett (1970) did so because she saw women's class affiliations as basically impermanent. Firestone (1970) saw women as united by their biology; she substituted the term 'sex' for 'class' and categorized

women as a 'sex class' as opposed to an economic class. Delphy (1977), in a more sophisticated analysis, rooted the problematics of defining women by class in their not owning the means of production and their economic vulnerabilities with marital break-up, even when married to men from the capitalist class. She located the material basis of women's oppression in patriarchal exploitation which, she argued, cuts across classes. Also see the discussions in Barrett (1980) and MacKinnon (1989).

27 On this, see especially Dixon (1978: chapter 6) and Caplan (1985).

28 There are of course aspects of a person's identity other than class which also can be divisive or adhesive, such as caste, ethnicity, and religion.

29 For illustration, see the discussion on female seclusion in chapter 9.

30 Moreover, notions about 'legitimate heirs' vary widely across cultures and are not linked everywhere to monogamy or wedlock, even among propertied households (as will be discussed in chapter 3).

Excerpted from Bina Agarwal, *A Field of One's Own: Gender and Land Rights in South Asia*, Cambridge: Cambridge University Press, 1994.

Bringing Land Rights Centre-Stage

A review of *A Field of One's Own: Gender and Land Rights in South Asia**

INDU AGNIHOTRI

This book seeks to bring the issue of land rights for women centre-stage, arguing that women's struggle for ownership and control over land can prove to be the most critical instrument for women's empowerment in South Asia. In view of the fact that recognition of women's need to have independent rights in land is itself an arena of struggle, the author envisages that this itself would be as important as getting land rights. This underlying assumption in the book is based on information from the field and the knowledge that despite gender sensitive and progressive legislation, few women in South Asian countries actually inherit land and, even fewer, control it. Agarwal makes some effort to establish how, in fact, women do not inherit land, despite a widespread belief in India and elsewhere that laws have been changed to grant women 'equal' rights in property, including where they did not grant the same earlier.

In the case of India, the Committee on the Status of Women in India (CSWI) had well scrutinised such 'claims' of having attained equality both on legal grounds as well as through extensive data/field observations. Since then, the women's movement has, time and again, pointed to the serious gaps between constitutional guarantees of equality and the actual provisions as per prevailing laws. Activists have repeatedly drawn attention to the fact that there are serious lacunae in the entire

---

**A Field of One's Own: Gender and Land Rights in South Asia* by Bina Agarwal, Cambridge University Press, 1994.

gamut of succession, inheritance and adoption laws which curtail women's right to equal claims on property. What Agarwal does is a seminal job indeed, to record the lacunae specifically with regard to claims to agricultural land because that seems to be the archetypal 'patriarchal' domain. The continued resistance to conceding women's right to agricultural land seems to be the last bastion, so to say, with both the field and the furrow being strictly guarded as a male preserve (with due acknowledgements to Leela Dube, Rajni Palriwala and other social anthropologists who have repeatedly drawn attention to the link between land, caste, symbolism and gender relations).[1]

Agarwal argues that side-by-side with social groups which have traditionally denied women land rights, there exist those communities and groups which also have a regional/geographical identity, where under prevailing customary rights and associated practices, women's rights in land were definitely given greater recognition in earlier periods in history. These included tribal regions/communities (not necessarily defined or demarcated by religion) and those traditionally recorded to be matrilineal/bilateral. Many of these, such as the garos and nayars in India, and communities in Sri Lanka, have been witness to a fairly quick process of erosion and a change to the patrilineal norm. This is despite the fact that legally, in all five countries (India, Pakistan, Bangladesh, Sri Lanka and Nepal) most women are today supposed to enjoy significantly greater inheritance rights in land than they did earlier. The problem lies with the issue of succession. Some of the different kinds of identifiable gender inequalities being: (a) smaller shares than men; (b) restrictive conditions on women's legal entitlements: (c) restrictions on women's ability to dispose of what they might inherit; (d) continued usage of uncodified customary law, such as in the north-east, where among patrilineal tribes, women's rights in land are severely circumscribed and limited to usufruct; and (e) specific gender biases pertaining to agricultural land.

In the chapter on 'Customary Rights and Associated Practices', there is first a lengthy discussion on what would today be encompassed by the Hindu Code Bill, as well as Muslim personal law. Only later, the focus shifts to tribals as well as specific communities which have recognised women's right to inheritance in Sri Lanka and in south India. The practices are discussed in terms of how these affect gender relations and are in turn affected by structural conditionalities. This chapter could have been enriched by drawing on the more specific ongoing studies of customary law and practices in the fields of history and sociology which, being region-based, often cull out varied information from an array of folklore, proverbs, contemporary sources as well as field studies.

In subsequent chapters, Agarwal draws cross-regional comparisons in the different countries of South Asia to identify the gap between law and practice, and the bogus reality of a 'voluntary' giving up of claims. She does this at the level and in the context of real-life processes, marriage systems and post-marital residence, practices of seclusion and control over sexuality. The role of the state and its attitude reflected in the trends that emerge at the macro level with regard to female labour participation rates as well as fertility rates are also examined.

The book, in its central argument, makes a strong case for land rights for women. It takes stock of a changing reality where a whole new area of debate has opened up with mounting pressure from the women's movement for a focus on land rights—a question which two decades ago was not even admitted in public policy discourse in most parts of South Asia. Agarwal rightly points to the dysjunction between public policy formulation and the rights encased in personal law. She contests the continued assumption in public policy of gender congruence in interests within the family. This is arguably premised on strongly vested male interests and the belief that (a) men are the breadwinners and women the dependents and (b) land distribution to women will further decrease farm size and fragment cultivated holdings. The last aspect is countered on the basis of the farm size productivity debate in the wake of the Green Revolution which had convincingly argued that land redistribution from big to small farmers would increase agricultural output or, in any case, give no reason to expect a decline.

This has given rise to a contradictory situation where acceptance of women's entitlement is on the one hand recognised in inheritance laws affecting private land, while the issue is generally not even discussed in development policy governing the distribution of public land. Thus redistributive land reform programmes spreading over the last three or four decades in South Asia (marked by different phases/faces in each country), remained modelled on the notion of a unitary male-headed household, with women figuring as title holders only in a typical situation, e.g. widowhood, as visible in most British records of the colonial period. The bias was replicated even in resettlement schemes in Sri Lanka, a country where inheritance systems have been known to be bilateral or matrilineal.

While discussing the absence of a gendered focus in redistributive programmes Operation Barga in West Bengal is taken as a case in point, where primarily men were registered. While the criticism on grounds of non-registration of women is perfectly valid, the critique mounted of the Left certainly needs to take note of the issues involved, especially since the Left-inclined women were some of the most outspoken in demanding land rights for women. This resulted in an intense debate around the question of how the slogan of land to the tiller was to be effectively implemented and the central question related to the establishment of the identity of the tiller. Could it be said 'that women do not plough' in any circumstance and what is the economic cultural symbolic significance of the very crucial task of ploughing which women are really not supposed to engage in on account of social taboos? Can women be disqualified on this ground alone? These are some of the issues keenly debated between women and Kisan Sabha activists in the Left, through the decade of the 80s and finally led to the acceptance by the Left Front of the slogan/demand for joint *pattas*' raised by the women's movement. Subsequent to this, joint *pattas* were distributed in a few districts such as Midnapur.[2] The discussion in the book does not reflect these debates. Also the critique of Operation Barga hangs in the air, so to say, in the absence of any kind of discussion of land reform *per se*. While pointing out the patriarchal bias in land reforms implemented by Left-led governments, it may have also been useful to explore what implications the abandonment of the land reforms programme altogether by other political configurations has on the economy in general and the lives of women specifically.

Agarwal's tract makes note of cross-community and regional differences as well as, to some extent, the impact of colonial interventions. The last point, though, has not been sufficiently well-argued. This is surprising for a book which is an update on the latest research (globally). In fact the virtual absence of use of archival source material weakens the historical basis of the claims made. The erosion of women's rights has proceeded along with other changes. The state has played no insignificant role in this. A systematic study of the manner in which legislation was framed during the period of British rule would effectively show how entire groups lost out on their rights in the very process of the establishment of the rule of law. While this was true of the established agricultural communities, it was also equally true of those practising shifting cultivation and nomadism. The enactment of a series of laws over the 19th and 20th centuries, including forest laws, put restrictions/curbs on a range of existing rights in arable land, forests, grazing land and rights to use of water. Even the restrictions had a differential impact. However, one could argue that in general the British pushed/adopted an ideology in favour of settled agriculture wherein preference was given to the male. In fact, parts of India, such as west Punjab, even saw attempts at imposition of the rule of primogeniture. While this was strongly resented and resisted, the easing out of women's rights was achieved with relatively greater ease in all areas of concentration of agricultural land.

A number of questions which would have a bearing on gender relations, however, get obfuscated in the absence of any discussion of the production process, the organisation of production and relations of production. Land becomes a matter of juridical rights, and has value only as property. The contrast is striking. More so, since the Marxist viewpoint, which Agarwal critiques, emphasises an enquiry into the relations of production to arrive at a more integrated picture of land, caste, class and gender. This would also appear to be crucial if the question of land rights has to be addressed beyond arguing for the rights of women from the standpoint of ownership alone. Can the argument for the rights of dalit and landless women be advanced if the dominant framework remains one of primarily identifying the *patriarchal* underpinnings of control of land and property? Must the framework of analysis not be widened if we wish to really identify the needs of the vast rural masses, including the women, who may stand elsewhere in relationship to the land? True, in view of the dominance of the settled agricultural community pattern, this focus gets primacy, but rural India offers an extremely rich variation of the intersection of land with women's labour. Aggarwal's single point agenda tilts the balance in favour of one form and mode of agricultural activity, somewhat in continuation of the prejudice reflected in British administrative records.

While the book brings out the tremendous advantages of a conscious academic exercise to make visible the gender based discrimination against women at the level of juridical/property rights at the same time, the limitations of the theoretical formulations made underscore the fact that 'feminist' vision cannot be substituted nor can a strong ideological argument cover up the grey areas in feminist theory.

In the context of the discussion focusing on how a woman's class is determined, the assertion that "there is an ambiguous character to women's class position" says nothing, really.

Agarwal questions the Marxist assumption that "women belong to the class of their husbands/father" in view of the "relatively vicarious character" of women's class privilege. She raises objections on two specific counts: (a) relocation through marriage/change in marital status which can drastically change women's class: and (b) since even women from propertied households do not own property. While Agarwal's reservations make a point, the issue remains problematic. Is class a descriptive category which can be interchanged/substituted with status or even wealth? What role does social location play in determining this and where would ideology figure in all this? As has been shown by fundamentalist outbursts and mobilisation in recent years, the processes of identity formation involve a complex interplay between, circumstantial/societal location, socialisation and emergent consciousness. It is a complex problem which defies any single answers or broad generalisations. Divisions between men and women, as well as between women and women can form the basis of immense social cleavages depending on social and political processes and to assume, as Agarwal does, that class divisions between women are "less sharp and divisive than those among men" can be an expression of extreme naivety.

To have greater relevance, the point would have to be developed further. Feminist writing on the class question has tended to highlight the patriarchal underpinnings of women's oppression/exploitation but other than Barrett, there has been an underplay of other aspects of the material reality and structures of oppression. MacKinnon's work has provided insights into the play of patriarchal power mediated through structures of state and the law. Pateman's work on liberal theory and the public-private dichotomy has re-opened discussion on aspects touching on citizenship. All these works have successfully highlighted specific aspects which Agarwal cursorily touches on and offers on more.

The case for women's right to land is built up primarily on the point of property in a juridical sense and as a means of security, given the reality of a conflict or incongruence of interests within the family. So land is a matter of contestation as a reference-point for generation of wealth determining status/class or as a 'giver' of security. The woman's case is being argued from the standpoint of her being socially disadvantaged and often a victim of dispossession or social discrimination. In a sense, this does not really go beyond the 'welfare' argument which Agarwal herself critiques and counterposes to 'empowerment'.

Nonetheless, the book, encyclopaediac to some extent, raises many questions. What is the efficacy of the slogan for land reform in today's context? The author does not, however, question the veracity of GOI's claim, for instance, that only 1.04 million hectares of land is available for distribution. This would constitute just 0.56 per cent of the country's arable land. Here, it may be useful to consider the point made by the women's movement that providing women with control over resources is necessary for a more meaningful notion of development itself. This is important in view of the assertion that the parameters of social policy as laid down in terms of central concerns are themselves warped (not just because it is male-centred). This argument needs to be spelt out in the specific context of land rights. It is not enough to point to the fact that nearly 40 per cent rural households are women-headed and therefore women should be given land. The question is: what goes into the making of macro-policies which lay the ground for the trends reflected in these statistics? How does a situation of excessive migration arise; and what does the absence of generation of employment in the vast areas of rural India signify, both in terms of economic growth/and social development? These questions have always been raised while making out a case for land reform and the argument was reiterated in the context of the 'economic reforms' initiated under the Structural Adjustment Programme. At this point it may be noted that those countries being held up as models, such as South

Korea, Japan, etc., in the current phase of 'modernisation' have all gone through a period of land reform.

The chapter of 'Struggle over Resources, Struggles over Meanings' begins on an interesting note. Here some voices from the women themselves begin to emerge. Agarwal has drawn on various studies, primarily from India and Nepal to point out how resistance to intra-family authority structures takes diverse forms. She emphasises that we cannot infer from *overt* behaviour alone whether women really accept the ideological justifications of male privilege and the inequitable distribution of resources and work burdens: whether compliant behaviour is only a survival strategy or that the truth lies somewhere between the two. This is an opening which needs to be given greater space. For, between the trajectory of victimhood and the blinkered vision reflected in state policy, women are seen as little more than 'abject subjects'. Through all these centuries while they have mediated/reworked relationships, they have also contributed their labour and interacted with land and nature. The release of creative energy has certainly not been an unbound process. There have been inherent tensions. But life has had a rhythm woven around nature as well as other human beings, including men. In *A Field of One's Own*, however, women stand alone, even when together. The fact that forging of alliances may be necessary if even the demand for land rights is to be made realisable is not even considered.

Agarwal, at one point, counterposes the demand for employment *vis-a-vis* the demand for women's title to land. The question is whether it ever arose in that framework within the movement. Rather, the formulations in charters/memoranda drafted by individual organisations and jointly by national organisations have seen these as linked and even complementary with prime importance being given to the slogan of land reform, accompanied by women's title and gainful employment. Agarwal herself notes that in fact one of the first policy level interventions in the current phase of joint activity gave centrality to the demand for joint *pattas* (*Indian Women in the Eight-*

ies: Development Imperatives, 1980); but few would have noticed that in a memorandum submitted at the end of a long campaign which ended in a massive march of 25,000 women to parliament specifically on the question of right to work, one of the topmost demands was that of land reform and joint *patta*.[3] This indicates that the understanding developed, at least within the Left-inclined sections of the movement, was that the question of women's economic rights had to be understood within and as part of an overall strategy for economic transformation and development itself.

The empirical substance in the book, nevertheless, is voluminous. Above all, it provides an update on the latest research on questions of land rights in South Asia from all the premier universities in the world. This is accompanied by a minefield of references spread over more than 40 pages, tables, maps and diagrams as well as an extremely useful list of definitions and a glossary. However, this reviewer was extremely surprised to find that in a book which somewhere in the introduction pegs the argument for land rights for women on a feminist critique of Marxism, out of the over 620 footnotes and 40-odd pages of referencing, not a single reference to the writings of Marx or Lenin could be located. The Index did not help in this regard. Surely, for the debate to go forward, feminists will have to engage in a more concre critical analysis of the Marxist understanding of the land question. But *A Field of One's Own* shall henceforth be compulsory reading for all those contemplating serious deliberation on issues of Land Rights for Women, be they activists or academics.

Notes

[1] Dube, L. and R. Palriwala (eds.), 1990. *Structures Strategies: Women, Work and Family*. New Delhi: Sage Publications.

[2] See Gupta, J. 'Land, Dowry, Labour: Women in the Changing Economy of Midnapur', *Social Scientist*, pp, 24446.

[3] *Women's Equality*. Vol. II, Nos. 3–4, July–December 1989, p. 18.

References

Barrett, Michele (1980): *Women's Oppression Today: Problems in Male-Female Analysis*, London: Verso.

Lerner, Gerda (1986): *The Creation of Patriarchy*, New York: Oxford University Press.

MacKinnon, Catharine A. (1987): *Faminism Unmodified: Discourse on Life and Law*, Cambridge: Harvard.

Pateman, Carole and Jacqueline Goodnow (eds.) (1985): *Women, Social Science and Policy*, Boston: George Allen and Unwin.

First published in *The Economic and Political Weekly*, March 2, 1996.

Gender and Land Rights
A Response

BINA AGARWAL

This is in response to Indu Agnihotri's review (*EPW*, March 2, 1996) of my book: *A Field of One's Own: Gender and Land Rights in South Asia* (Cambridge: Cambridge University Press, 1994). When I heard that Agnihotri was to review the book, I welcomed the idea. A positive response to the issues the book raises, from someone with a long-standing commitment to improving women's situation, and active in the All India Democratic Women's Association (with links with the CPI(M)), could further advance these issues in policy and political agendas. And indeed Agnihotri has written a long and serious review, affirming the importance of bringing the question of women's land rights to center stage.

And yet the review contains so many misrepresentations that one is left feeling that Agnihotri approached the book not in a spirit of dialogue with someone who shares her concern with the problems of the disadvantaged, but rather as an adversary and a defender of the "faith".

While I don't normally respond to reviews of my books, in this case I feel I owe it to the readers of *EPW* to counter some of the most important misrepresentations, and to spell out my differences on the question of "joint pattas" which Agnihotri and some others are advocating. The length of this response has been necessitated both by the length of Agnihotri's review and the need to quote relevant passages in the book to clarify my own arguments.

On women's class position

Agnihotri accuses me of not taking cognizance of "the immense social cleavages" "between men and women, as well as between women and women". She dismisses my argument that "there is an ambiguous character to women's class position" as "saying nothing". And she sees my statement that class divisions between women could be less sharp and divisive than those among men as "an expression of extreme naivety". She ignores the discussion *prior* to these arguments, thus putting them out of context. She also ignores the book's extensive discussions of class and caste divisions between women, and how these divisions might obstruct collective action.

In fact, the book centrally addresses the importance of recognizing class differences between women, while also arguing that a woman's class position cannot be derived simply from the household's class position as has been the standard assumption in Marxist and other social theory. Consider a few of the relevant passages:

Chapter 1 (Text: pp. 14–15; fn 32: p. 15):

In fact, neither deriving women's class from the property status of men nor deriving it from their own propertyless status appears adequate, although both positions reflect a dimension of reality. Women of large landed households in South Asia do gain from their husbands' class positions in terms of their overall living standards, their typically lower work burdens, the social status and influence they can command in relation to other village women, and so on. Hence property mediates relationships not only between men and women but also between women. At the same time, there are significant commonalities between women which cut across derived class privilege (or deprivation), such as vulnerability to domestic violence; all women's responsibility for housework and childcare (even if not all women are obliged to perform such labour themselves—the more affluent ones can hire helpers); gender inequalities in legal rights; and the risks of marital breakdown due to which even women of rich peasant households can be left destitute and forced to seek wage work, reflecting their propertyless state and economic vulnerability *as women*.

In other words there is an ambiguous character to women's class position.

This complexity impinges with critical force on the possibilities of collective action among women.... Class differences among women, derived through men, can be and often are divisive in terms of relative economic privilege or deprivation, the associated ability (or lack of ability) to dominate women's groups, perceptions about which aspects of gender relations need challenging, willingness to engage in collective struggle, and so on. At the same time, the noted commonalities between women's situations and the relatively vicarious character of their class privilege make class distinctions between them less sharp and divisive than those among men, and could provide the basis for collective action on several counts (as will be elaborated in chapters 9 and 10). [There are of course aspects of a person's identity other than class which also can be divisive or adhesive, such as caste, ethnicity, and religion.]

Again Chapters 9 and 10 contain long discussions on class and caste cleavages between women; for example, consider these passages from chapter 10 (pp. 490–92):

A particularly contentious issue [regarding the potential for collective action] relates to class (and caste) differences and associated conflicts of interest. For instance, women of middle and rich peasant households are likely to enjoy several class-related advantages over women of poor peasant households in exercising their inheritance rights. We might expect them to be better informed of their legal rights due to higher literacy levels; to have greater access to the judiciary, bureaucracy and local decision-making bodies; and to have more economic resources at their command.... Such women may thus need less support in exercising their inheritance claims than would poor peasant women, and their incentive to cooperate with poorer women may consequently be weaker.

Also certain types of legal changes, such as redistributive land reform enactments, which benefit tenant or agricultural labourer households at the cost of landowning households, are likely to be associated with conflicts in interests (stemming from class, sometimes overlapping with caste, differences) between the women of these households. This would impinge adversely on the possibility of cross-class/caste solidarity between women....

These and other conflicts of interests among women... cannot be ignored. They suggest that women's organizations which are class (and caste) homogeneous and cater to poor, low caste women have a greater chance of ensuring the latter's participation. The experience of grassroots organizing across South Asia also bears this out. Forging cross-class/caste solidarity appears to have more promise around issues such as domestic violence, but even here experience suggests that social and economic homogeneity is helpful. The dilemma is that in order to overcome the obstacles in women's path for realizing rights in land, both cross-class and cross-regional mobilization is likely to be necessary.

Here I would like to argue that despite the noted sources of conflict, there are significant areas of mutual benefit which could yet motivate collective action by women across class/caste lines. One is legal reform. Women of all classes with a stake in family land..., whatever its size, stand to gain from more gender-egalitarian personal laws governing the inheritance of landed property. And the percentage of such women in South Asia is not small: despite the highly skewed distribution of land in the region, the large majority of rural households do own some land.... Similarly, a wide spectrum of peasant women belonging to large and small farmer as well as tenant households (even if not to agricultural labour households) would benefit from certain changes in land reform legislation [to eliminate gender inequities].... Such legal reforms could form the basis of a joint struggle. That women with divergent concerns can cooperate strategically for legal change is also borne out by campaigns in recent years to amend dowry and rape laws in South Asia, for which women's groups successfully came together to form common fronts, despite significant differences in their ideologies, agendas, and class/caste compositions ....

Some optimism on the possibilities of cross-class/caste links is also generated when we consider the important role played by many urban middle-class women activists in promoting issues affecting poor rural women. Many women's organizations in South Asia which are constituted of working class or poor peasant women have been spearheaded by middle-class activists.... More generally, understandings forged through debates conducted in academic and other middle-class forums have helped to legitimize and promote gender-progressive ideas and movements ....

In other words, although it would be grossly unrealistic and romantic to suggest that economic and social differences will not be barriers to collective action across class and caste lines, it would be unduly pessimistic ... to argue that no joint action is possible by women divided along those lines. The strategic question is that of identifying those issues on which there would clearly be gain ... for women of diverse socio-economic backgrounds, and those on which a conflict of interest is likely to dominate.

Thus for Agnihotri to say that I do not recognize the social divisions among women, or between women and men, is a gross distortion. At the same time, I would like to ask Agnihotri: are such cleavages insurmountable in all contexts? If that were so, what role would middle class university-educated activists have in movements of the working class or the rural poor? What contribution could the Left intelligentsia make in the process of radical social transformation? There are innumerable examples of middle class activists and academics who have played important parts in such transformative movements, and Marxist theory (particularly Lenin's!) has had a place for this.

That I think class and social divisions among women may be less divisive than those among men, is a matter of judgement. I base mine on many years of participating in the women's movement in India, and some familiarity with feminist movements in other countries. Perhaps Agnihotri has a different reading of this experience. If so I'd like to hear why. But distorting my views and calling them "naive" cannot substitute for argument.

The colonial state and erosion of land rights

Agnihotri says that I have not adequately recognized how the erosion of women's land rights is related to other historical processes, particularly the actions of the colonial state. She proceeds to elaborate how laws framed during British rule led to entire groups losing their rights, including those practicing shifting agriculture, forest dwellers, etc., and reproaches me for not using more "archival source material" to trace these changes.

Let me refer Agnihotri to my lengthy discussion on the Garos (running into 15 printed pages of Chapter 4) which is precisely on this issue. It traces how legal, administrative and technological interventions by the colonial (and post-colonial) state led to the transformation of a community which had been virtually classless and relatively gender-egalitarian (with land being held communally under shifting agriculture and non-inheritable), to an increasingly class- and gender-differentiated one. This analysis was based on available archival material in English (there wasn't much, and I doubt much more could be dug up in English) as well as on field visits and interviews with elderly village women and men, forest and land reform officers, and scholars in Shillong, Guwahati and the Garo hills. None of the then existing studies of the Garos to my knowledge had traced in this way the interactive effects of state interventions, technological change, kinship structures, production relations and gender relations (see Agarwal 1991 for the fuller analysis).

Again the discussion on the Nayars and the Sinhalese in Chapter 4 dwells at some length on colonial and post-colonial state interventions in changing laws and rights for men and women. The entire chapter runs into 40 printed pages. It must take a very cursory read for a reviewer to miss this discussion on a subject which is clearly close to her heart!

Of course a historian writing a monograph on the Nayars or Sinhalese in the 19th century would wish to draw upon more detailed archival sources, and in the original languages, but this is not a book on only one community or region. Instead of nit-picking about particular bits of source material (and nowhere does Agnihotri give references on exactly what archival material she has in mind or how it would change my argument), Agnihotri might have recognized the book's contribution to interdisciplinary inquiry (covering economics, law, anthropology, history, sociology, geography, and political science). It would indeed be a happy day if many more scholars engaged seriously with writings beyond their own disciplines.

Feminist theory

Agnihotri refers to "grey areas" of feminist theory and implies that the book has little to offer on this count. I am not sure what she means here. Chapter 2 on "Conceptualizing Gender Relations" is entirely theoretical. It critiques as well as builds on bargaining theory to illuminate how gender relations get constituted and contested, both within and outside the household. It is theory that economists, and increasingly social anthropologists and political scientists studying social relations (including gender), would readily recognize.

I entirely agree with Agnihotri (and many others before her) that merely tacking on feminism to Marxism has not taken us very far, and I choose not to do so, although my work is certainly indebted to Marxism. For furthering our understanding of gender inequities, however, I find theoretical developments, such as the bargaining approach, particularly illuminating. I also chose not to spend much time on Catherine MacKinnon's theory of the state (which Agnihotri is unhappy I only touch upon). MacKinnon (1989) characterizes the state as a male institution: "The state is male in the feminist sense: the law sees and treats women the way men see and treat women". I am surprised that Agnihotri appears to endorse this position (which could be read as bordering on essentialism), and is not unhappy with MacKinnon's relegation of "class" to the sidelines in her characterization of the state.

My own view of the State, as outlined in Chapter 2 (p. 79) is:

[Here] the State is not being seen as a monolithic structure which is inherently, uniformly or trans-historically 'patriarchal'. Rather it is a differentiated structure through which and within which gender relations get constituted *through a process of contestation*. Such a conceptualization does not deny the empirical realities of State-functioning in South Asia as having been, in greater or lesser degree, more gender-retrogressive than gender-progressive. But it does mean that the State could be and has been in some degree subject to challenge and change in this respect.

Land ownership vs control and land as property

Agnihotri criticizes me for allegedly "arguing for the rights of women from the standpoint of ownership alone", and treating land only as a matter of "juridical rights". These are again misrepresentations.

To begin with, the book's focus is not only on women's land "ownership", but also on property control. In Chapter 1 (pp. 13–14) I argue:

[Another issue that] needs emphasis is that of property *control*. Property advantage stems not only from ownership, but also from effective control over it. In societies which underwent socialist revolutions, while private property ownership was legally abolished, control over wealth-generating property remained predominantly with men; any positive effects on gender relations that could have stemmed from the change in ownership if accompanied by gender-egalitarian mechanisms of control, thus went unrealized. Indeed in most societies today it is men *as a gender* (even if not all men as individuals) who largely control wealth-generating property, whether or not it is privately owned, including as managers in large corporations. Even property that is under State, community, or clan ownership remains effectively under the managerial control of selected men through their dominance in both traditional and modern institutions: caste or clan councils, village elected bodies, State bureaucracies at all levels, and so on. Also in most countries, men as a gender exercise dominance over the instruments through which their existing advantages of property ownership and control get perpetuated, such as the institutions that enact and implement laws, the mechanisms of recruitment into bodies which exercise control over property (private or public), the institutions which play an important role in shaping gender ideology, and so on.

Of course, as Agnihotri emphasizes, issues of production relations are important as well. The point, however, is that the organization of production and relations of production are crucially (albeit not only) linked to who owns/controls the means of production. Indeed, I am surprised that Agnihotri as a Marxist feminist should so downplay this link. In any case, I fail to see how all this can be interpreted as emphasizing "juridical rights" alone. In fact much of the book (Chapters 1, 3, 6, 7, 8, 10) is devoted to explaining why there are such large gaps with respect to women's land rights between law and practice, and between ownership and control.

On a related point, for Agnihotri to suggest that I build my case for land rights only in terms of welfare misses the point stressed again and again in the book. As the first chapter makes clear, the case for women's land rights stands on four main pillars: welfare, efficiency, equality and empowerment. And while the welfare and efficiency arguments are concerned with women having some land in absolute terms, especially in a situation of poverty, the equality and empowerment arguments are concerned also with women's position *relative* to men, and particularly with women's ability to challenge oppression within the home and in the wider society. The entire Chapter 2 is focussed on how effective property rights would increase women's bargaining power in different arenas: the family, the community, the market, and the State.

Similarly, Agnihotri's characterization of my discussion of land rights as tilting "the balance in favour of one form and mode of agricultural activity", is incorrect. At several points in the book (including Chapter 1, pp. 22–24) I emphazise the importance of village common land (such as still exists), for poor women's subsistence, and discuss the prospects of non-farm employment. But agriculture is still the most important source of livelihood for rural women in South Asia, and the gender gap is increasing as more and more men move into rural non-farm employment, while women remain in agriculture (the feminization of agriculture), but without land titles. Moreover, many viable non-farm activities also need access to at least some land.

A single point agenda?

Agnihotri takes me to task for having what she sees as a "single point agenda". This misses the point of the book. The book does not present a single point agenda; rather, it *prioritizes the agenda*. I argue that the gender gap in property is the single most important economic factor affecting women's economic, social and political status, and that "it could prove to be the single most critical entry point for women's empowerment."

For too long now the demands of activist groups and policy statements by state and central governments have been like a smorgasbord: every issue under the sun gets thrown in, so that we have a long list of ills but seldom priorities for action. Surely the aim of theory and analysis is to sift through this confusion and suggest what might be the most central linking issue?

As I see it, women's command over property, especially agricultural land, is vital for reducing other social and political inequalities. Every chapter in the book emphasizes the interlinks between property and other aspects of women's lives. The obstacles to realizing women's rights in land are recognized as being multiple and complex, including legal, administrative, social, and ideological. Chapters 1 and 9 also bring out how peasant women themselves link property rights with issues of identity, dignity and social status. It is precisely because property is connected with so many aspects of women's lives, and in such fundamental ways, that women's struggle to gain effective command over land has such an important transformative potential in South Asia.

Also as I argue in Chapter 10 (p. 477):

The present analysis indicates that today change will require simultaneous struggles over property, over the norms governing gender roles and behaviour, and over public decision-making authority. It will mean contesting the existing hierarchical character of gender relations, within and outside the household, based on highly unequal access of women and men to economic, political and social power. In the countryside, the distribution of landed property is both a crucial contributor to these dimensions of power and an outcome of the initial distribution of such power. This interactive effect of landed property and rural power makes for a deadlock which is often difficult to break. At the same time, the very breadth and depth of the obstacles make land rights a critical entry point for challenging unequal gender relations and power structures at many levels. The struggle for land is thus important in terms of not just the end result, but the very process necessary for the realization of that result, which can be (and indeed would need to be) one of women's empowerment at multiple levels along the way.

Does this sound like a single point agenda?

Women's demands and land reform

Agnihotri suggests that the issue of women's land rights has been raised consistently, for some years, by large numbers of leftist and feminist activists. Would that it were so. While it is true that land rights for women have been mentioned here and there by activist groups (the book quotes a few documents from the 1980s which do so), and were raised centrally in a few movements such as Bodhgaya, the fact remains that this issue has failed to receive the critical and central attention it deserves from most gender-progressive groups. I am of course glad to hear from Agnihotri that the question has been debated within the Left between women and Kisan Sabha activists. But it still needs answering why despite such debates, we see so little in terms of results, and why Operation Barga so completely bypassed women's claims. At the same time I think Agnihotri is being unduly sensitive about my passing criticism of Operation Barga. The main point I was making is that women's rights in land have not been part of the land reform agenda of any political party, including communist ones. I do point out, though, that the CPI(M) is the only party whose election manifesto (in 1991) explicitly promised to take measures to ensure women's equal rights in landed property. Nevertheless, the question of implementation remains.

Only a woman's issue?

Agnihotri says that the importance of forging alliances between women's groups and other progressive groups is something I have "not even considered". Nothing could be further from the book's thrust. Again and agin the book stresses the important role of gender progressive organizations (and not just of women alone) in transforming patriarchal structures. Gender-progressive is defined as relating to laws, practices, policies, etc., which reduce or eliminate the inequities (economic, social, political) that women face in relation to men; the term is also applied to individuals and organizations (be they constituted of men or women) that work toward this end (chapter 1, fn 18, p. 9).

In fact I include within the fold of the broad "women's movement" (Chapter 10) those mixed-sex organizations which include women's concerns as part of their agendas. I point out that a more gender-sensitive approach among some mixed-sex groups has appeared particularly since the early 1980s, alongside a more general spread of gender awareness among activist, academic, and government circles. Although the number and reach of gender-progressive organizations and individuals vary across South Asia, they constitute a noticeable presence in all countries of the region.

The importance of forging alliances is noted particularly in Chapter 10 (p. 502–3):

Especially since the mid-1980s.... there is an emerging recognition among many women's groups that the struggle against gender inequalities cannot be waged in isolation from struggles on many other fronts, including those for democratic rights, against communalism, and for development policies that are environmentally sustainable, egalitarian, and politically participative. One outgrowth of this recognition has been attempts by women's groups to forge links with other progressive groups to provide a wide-ranging critique of the economic and political system and a broader base for agitation. In India, for instance, several (especially left-oriented) women's groups have participated actively in campaigns for civil and democratic rights, for environmental protection and regeneration, and against communalism, along with mixed-sex groups formed primarily around these concerns. In Pakistan, the Women's Action Forum was also a part of the movement for the restoration of democracy in the 1980s. In Sri Lanka, a number of women's organizations have been working for peace and secularism in a society torn by ethnic strife; and so on.

I also find it curious that throughout her review Agnihotri refers approvingly to the wisdom and foresight of "left leaning women", "the Left", and "the women's movement", as if these groups stand quite separate from many of us who for the past decade and a half have been part of the women's movement, the environmental movement, and movements for democratic rights. Agnihotri states: "Here it may be useful to consider the point made by the women's movement that providing women with control over resources is necessary for a more meaningful notion of development itself". It is strange to have one's own arguments, made over a decade or more, returned in this way!

Let me now come to the issue of "joint *pattas*" which Agnihotri says has the support of the women within the Left and many other groups.

Joint, individual, or group *pattas*?

As argued in the book's chapters 1 and 10, I believe joint *pattas* cannot adequately address the problem of women's lack of effective land rights.

To begin with, the bulk (about 86 per cent, by my assessment) of India's arable land is already privatized; thus to make a dent in women's property needs, the question of inheritance is central. The *pattas* that are distributed are largely from public land and in some small degree from private land, acquired mostly under the land ceiling laws. In whichever way we calculate available "ceiling surplus land", it would still come to only a small percentage of total arable land in the country.

Nevertheless the issue of public land distribution is important. Here while joint *pattas* are better than no *pattas* at all, many of the advantages of women having land would not accrue with joint titles. For instance, with joint titles women would find it difficult to gain control over the produce of the land, or to claim their shares in case of marital breakup; and they would be less able to escape from situations of marital conflict or violence. As some Bihari women told me: "For retaining the land, we would be tied to the man". Wives may also have different land use priorities from husbands which they would be better able to act upon with independent land titles. Moreover, joint *pattas* take no account of women who live outside the context of marital relationships. Individual *pattas* would give these and other women greater autonomy.

At the same time, both individual and joint *pattas* carry other risks such as of the land being appropriated by a rapacious moneylender. In addition, there is the dilemma of who would later inherit the land. In the Bodhgaya movement in Bihar most women who received land said they would bequeath it to sons or daughters-in-law rather than to daughters, since the latter would leave the village on marriage.

An alternative to joint titles with husbands, as well as to individual titles, would be for poor peasant women to receive land as a group, as discussed in Chapter 10, pp. 487–8:

> [W]omen of each participating household [could have] use rights but not the right to individually dispose of the land. The daughters-in-law and daughters of such households who are resident in the village would share these usufructuary rights; daughters leaving the village on marriage would lose them, but could reestablish their rights should they need to return to their parental homes, due to marital breakup or widowhood. In other words, land access could be linked formally to residence, as was the case under

some traditional [tribal] systems... the difference being that here the land would belong not to a joint family or a clan, but to a group of poor peasant women. This would strengthen women's ability to retain control over the land. Collective ownership would also be a means of creating, or (as in some tribal contexts) preserving, a more communal and egalitarian basis of land access. More generally, containing the trend toward the individual privatization of what is currently communal land, especially village common land, would help protect the welfare interests of poor households, and especially of women in these households. ...

Group ownership of land need not of course imply joint management, just as individual ownership need not preclude joint management. For instance, women jointly holding ownership rights in land could cultivate the land either in separate plots allocated on a household basis or cooperatively as a group, with each woman putting in labour time and sharing the returns. Or there could be some combination of individual and group management, such as family-based female cultivation along with joint investment by the women's group in capital equipment, and co-operation in terms of labour-sharing, product marketing, etc.... Women functioning in groups would [also] be in a better position to mobilize resources either from among themselves, or through available governmental or non-governmental schemes [for investing in irrigation and other inputs]. Group investment when linked with group management could further strengthen women's hands in this respect.

Some cases of successful joint land management by groups of women already exist in India and Bangladesh, relating both to village wastelands and the cultivation of private land. In such initiatives, the economic and social homogeneity of the groups and the fact that they involve those who had little or no land to start with, would help guard against some of the pitfalls encountered, for instance, in attempts to promote cooperative farming in India in the 1950s: in that experiment the cooperatives were typically class and caste-heterogenous and mostly involved farmers long used to individual cultivation.

In August 1995, at a meeting of elected women panchayat representatives in Madhya Pradesh, when I raised the issue of groups of women holding land as versus joint *pattas*, many of the women expressed immediate enthusiasm for group ownership. They said this would ensure that male relatives would not be able to take over the land and women could pool resources to invest in capital equipment.

I wish that Agnihotri had seriously discussed this alternative. In any case, I hope it will be considered as an option by rural women's movements and other groups in the future.

Let me end by emphasizing that the spirit of this response is not one of confrontation with Agnihotri. I appreciate her recognition of the seriousness and scale of the study and the issues raised therein. Rather my purpose is to ensure that dialogue on this question can be extended, rather than mired by incorrect readings. Indeed, one important objective of the book was to have the issue of land rights taken up seriously by gender-progressive groups and political parties. Perhaps Left political parties and groups could play a vanguard role in this regard. But I do believe that with such difficult tasks ahead, it is important to build alliances across a broad spectrum of individuals and groups, not just with members of one's favourite organization or political party. Misrepresentations and unnecessarily adversarial postures serve neither the cause of scholarship nor that of activism.

References

Agarwal, B. (1991): "Tribal Matriliny in Transition: Changing Gender, Production and Property Relations in North-East India", ILO (Geneva) Working paper No. WEP10/WP50.

MacKinnon, C. (1990): *Toward a Feminist Theory of the State* (Cambridge, MA: Harvard University Press).

First published in the *Economic and Political Weekly*, June 8, 1996, Vol. 31, No. 23, pp. 1417–1420.

Widows and Property Rights:
A Study of Two Villages in Bihar

SEEMA MISRA & ENAKSHI GANGULY THUKRAL

Introduction

Do widows have property rights? This is the issue which we address in this chapter. For an in-depth and clear understanding of this issue, four broad questions are dealt with:

(i)   What is the formal law dealing with widows' property rights?

(ii) What are the perceptions of the widows themselves, and the perceptions of society, regarding their rights?

(iii) What is the actual practice regarding widows' property rights?

(iv) How do officials deal with widows' rights, in actual practice?

The findings as presented in this chapter are based on a study of two villages, Aropur and Hariharpur of Saraiya block in Muzzaffarpur district of Bihar. Since we have drawn our case-studies from only two villages, we realize that our findings may not be fully representative, especially because we were unable to study cases from all religions. We spoke to 16 Hindu widows, their families and the land and revenue officials at the block level. There were no Muslim widows in these two villages, ...

These 16 women were part of the sample of 70 widows selected for a larger study on 'Widows of India'. These 16 women belonged to different castes and economic backgrounds. No questionnaire was used. It was easy for us to speak to the widows since there had already been contact with them and we approached them through the local activists who had done the initial survey. In our conversations with the widows and their families, we dealt with similar questions as were dealt with in the earlier study but went into greater detail. In the initial sample too, there had been no Muslim widows. ... Our findings, however, largely pertain to Hindu widows and how law and society treat them ... .

Hindu widows and society

The widows' legal right to property is based in personal or religious laws. However, the following questions still remained: What rights do the widows see themselves as having with respect to property? What are the societal perceptions? Are these perceptions synonymous with what the personal laws say? Does actual practice reflect these perceptions? In case a widow has no property in her marital home or is unable to get a share of her husband's property, can she stake a claim in her parental home?

We found that the widows reflected the societal perceptions. All widows, irrespective of caste or economic background, had the same perceptions, which were: the widow is considered to be the rightful heir to her husband's share of the property after his death; all her rights are in her marital home; a widow or any woman has no property rights whatsoever in her father's home.

The law that is followed in the village is the system recognized by the community, that is, the customary law. For day-to-day functioning, the societal rules are upheld. If these happen to be similar to or coincide with the formal statutory law then it was all very well. Even if they did not, nobody seemed to be perturbed. People take recourse to statutory law only when they think it would be to their advantage in a dispute. But even this is very rare.

When we spoke to the widows, there was a vehement declaration of their rights in their marital homes. Irrespective of caste, all the widows held the same opinion that after the death of their *malik* (guardian), as they referred to their husbands, they had the right to his share of the property. They were very emphatic about this, irrespective of whether they actually got these rights or not. **Gulinder Devi** said that she had full *haq* (right) over her husband's land. She said that she had this right irrespective of whether she had children or not. If a widow had no children she could do whatever she wanted with her husband's property, even sell it and go on a pilgrimage. Rampari Devi, a Brahmin widow, had given her elder son's widow, Sunila, a share of the property, even though she only had a daughter. When questioned, she said that Sunila was given property because her husband was a shareholder *(patidar)* and it did not matter whether she had any children or not, or what the sex of the child was.

However, we found that despite the women's perceptions of their rights to property, they did not have real control over the property. Whether they could actually exercise their rights depended on a number of factors, including the age of the widow, whether she had children, the sex and age of the children, the status of her parental family, the attitude of her in-laws, whether the land had been partitioned before the husband's death, whether the widow remarried, and where she lived.

In brief, widows with adult sons typically forfeit their property rights to their sons; widows with minor sons are generally able (with some difficulty) to claim use rights over their husband's share of property; and widows with daughters only are often able (with significant difficulty) to claim use rights over their husband's land; but childless widows are least likely (and not without great difficulty) to claim use rights over their husband's share of the land.

Prabha Devi, a Bhumihar Brahmin, had three minor sons when her husband died. Prior to his death, his brothers had already asked for a partition. Her husband received his share of three *bighas* (unit for measuring land) of land. She had to sell some of the land to cover the medical expenses of her husband's illness. She had also mortgaged 11 *kathas* of land to meet the expenses. When her husband died she got no help from her brothers-in-law. She managed the land entirely on her own to support her children.

Siyapati Devi, a Koeri, was only 23 years old when her husband died. She had three children. A year after his death when she demanded a partition from her brothers-in-law, there were fights in the family. Finally the caste panchayat (a body of five elders) facilitated the partition and gave her a share equal to that of each of the brothers-in-law. When we spoke to her the land was still in the name of her father-in-law. The decision to mortgage some of the land to cover the medical costs for her elder son, who eventually died, was hers. She was also very confident of the community's support if any of her brothers-in-law tried to appropriate her land, because she had *kabza* (control) over the land and paid the revenue. She felt that women who could not get *kabza* of their lands were *burbak* (idiots). 'How can you not have control if you live there?', she asked.

Laxmi Devi, a Kurmi, had been widowed five years ago and had three minor children. Her father-in-law refused to give her any share in the property. He said that as long as he lived he would not give her a share. Actually, partition had not taken place between him and his brothers as yet. He was not even willing to help her bring up her children. She and her elder son, who was 14 years old, earned their livelihood by engaging in wage labour.

Thus, it was fairly clear that while, in principle, both the society and the women themselves saw the widows as having a right to a share in the husband's property, in practice, these rights were limited and restricted. The entire system of widows getting property rights was based on the understanding that they were given property not for themselves but to enable them to maintain the patriarchal lineage. That is why it was easier for a widow with sons to get a share of the property. But her rights to this share were, essentially, only usufructuary rights.

In case her son was a minor she could use and maintain the share until he was ready to take over the property. She was only allowed to sell or mortgage the property to further the interest of the family or to meet the husband's obligations. For example, land could be alienated for a daughter's wedding or for sickness in the family or to pay off debts. A widow would however face a lot of opposition from her husband's kin group if she disposed off the land for personal use or for any other reason that was not considered valid by the lineage. **Shivkali Devi,** a widow, had sold most of the 'property she had inherited from her husband to pay off a loan she had taken from her husband's brother at the time of her husband's illness. That is why no one objected.

If a widow wanted to sell property, the unwritten rule was that she would first ask her brother-in-law to buy it. In case he was not interested, she would then sell it to someone in the village itself. It would not be acceptable to the village community if she sold it to an outsider. To be fair, even the men would face opposition from the kin group if they alienated property outside the interest of the lineage. For example, it would not be socially acceptable if they willed the property to someone other than a family member. This applied both to ancestral and self acquired property.[1] The use rights and duties of the widow appear to be the same as those of the *karta* or manager of the joint family. The *karta* is the senior-most male member of the joint family. He has to look after all the members of the family and manage the family's property. He can alienate the property only for the benefit of the members of the joint family or to meet the family's obligations. The present status of the widow, as we observed, seemed to be an improvement on her traditional status where she was only given maintenance and shelter by the family, while the property was still controlled by the oldest male relative.

Rampunita Devi was the only widow we met who had given the property to someone outside her husband's family. The village community did not object because she did so after the husband's family had put her in dire straits. Her husband's brother had put pressure on her to transfer the land to his son's name. He and his wife had been worried that she might give the property to her niece Subhadra (her brother's daughter) whom she had raised. When she refused, her brother-in-law and his wife began harassing her. Ultimately they had tried to kill her and she had had to move to an adjoining village. She had originally intended to give the property to her husband's brother's son. She was only holding on to it in the hope that her brother-in-law would at least look after her as long as the property was in her name. It was only after her brother-in-law's family tried to kill her that she gifted the land to her niece.

A woman widowed at an older age with adult sons generally has no control over the property. Her sons manage it and take all the decisions themselves. If there is a partition between her sons then she is rarely given a share. It is felt that she only needs to be fed and looked after by her sons. If a widow complains, the village community will pressurize the sons to look after her but rarely will they give her a separate share. **Laxmi Devi**, a Bhumihar widow, said that while she had gone to her *naihar* (parental home), there was a partition between her three sons and she did not get a share. When she returned she asked the *panch* (the community elders) who had arbitrated the partition, for her share. They asked her what she would do with a share and was told that she should be satisfied that her sons would feed her. Most of the widows also did not feel the need for a share from their sons.

After the death of Raghuni Bethav, a dhobi, his *jajmani* (clients) were divided between his wife **Badam Devi** and their sons. For a while, she lived alone and earned her own living. She had also inherited some palm trees. But at the time of partition of the house, her sons did not give her a share. As she grew old, she had to depend upon her sons for food, money, etc. They did not give her money on a regular basis.

Kailasu Devi, another elderly widow, was very angry with her son and daughter-in-law for not looking after her and not giving her enough respect. She had a long list of grievances against them. The main one was that she was the *sardar* (head) of the family but was not accorded due respect. But when someone in the village offered to buy off some land, she refused because she did not want to reduce her son and grandson's share and was also worried that the community would not approve. Even **Gulinder Devi,** who was so emphatic about her rights to her husband's property, said that she saw no logical reason to ask for a share from her sons.

In the case of **Rampari Devi,** a Brahmin widow, the land was in her own name. She asked for a share when partition took place between her elder son's widow and her younger son. But her daughter-in-law did not want to give her a share and so her son dissuaded his mother from insisting on this. In this case Rampari may have asked for a share just to reduce her daughter-in-law's share from half to one-third.

A widow without children has little chance of getting any share of her husband's property. Her husband's kin group generally does not feel that she requires a share. This was best illustrated by the example of **Rampunita Devi** as discussed earlier. Because of the torture she was subjected to, she had transferred the land to her niece's name. Though she and her niece were in possession of the land, they were having difficulty cultivating it, as the brother-in-law uprooted the crops. Besides, no one was willing to take the land on *batai* (share-cropping). The brother-in-law had also filed a case questioning the transfer of land by Rampunita to her niece. In this situation the village community did help Rampunita Devi, as there was a sense of outrage because of the attempt to kill her. But would the community have supported her under normal circumstances, or if she had not been given a share and had demanded it?

The general opinion is that a widow with no sons but only daughters can manage to get her husband's share of the property. This is so because the daughters have to be looked after and married. The widow can sell or mortgage the land to get her daughters married off. Of course, this is done to ensure that the entire burden to marry the daughters off does not fall on the brothers-in-law. We came across one such widow with a daughter who had received a share of the property. She had asked for partition and was given a share of land equal to that of her brother-in-law. This was **Sunila Devi**, Rampari Devi's young daughter-in-law, whom we have mentioned earlier. Since she did not stay in the village we could not talk to her, but we spoke to her brother-in-law and mother-in-law. A number of factors may have contributed to her getting a share. First, she was educated and worked as an *anganwadi* (creche) teacher; second, her in-laws agreed that she had a rightful share, and lastly, the fact that her parental family was influential cannot be entirely discounted. The in-laws held no grudge because she had taken her share. What seemed to upset them was that after having opted for partition, she had asked her own brother to manage her property, who in turn had given it to a third person on *balai*. They felt slighted and said that she should have let her brother-in-law manage her land. They also felt that since she was given her share of the land and her mother-in-law had agreed not to take her share because Sunila has objected, she should now share the responsibility of looking after her mother-in-law. Rampari Devi said that, after all, Sunila's husband would have had to share this responsibility in case there had been a partition in his lifetime.

The place of residence was one of the most crucial factors which determined if a widow got her husband's share of the property or not. Only as long as the widow stayed in her husband's village, would she get her share. But she did not have to live with her in-laws. If a woman went back to her *naihar* (parental home) after she became a widow, then she could not stake a claim to her husband's property. All the women we spoke to said that they did not go and stay in their parental villages after their husband's death to ensure that they could retain title to the deceased's land. Sunila Devi was the only one who had managed to get her share in spite of living away from her marital village. But this was an exceptional case.

Remarriage was another important factor that determined whether a widow was given a share of her husband's property. If a widow was remarried she would not get any share of the first husband's property. Traditionally, remarriage of widows was prevalent in all the castes except in some upper castes like the Brahmins, and Bhumihar Brahmins and Banias. But most of the widows belonging to the remarrying castes were not in favour of remarriage. **Siyapti Devi** (Keori caste) felt that it was wrong for both men and women to remarry. She said that marriage should be a once in a lifetime affair. **Shivkali Devi** who belonged to a backward caste (Mallah) said that her first husband had died leaving her alone to handle all the problems and responsibilities, and there was no guarantee that a second husband would not do the same! Moreover, they all knew that remarriage meant forfeiting their share in their previous husband's property.

Despite the fact that the widows were very categorical about their rights, and that some had even demanded a partition from their in-laws, that it was they who were also managing the property on their own, and that some of them had even gone to the land registry office to sell the land, etc., it was found that widows rarely got their own names entered in the land records. As long as there was a male in the family—husband or son—the women saw no reason to put their own names on the land records.

Even a confident and outspoken woman like **Siyapati Devi** said that though currently the land was in her father-in-law's name, when changes in land records were made, she would put the land in her son's name. She said that if she had only a daughter, then she would have put her own name on the land records, but since she had a son, the question of registering the land in her own name did not arise. **Prabha Devi** who had managed the land for 15 years also said that she would put her four sons' names on the land records. **Kailasu Devi** said that she had asked her husband to put the land in her name before dying. But he had not felt the need to do so. Instead, her husband had reasoned that since they had only one son, the property should be in his name and he would manage the property and look after her. In spite of the strained relations between her son and herself as has been noted earlier, Kailasu Devi would do nothing to harm his interests. **Premi Devi**, a Kahar by caste, had only one daughter and no sons. She has transferred the land to her son-in-law's name. The only women who had their names put on the land records were Rampunita Devi and Sunila Devi. It will be recalled that Rampunita Devi was a childless widow and her father-in-law had put the land in her name. Sunila Devi, on the other hand, had only a daughter.

On the whole, the widows had very little to do with land records as property was usually partitioned orally. In the perception of the village community, partition had taken place if the heirs had mutually decided to separately cultivate and manage the land. In such a situation they would also live separately. Very rarely was a partition formalized by changes in the land records. This meant that the land was divided amongst the heirs (*patidars*) verbally and they cultivated the share of land allotted to them. The household was also divided between the heirs at this time. The rooms in the house were portioned off and each heir now had a separate kitchen. But all of them still shared the same courtyard. Once partition had taken place, a person could even sell his portion of the land. This was also allowed by the local land revenue officer, the *karamchari* or *patwari*. Once an oral (*maukhik*) partition occurred, all the heirs would begin paying the revenue separately. There were a number of families where the land records were still in the grandfather's or great-grandfather's name, even though partition had taken place a few times over, and the only proof of partition having taken place was that the shareholders were paying the revenue separately.

When a party wanted to get the partition formalized by making the necessary changes in the records, they had to make an application to the circle officer (the highest land revenue officer in the block). After making enquiries the circle officer would ask the *karamchari* to make the necessary changes in the records.

Widow's rights in her parental home

There was no notion whatsoever of a woman (widowed or not) having any property rights in her parental home. Since it was believed that a daughter must get married and leave the house to go elsewhere, it was felt that there was no point in giving her any share of the property. The family's duty towards the daughter was seen to be restricted to marrying her into a good family and paying dowry or *tilak*, to enable her to have a 'good marriage' which was to be her share of the property. Often a portion of the land was sold to pay the dowry. Apart from this, it was completely unacceptable to almost everybody that a girl should be given any share in her father's property nor could anyone cite any case of a girl asking for a share.

Very few people knew that the formal statutory law gave daughters the right to a share. They all thought that giving girls a share of the property was wrong and would mean depriving the brothers of what was meant to be rightfully theirs. They clearly stated that they would never, of their own accord, give their daughters a share of the land or property. If a daughter wanted to share she would have to go to court and that would mean her doing so at the cost of breaking off all relations with her parental family, and ruining her relationship with her brothers. She would not be able to visit her brothers' homes after taking a share. All the widows we spoke to also said that they would not give their daughters any share.

Rajkali Devi said that only a *dayan* (witch) would ask for a share from her brothers. She said that because a girl belonged elsewhere, she would not give her a share. She knew that a girl had rights, but felt that only a girl who was selfish and did not want to see her brothers become prosperous would claim her share. **Shivkali Devi** said that her daughter was very dear to her but she would not give her a share, as she would go to someone else's house. About herself, she said that she would not ask her brother for anything. She only wanted to be treated well and looked after when she went to visit him. One educated girl in the village, while trying to rationalize why she should not get a share of her father's property, said that since her father had paid a significant dowry at the time of her wedding, she could not ask for a share of her father's property. Interestingly, her sister, who had been married without any dowry, also said she could not even think of asking for a share.

Kamalkanth Chowdhary, a knowledgeable and well-read man, knew that since 1956, the law gave girls rights to their father's property. But he said that, in practice, a good family is 'bought' for the sisters and daughters by giving *tilak* which is their share. 'Besides they have rights in their marital home', he added. He himself had no children, so he said that his property would go to his nephews and not his nieces. As a result, even if a widow was unable to support herself, or denied her share of the inheritance in her marital home, the social compulsions being what they were, she would not demand a share as a right in her parental home. Clearly she may, if the situation so demands, take assistance from her brothers, and in an extreme situation even go and stay as a dependent in his house, but under no circumstances should she demand or ask for her share of the property … .

Conclusion

The widows see themselves as having a right to their husband's land and property. However, in actual fact, they do not exercise complete ownership rights. Instead of these rights, they have limited use rights over the property, in that they can dispose of it only within the parameters laid down by the husband's patrilineage. The women themselves see this limited societal-conditioned control as actual control and there seems to be no contradiction in their minds regarding this. Though this situation may be an improvement from the time when all that the widows could expect in their marital homes was access to shelter and some food, there remains an inconsistency between perceived and actual control. The rights of the widows in their marital homes (*sasural*) appear to exist merely as a reinforcement of the patrilineage and property of their husband. In this system, it is difficult to find space that would accommodate any challenges to the structure; challenges, for example, from a daughter, widowed or otherwise, asking for rights to parental property; or from a widow, who in spite of the presence of male heirs, insists on registering her name in the land records; or from a widow without children asking for a share and then selling it to buy property in the city.

Notes

[1]   Interestingly, at the village level there was very little distinction made between the two types of property. All property was treated as ancestral property.

First published in Martha Chen (ed.) 1998. *Widows in India Social Neglect and Public Action*, New Delhi: Sage Publications Pvt. Ltd.

Haklenewali: Indian Women's Negotiations of Discourses of Inheritance

SRIMATI BASU

Indian women have substantive (though not fully equal) legal rights to inheritance in the postcolonial era, but rarely lay claim to the natal family property they are legally entitled to, most often citing ideological hindrances. An unpacking of refusals of property shows not a passive acceptance of cultural prescriptions, but rather, the negotiation of material, social and emotional needs, a complex mix of consternation, affection and optimized survival strategies. As Brettell argues in her analysis of nineteenth-century property bequests in Portugal, property transactions "both shape and are shaped by relations between men and women, parents and children, brothers and sisters," constituting "moments when the rights and obligations between people are negotiated" (1991, 447).

Indian women's putative claims to natal property are often inscribed in images of overreaching greed, selfishness, lack of empathy and love for the natal family and a desire to cause family conflicts. Sushila, in an interview, described what she imagined her brother, sister-in-law, and other relatives would say if she ever tried to claim her legal share of natal family land in the village: "*wo ayee hak lene*" (there she comes, to claim her rights). This tension between the fairness represented in enforceable legal equity and the invaluable family ties which allegedly rise above legality may explain the hostility directed towards the "*haklenewali*", the woman who claims her "rights". The transgression lies in her "demand" to break cultural taboos in favour of legal guidelines. The myth that women are waiting to seize their rights, grab property and destroy their natal family base is frequently used to set up legal avenues disinheriting women without their knowledge, to indefinitely delay property division and, most often, to offer women token amounts in lieu of substantive property.

The spectre of the *haklenewali* seems to have been effective: there has not only been no dramatic transformation in social hierarchies, in fact there has been little change in inheritance practices in over forty years of the Hindu Succession Act's existence. Numerous studies show that the inheritance provision for daughters is rarely availed of; that women generally turn down shares of natal inheritance.[1] Why are they averse to taking advantage of legal provisions that would benefit themselves and their nuclear families? Women frequently cite reasons relating to gender roles, kinship and family responsibilities to justify this situation.

The situations described in this paper are based on the interviews I conducted in New Delhi between 1991 and 1993, in three neighborhoods of varying socioeconomic profiles I call KE, KC and SN. In what positions were these women likely to become actual property owners? Marital property was the most likely route: in this sample, some of the middle-class women, many of whom had contributed gold for purchasing their residential homes, had titles in their names, and a large number of the poor women had temporary huts in their residential colonies registered in their names, although these had dubious legal or monetary value. Neither group had legal ownership or control over their husbands' family property in the husbands' lifetimes. As widows, a few women became de facto owners and managers of family property, or received a share of affinal property if they had lived in joint patrilineal households. No women with brothers had been given any natal property; a few brotherless women expected to inherit. One other atypical route was for the chain of inheritance to be diverted in favour of women in cases where they had been care-givers to elderly neighbours or relatives who would not customarily have been their responsibility.

The socioeconomic profile of the three neighbourhoods is indicated below:

KE	Middle Class	Eg. Senior government officials, engineers
KC	Lower Middle Class	Eg. Small shopkeepers, lower-level government servants
KN	Squatter colony: workers in informal sector	Eg. Petty traders; construction labourers

The sample included an equal number of families from each of these neighbourhoods.

Among the women I interviewed, no women who had brothers had received, or expected to receive, natal property (typical of other studies of inheritance practices). Women's responses evoked different paradigms for achieving a fair social distribution of resources. Most numerous was the fear that taking natal property would lead to rifts with brothers and sisters-in-law (41.7 per cent of the women in all, by 50 per cent of women in the highest income group in this sample), that leaving women's share as part of their natal family's assets allowed family relations to be harmonious and supportive. Next in importance were responses that brought up the idea that marriage placed women in a different mode of entitlement: that women got dowry and other gifts instead of property (38.3 per cent); and that daughters "got" marital and affinal, rather than natal, resources (38.3 per cent). While 23.3 per cent of the women opined that women could get property in Hindu families if they were brotherless, as per alleged scriptural prescriptions, others saw themselves as being generous (rather than afraid) in being able to keep their natal family more prosperous by not withdrawing their share (20 per cent). In addition to these rationales based on the idea of women's separation from the natal family at marriage, other paradigms invoked property being a reward for elder-care (10 per cent), or property as a compensation for a daughter's economic hardship (6.7 per cent of responses).[2]

The tensions within the responses is further demonstrated in the discrepancies between women's reactions to their own natal property versus their views on how they would distribute property *ideally*. Many of the same rationales appear in both, but in different proportions. In all, 66.7 per cent of the women supported ideas of not discriminating between children by gender in distributing property, whether by including them all as heirs, or choosing heirs based on need or ability, rather than gender. In sharp contrast to the previous question, where only 18.3 per cent of women in all contemplated taking natal property in equal shares, 53.3 per cent thought that, ideally, both daughters and sons should get property in equal shares.

Equal love: conceptions of equitable distribution

If parents gave both daughters and sons something then both might think that their parents loved them. Reena, SN[3]

Notions that daughters should be equally included in property distributions were the commonest way in which women conceptualized ideal inheritance. Reena's response above illustrates a theme running through women's ideas about giving and getting equal property: showing and earning love. Women's rights to property are often viewed as being a "modern" and feminist demand, appearing proportionate to education and high social class (connoting more "enlightened" views) and irrelevant to the majority of women. The voices of Reena and many women in her neighborhood refute the eliteness of the above claim. Women from the poor neighborhood, SN, were the ones who supported equal distributions of property in far greater proportions (as high as 60 per cent followed by KE, the wealthiest neighbourhood, with 50 per cent). In this sample, high education and class were definitely not correlated with ideals of women being equal inheritors of property, and it was not women's own "backwardness" or disinclination that was keeping them from sharing natal assets.

Furthermore, the images used by SN women revealed a significantly different paradigm for claiming property, evoking neither the alleged brashness of rights-based claims nor the pathos of victims' needs associated with demands for legalization of women's rights to property. Instead, inheritance issues were coded in emotional and affectional terms. For example, several of the women who unqualifiedly supported equal property for sons and daughters used their experiences of motherhood and images of the womb as a symbol of equal entitlement for all children. As Meena, 22, and mother of two daughters, put it:

> If parents make equal shares of everything for all their children, then no one can say they have been given less or more, they can say that the parents having given birth to them all, gave them all equal shares. After all, daughters and sons come from the same cells in the body, not different places, and one feels the same empathy/tenderness ("*darad*") for both.[4]

In such comments, the economic dimensions of property were muted; women's profound connections to their natal families were emphasized. While it is impossible to tell if this was a conscious strategy on the women's part, this line of argument provided a much more comfortable entry to the discourse on property because it did not evoke the spectre of the woman rudely claiming her "rights". In defiance of dominant ideologies which proclaim women's complete severance from the natal family upon marriage, it also emphasized the importance of ties of birth for women and hinted at the need to feel recognized by natal kin through gifts of property.

In contrast, women from KE and KC often used calculations of relative amounts in justifying their choices, focusing on a more precise financial division. Ritu, a 35-year old lawyer with one son, said, "Parents should divide property equally, or proportionately depending on marriage expenses. But now-a-days they spend a lot on sons' weddings too, so it should be equal".[5] Uma, a 27-year-old mother of one son, proud of her dowryless wedding and aware of her lesser claims on her mother's house compared to her brother, contended that if she had daughters she would prefer to give them no dowry but equal shares of property instead.[6] Here equity of assets was far more of a direct concern. Although talking about women's "rights" was just as socially taboo in these milieus, tangible economic fairness apparently could be voiced as a standard.

"Naihar Tut Hi Jaye" (The natal home is broken for me): fears of natal abandonment

A significant number of women (41.7 per cent) also evoked the theme of a daughter's love and love for a daughter in delineating their rights to property by calling upon apprehension rather than affection, saying they would not claim full or any shares of natal property because they were afraid this would sour relations with their brothers or cause their brothers' wives to hate them, and that, as a result, they would no longer be welcome in their natal homes. This attitude marks one of the dominant metaphors mediating women's refusal of property (Teja 1993, 70; Hershman 1982, 75). There was also a close connection between these feelings and the apparently obverse ones, the desires for continuing to be part of the natal family by actively contributing to its prosperity or being available for its crises. Significantly, these attitudes articulate women's desire for closeness with the natal family with an agency that is invisible in, and indeed contrary to, the discourse on women's needs and feelings.

The opening phrase heading this section (quoted from a well-known folk song) illustrates the dominant discourse whereby the wedding is represented as the event that marks the watershed of the woman's pleasures, affections, loyalties and memories.[7] Ties to the natal family are supposed to be severed, and she is to become an inseparable part of the affinal family. The *bidai* ceremony, when the bride leaves her parents' home after the wedding, is an occasion of bitter-sweet sadness over the cutting of deep emotional ties.

Without dismissing the parents' sorrow at this rite of passage, made worse by rituals of eternal severance, it is difficult to miss that the mourning veils the consolidation of patriarchal property relations. As Kolenda (1984) demonstrates in her study of two Hindu communities, groups (often north Indian) which ritually sever the woman's natal connections upon marriage tend to pack her off with dowry and little subsequent inheritance, while those who have no concept of "losing" the woman upon marriage and who believe couples "belong" to both families often give land to daughters to persuade them to live nearby and help the family. Among the communities studied here, the woman's complete change of identity underlined by Hindu wedding rituals that permanently alter her name and caste (and even religious and funerary affiliations), along with the concept of *kanyadan*, the gift of the daughter, symbolize her severance. Thus, property comes to be the brother's, because he remains "in" the family.

Yet, contrary to these hegemonic expectations, many women do not internalize this severance from the natal family in the ways represented by the songs; if they cry "the natal home is broken for me," they do so with regret, longing to keep that tie unbroken, to retain their connections with the family associated with love, as opposed to the affinal family which represents the realm of dutiful work (Jeffery and Jeffery 1996, 155). Numerous studies that examine north Indian Hindu women's relationship to their natal families emphasize repeatedly that women challenge the notion of "losing" their natal families and affirm profound emotional connections with them. Raheja contends that women's assertions of their natal connections are not just about sharing wealth and resources of their families, but "a poetic discourse on power and the possibility of women's resistance to patrilineal authority and patrilineal pronouncements on female identities...contesting the power relations that make them so vulnerable when they marry and go away" (1995, 26).

One of the commonest traces of such love for the natal family is seen in the fear that claiming property will break the last residual ties with the natal family and that women will no longer be welcome in their brothers' homes. The *haklenewali*, the woman who "takes her rights", is evoked here as someone best avoided so that natal links are not broken. As one woman explained, "where the sister takes her share, all those things [gifts, respect] are not there any more; they say 'now you've got your share so go away, why are you back here again?'"[8] The connection to the natal family can be seen, in such a remark, as a concrete fund, and taking property exhausts that link, cutting women off from customary gifts, emergency shelter, and even affection.

The severe wrath faced by women claiming property described by my respondents show that these were not idle threats. To prevent such rifts, some women tried to leave a residual share in the natal family fund by not separating their portion, as among Rehana's aunts who told their brothers to keep the land and farm it, and that they would visit and take crops once in a while.[9] But several others (20 per cent of the middle-class women, plus 3.3 per cent of women from the poorest area) legally signed over their portions to the brothers to emphasize the affectional connection over the material one. This was usually done at the brother's request to show good faith, but was in fact a legal safeguard, an official insurance against the woman's claims surfacing later.[10] It is important to note that, given the paucity of *actual* gifts or sustained help from the natal family, no economic consideration was usually expected in return; women usually made such "gifts" because of the fear of loss of the *emotional* space represented by the natal family, the fragile realm already threatened by marriage and residential separation. Bringing up property and hence monetizing the brother-sister relationship was seen as undesirable, i.e. brothers resented any financial claims made by sisters, and could apparently be munificent based only on "pure" love. Brothers' relationships, on the other hand, were not perceived to be adversely affected by having to divide property.[11]

Fear of incurring the wrath of brothers' wives figured prominently in women's reasons for staying away from natal family property. It was alleged that mothers could no longer give gifts once sisters-in-law came into the family, because they claimed rights over all possessions; and that women would no longer be welcome in the natal home managed by sisters-in-law if they had asked for property. The putative jealousy of daughters-in-law has a rational basis: if women are supposed to get property only through their in-laws, as daughters-in-law they might well feel possessive towards their only sanctioned (albeit indirect) access to resources (Jeffery and Jeffery 1996, 142). Some women did indeed express resentment at the idea that their husbands' sisters might diminish the property of their in-laws, such as Pushpa who said about her sisters-in-law, "Why should they take anything? *I'm* not going to give them anything from my share."[12] But the jealous sister-in-law can also be regarded as the metonymic transformation of the wrathful brothers themselves (the wrath supposedly brought on by sisters demanding property). With sisters-in-law being the only "strangers" to women in the natal home, it seemed emotionally more comfortable for women to scapegoat them as the disapproving ones, thus preserving parents and brothers as sources of love and generosity, and denying the collusion of their own relatives in erasing their natal connections.

Women's fear of estrangement as the motivation of their refusal of natal property is a widely articulated belief, but there is also a positive face of that desire: women's active urge to contribute to the well-being and prosperity of that family. Ritual connections with brothers observed by north Indian women, such as the wearing of two toe rings for the husband and brother to symbolize natal and affinal connections (Wadley 1995, 97) or the similar mourning rituals for husbands' and brothers' death (Raheja 1995, 34), signify the most profound of emotional ties. Thus, in what Moors terms the "problems of dependence and the pleasures of identification," women may not take shares of inheritance as this is one way to retain rights in her natal family, 'to share in its status and feel a special closeness to their natal household," which "enhances the(ir) status and by implication her own and accentuates their obligations towards her" (1995, 53–54). 20 per cent of the women claimed that they wanted their brothers to have all the property not because they were afraid of soured relations, but because they did not want to diminish the resources of the natal home further and wanted it to flourish as much as possible. Whether these women had independent financial resources to help their families or not, they could contribute passively by "not taking". As Pramila put it, women want that *"mera naihar bana rahe"* ('my natal home remain prosperous/well-endowed).[13] They take pride in this first home being joyful and smoothly run, and indeed draw esteem from preserving that part of themselves. The related notion that the natal home should continue to exist as a site of love and indulgence in a world of duty and work also powerfully propels the distribution of property. Lata stressed the seemingly contradictory idea that her daughter would lose if she and her brother divided up and sold the parents' apartment in KE, because she would no longer be able to come back to the emotional space represented by a natal home.[14] In these instances, the poignancy of feeling towards the natal family completely undercuts the ritual, patriarchal prescription of severance, and reveals women's ambitions for, and dependence on, ties of blood.[15]

Property as payoff: elder-care and other family responsibilities

"Both daughters and sons should be given something. But furthermore the son, or daughter, who looks after the parent the most should be given the property, because usually all the others have separated themselves, are living and eating by themselves and do not even ask about the parents. Just when it is time for the parents to give things [before dying], they

all show up and start calling them "mother" and "father"; then all they have to do is to put them on the funeral pyre, feed some people at the funeral to hide their shame, and get ready to take the property and live it up" (Parvati).[16]

An alternative paradigm to viewing inheritance as the transmission of family wealth over generations is the commonly recurring standard of elder-care—that elderly parents give children property as a reward for tending to their physical, financial and emotional needs. While only 10 per cent of respondents overall (none from SN) pointed to it as a rationale for property division, one SN woman had actually received all of her mother's property in exchange for care-giving, and many other instances of elder-care awards across generations were cited by the respondents. Though not the commonest basis of property division, this was nonetheless an important path of non-customary property devolution.

Parvati, a widow of 50, who was often perturbed by her four sons' allegedly selfish lack of attention to her needs, framed the concept of property division based on elder-care in the gender-neutral way cited above. But the rationale of elder-care was more commonly used to justify male inheritance, by invoking the customary gendered division of labour among siblings whereby sons are supposed to be responsible for elderly parents' financial needs, medical crises and even funeral costs. Ironically, the consistent application of the elder-care principle has the potential to be especially significant for women, who more often take on care-giving, marking one of the negotiable spaces for women to get property in defiance of norms of male inheritance. And yet, the standard of elder-care can also be one of the most intransigent bases to deny women property, if customs against accepting help from married daughters set the standard. To understand whether property indeed devolves precisely in proportion to elder-care, or whether this rationale is simply a screen to justify giving property to sons, explicit elder-care rewards and the barriers to women assuming these responsibilities need to be examined closely.

Using property as a reward for services rendered or for potential responsibilities (as 1.7 per cent of the respondents did) is of course the obverse of the view that property is a gift of love towards all children (and also distant from the perception that ancestral resources are carried on through inheritance). Parvati's comment makes explicit the vulnerability and fear of abandonment that runs through the idea of using property to pay care-givers, fears especially tangible for people with meagre resources. For instance, Durga related that her mother was afraid to cash in the remainder of her natal family's land in Bangladesh, fearing that if she went with her sons and they took the money, they might then abandon her and she would no longer have the inheritance to hold over them.[17]

Numerous examples of women receiving property in return for taking on elder-care, in preference to customary male heirs, bear evidence of male heirs' abandonment of the elderly despite lip service to sons' responsibility in this area. A dramatic instance where property was left to non-kin or neighbours who had been care-givers was that of Kavita's mother: she looked after a widow in the neighborhood, who left her land to Kavita's mother and brother.[18] In other cases it was daughters who had looked after mothers and been given family assets, e.g. Uma's paternal aunt who had lived in the rural home in Bihar with Uma's grandmother, and was treated as de facto owner of that house and property, while Uma's father had opted to live in the city and travel abroad.[19] In one of the clearest cases of commodification of elder-care, Bindu's mother had come to live with Bindu and her family, and had given her her savings of Rs. 15,000 because she had agreed to look after her.[20] None of the other sons or daughters received anything. Bindu's mother had lived earlier with one of her sons, but when he died the other married sons had not been willing to assume responsibility for her. Thus, Bindu received the privileges of being a default/surrogate son by looking after her old mother, and she felt she had lived up to the responsibility she had assumed by paying entirely for her mother's funeral (typically a son's job), and also taking care of her mother's food, clothing and bodily care while she was alive.

Given the gender division of labour whereby women are responsible for domestic work, including the management of intimate body fluids as part of child- and elder-care, it is not surprising that women had the advantage in getting unexpected elder-care awards. Several women drew connections between the provision of elder-care and inheritance, and wanted daughters to be included as equal heirs, evoking the superior quality of daughters' care-giving. For instance, Maya, with two married sons and a married daughter, proclaimed that "she [the daughter] plays an equal role in taking care of her parents, helps in their troubles, she comes by when her mother feels sick, so she should have a share".[21] Madhuri, having experienced only daughterhood and not marriage or parenting, was even more extreme: "When do sons help now-a-days?", she asked, "It is the ... daughters who take much more care of parents; they might get some share of property but they help more than sons do".[22] If property division were indeed proportionate to elder-care, women could thus have a favourable claim based on their physical care (if not financial assistance).

However, as the portrait of property divisions showed, women rarely inherited any property, and the examples of property awards cited above were highly atypical; only one of the 60 respondents (plus women in 6.7 per cent of the respondents' families) had inherited anything in this manner. Much more commonly, elder-care was supposed to be the province of the sons, and property dispensation was believed to reflect that responsibility, whether or not particular sons got property specifically as a result of eldercare.[23] Ritu and Vimla's husbands, for example, had both been the youngest sons and care-takers of their parents, and inherited the parents' residences by family consensus.[24] However, elder-care was not necessarily the only basis for distributing property in those families; Vimla's husband's brothers (and not his sisters) had received other property from their father. On the whole, all males were heirs and all females disinherited. As with many other families, one brother was responsible for the bulk of the care-giving, but all the males shared the property under the banner of sons undertaking elder-care. Among the kin of the SN women, it was very common for a parent to be living with one of the sons in the village, while other sons gave some crops or cash but were clearly not the primary care-takers; however, all males expected equal shares of land.

The persistent trope of the daughter's emotional and financial severance from her natal family upon marriage and the son's continuing responsibilities and privileges in the family strongly affect women's refusal of property. The belief is that daughters have no claims if they do not assume any corresponding responsibilities. Brothers' sole right to property is often seen by sisters themselves as a justifiable return for all the duties that are habitually assigned to the sons. As Kiran, a relatively newly married woman with an infant son living in the husband's "joint" family, said,

> My brother is the one who is going to be useful to my father and be with him in his times of joy or sorrow, so that is why he should have it [property]. We are away in our own homes. If my father runs into any problems, my brother is the one who will have to worry about it. We can maybe go there, but we can't help if they need money.[25]

Kiran's comment was typical of many women who implied that they *should* forfeit property because they were unable to help their parents, due to lack of financial resources, residential patterns, and most strongly, ideological restrictions. Kiran explained, "Among us the 'duties' have been fixed. We can worry about them [parents], if they really need help we could think about helping them in the time of trouble, but we are supposed to be 'attached' to our *own* [i.e. affinal] homes first". Suman also pointed out that her natal family had recently had many crises involving divorce, illness, etc., and although she was worried, she had not felt able to leave her allegedly primary responsibilities, her tasks in the nuclear family, to be with her parents in another city. However, her brothers had to go since their presence was expected in hard times.[26]

What is unfair in this customary division of duties is not that those who do actually expend resources are duly compensated, but that daughters are not permitted to share in eldercare (and hence property), in accordance with ideological proscriptions. In many cases this ban was framed in terms of the Hindu wedding ritual of *kanyadan*, translated as "gift of a virgin daughter," in which the giving away of the daughter constitutes a holy act for the father.[27] This is supposed to be the supreme selfless gift, to which the bulk of other material gifts are merely supplementary. As I learnt from some of the middle-class women (21.4 per cent of KE and 31.3 per cent of KC respondents), the act was interpreted in their families as one in which the daughter is given away along with the dowry with no rights retained in her, and so parents accept nothing from her—starkly symbolizing woman as property.

It appears quite significant that no women from SN brought up notions of *kanyadan* and the resultant blocking of any help from daughters. No similar taboos were ever mentioned; in fact, there were several instances where married women gave their families ongoing financial and other help. In contrast to KE where no cases of helping natal families were mentioned, and KC where two women narrated instances of sisters helping with family weddings and other financial crises (and only one woman gave her parents some financial support), there were several kinds of help proffered by the SN women. Among 13.3 per cent of 30 respondents and in many other households in the neighborhood, the woman's parent, brother or sister lived in her nuclear family. In 10 per cent of cases, women paid for natal family funerals, debts and legal expenses out of their own earnings; Medha described her motivation in doing this as wanting to be by her brother's side helping him through troubled times, an act of love and support.[28] Besides financial help, other assistance was provided by Deepa and her sister who would take turns staying with their father in the village a few months at a time, doing the cooking and domestic work because there were no women in their natal household.[29] There were clearly no cultural proscriptions against the women's natal family members staying or eating.

Although there were fewer restrictions on sources of help among SN families, no women had been given shares of property despite their assistance. Also, a much smaller percentage of SN women as compared to KC women (only 10 per cent as compared to 25 per cent) believed that elder-care should play a role in the dispensation of property. The conclusion may be drawn that in this group, elder-care was a matter of assisting one's natal family based on social and affectional ties and not on financial considerations.

Although relatively few respondents mentioned the ideological relevance of elder-care in delineating how property should be distributed, several instances of actual inheritance showed that women did inherit property in dramatically unusual ways as a result of care-giving. However, because of strong ideological proscriptions, women did not usually provide elder-care and did not, typically, expect inheritance in return when they did so. While only some of the sons (and daughters-in-law) actually did the care-giving in most cases, the rights of *all* male heirs to inheritance were nevertheless proclaimed to be connected to elder-care. The issue of elder-care thereby functioned as a screen for disentitling women from property; that is, sons inherited more in accordance with ideological prescriptions about sons undertaking the bulk of elder-care, whether or not they actually did any care-giving.

Conclusion

In delineating how property should be divided, some women echoed the patriarchal ideology that seemed contrary to their material interests, but often revealed their own dissociation from such beliefs while underlining their socioeconomic powerlessness. Furthermore, in naming connections between inheritance and factors like elder-care, dowry, or long-term financial help, women demonstrated a process of sense-making in which they weighed their realistic possibilities of intervention against financial options. Without a broader change in socioeconomic relations, it would be difficult for women to proffer substantial help to the natal family and get property in return, and thus dowry from the natal home along with the "protection" supposedly offered through marriage was the safest economic route, whereas radically different actions could leave them too vulnerable. Most remarkably, the images used by these women, particularly images of love from and towards parents, demarcated a realm of feeling escaping from, and indeed contrary to, dominant discourse, a construction of entitlements very different from and yet at least as powerful as the notion of individual jural rights.

Ultimately, it is useful to remember that these women did not inherit either natal or affinal property. In celebrating the spaces of discursive leakage, one ought not to forget the resilience of hegemonic discourse. Despite exceptional cases of women receiving family property and subtle negotiations by women to retain natal ties, patriarchal principles of inheritance remain stable. Studies of women and land have shown a positive correlation between owning even a small piece of land and a dramatic sense of empowerment with regard to legal rights, credit or income generation, healthcare etc. (Agarwal 1994). In this study, however, women neither received much family property nor expressed the wish to get much. While some women did appear to negotiate to create space for themselves, we ought to bear in mind how little property or substantial economic assets they actually owned, and how that limited their opportunities and aided their impoverishment and dependence.

Notes

[1] Agarwal 1994, Basu 1999b, Magu 1996, Sethi and Sibia 1987.

[2] There was no strong statistical correlation between age and attitudes towards taking natal property. Certain variations in responses between neighborhoods did seem connected to socioeconomic circumstances, e.g. differences in education, prevalence of particular ethnic groups, or rural vs. urban upbringing.

[3] Interview, SN, 12/30/92.

[4] Interview, SN, 1/7/93.

[5] Interview, KE, 12/13/91.

[6] Interview, KE, 2/24/92.

[7] See Sharma (1980, 137) and Chanana (1993) for a further discussion on the significance of wedding songs. The ideology of the woman's severance from the natal family has been documented in various studies (Sax 1991, 77–81; Raheja and Gold 1994, 83–5).

[8] Bharti, a married woman with two brothers, Interview, KE, 12/9/91.

[9] Interview, SN, 12/27/92.

[10] These signed releases sealed the woman's refusal of property even where the brother did not fulfil his part of a specific bargain.

[11] However, such notions of brotherly love being untainted by economic transactions was not borne out by the many stories about brothers' resentment over having to share resources (also Jeffery and Jeffery 1996, 45).

[12] Interview, SN, 12/21/92.

[13] Interview, SN, 12/30/92.

[14] Interview, KE, 12/3/91.

[15] In the rural areas, the natal home is literally a much freer and more comfortable place for women, because (even married) daughters do not have to veil themselves or not speak to elders or non-family like daughters-in-law. Besides, the load of domestic work is usually negligible while they are visiting, although in some cases daughters specifically come home to help with crops. Sharma (1980, 19) also shows the central difference between natal and affinal worlds for women, an opposition not particularly significant for men.

[16] Interview, SN, 12/25/92.

[17] Interview, SN, 12/28/92. Durga's mother's situation is a vivid illustration of a trend recently uncovered by researchers (Chen and Dreze 1992; Gulati 1993), that widows with even minimal property tend to be treated with more care and respect in their families as compared to the widespread neglect of widows without property.

[18] Interview, KC, 2/7/92.

[19] Interview, KE, 2/24/92.

[20] Interview, SN, 12/8/92.

21   Interview, SN, 1/8/93.
22   Interview, KC, 2/12/92.
23   Wadley's research shows that the most important economic resources for women were land, which they rarely got control over, and sons, through whom they could have a place to live and eat and be protected from the ill-treatment of the affines and the natal family (1995, 114). In the present study, a son often, though not always, took on elder-care.
24   Interview, KE, 12/13/91; Interview, KC, 2/17/92.
25   Interview, KC, 2/11/92.
26   Interview, KE, 12/5/91.
27   In some families this may be done by the maternal uncle and is a sign of the mother's family's participation.
28   Interview, SN, 12/23/92.
29   Interview, SN, 1/5/93.

Bibliography

Agarwal, Bina. 1994. *A Field of One's Own: Gender and Land Rights in South Asia.* Cambridge: Cambridge University Press.

Basu, Srimati. 1999a. "Cutting to Size: Property and Gendered Identity In the Indian Higher Courts." In *Signposts: Gender in Post-Independence India,* ed. Rajeswari Sunder Rajan. New Delhi: Kali.

———. 1999b. *She Comes to Take Her Rights: Indian Women, Property and Propriety.* Albany, New York: State University New York Press.

Brettell, Caroline B. 1991. "Kinship and Contract: Property Transmissions and Family Relations in Northwestern Portugal." *Comparative Studies in Society and History* 33.3: 443–65.

Chanana, Karuna. 1993. "Partition and Family Strategies: Gender-Education Linkages Among Punjabi Women in Delhi." *Economic and Political Weekly.* 28: WS 25–34.

Chen, Marty and Jean Dreze. 1992. "Widows And Health In Rural North India." *Economic and Political Weekly* 27: WS 81–93.

Chowdhry, Prem. 1994. *The Veiled Women: Shifting Gender Equations in Rural Haryana 1880–1990.* Delhi: Oxford University Press.

Jeffery, Patricia and Roger Jeffery. 1996. *'Don't Marry Me to a Plowman': Women's Everyday Lives in Rural North India.* Boulder, CO: Westview.

Kolenda, Pauline. 1984. "Woman as Tribute, Woman as Flower: Images of 'Woman' in Weddings in North and South India." *American Ethnologist* 11: 98–117.

Hershman, Paul. 1981. *Punjabi Kinship and Marriage.* Delhi: Hindustan.

Magu, Poonam. 1996. "The Hindu Succession Act—Has It Really Helped Women?" *Legal News and Views* 10.8: 1–3.

Moors, Annelies. 1995. *Women, Property and Islam: Palestinian Experiences, 1920–1990*. Cambridge: Cambridge University Press.

Raheja, Gloria Goodwin. 1995. "'Crying When She's Born, and Crying When She Goes Away': Marriage and the Idiom of the Gift in Pahansu Song Performance" in *From the Margins of Hindu Marriage: Essays on Gender, Religion and Culture*, ed. Lindsey Harlan and Paul B. Courtright, pp. 19–52. New York: Oxford University Press.

Sax, William S. 1991. *Mountain Goddess: Gender and Politics in a Himalayan Pilgrimage*. New York: Oxford University Press.

Sethi, Raj Mohini and Kiran Sibia. 1987. "Women and Hindu Personal Laws: A Sociolegal Analysis." *Journal of Sociological Studies* 6: 101–13.

Sharma, Ursula. 1980. *Women, Work And Property In Northwest India*. London: Tavistock.

Wadley, Susan S. 1995. "No Longer a Wife: Widows in Rural North India" in *From the Margins of Hindu Marriage: Essays on Gender, Religion and Culture*, ed. Lindsey Harlan and Paul B. Courtright, pp. 92–115. New York: Oxford University Press.

Conjugality, Law and State: Inheritance Rights as Pivot of Control in Northern India

PREM CHOWDHRY

The inheritance rights of women, whether partial or absolute, are very intimately connected with an important aspect of conjugality, that is, widow remarriage. The present paper seeks to establish this relationship and the crucial role which the state has played in controlling and regulating it, both in colonial and post-colonial periods, with special reference to the Haryana-Punjab region of northern India. I will argue that the custom of widow remarriage, as practiced in this region in its *karewa* or levirate form, remains in a decisive way the most effective device to prevent women exercising their right in inheritance as widows. A levirate marriage brings an otherwise independent woman of property once again under male dominance, without endangering the established kinship patterns.

For widows, however, the ostensibly progressive custom of remarriage remains a highly repressive one; with rights of inheritance, as well as desire for relative autonomy, not only economic but also sexual, taking precedence over the socially recognised remarried status. Yet, the colonial state, which selectively adopted customs and made them legally enforceable, was blatant in its attempts to encourage widow remarriage through administrative and judicial agencies. The post-colonial state has reinforced it, though indirectly and unintendedly, through present day legislation, such as inheritance laws, or more directly through executive and administrative directives of later day pension and award claims.

The state's attempts at a positive intervention in promoting greater gender equality for women in the sphere of inheritance has had an almost paradoxical consequence for widows, leading to the strengthening of *karewa* which is in direct contradiction to her inheritance claims. The absolute ownership rights granted to her under the Hindu Succession Act, 1956, have generated patrilineal fears and greed. This in turn has activated the customary socio-cultural constraints on widows which has made the Act infructuous in actual practice. This analysis attempts to highlight how the law's guarantees in principle were effectively undermined in practice through the threats and compulsions exercised by the widow's conjugal family members to perform levirate. Any breach in levirate, whether sanctioned in the form of *punar vivah*, or unsanctioned, in the form of runaway matches, has meant in effect the widow being deprived of her inheritance, notwithstanding the law. The strengthening hold of *karewa* has also underlined all the repressive aspects of conjugality which range from a forcible remarriage, an unmatched and undesirable alliance, to polygamy and the harsh reality of being a co-wife against the legal requirements of monogamy. Condemned outright by women for its repressive fall out effects, levirate continues to grow in popularity and acceptance, sanctified through a combination of patriarchal needs, custom, law and the state.

Curiously, the actions of the state are contradictory. It not only subverts the more positive facets of widow remarriage practice, but is also privy to the subversion of the revolutionising effects of the 1956 Act of succession as well as other legislative measures.

I. Custom of *karewa*: remarriage, inheritance and law

The custom of widow-remarriage as followed in Haryana and Punjab had special features of its own. Known as *karewa, karao,* or *chaddar andazi,* the custom was a throwback to the old Rig-Vedic *niyog* (levirate marriage) which was prevalent in the geographical region of Haryana-Punjab and associated with the early Vedic Aryan settlements.[1] *Karewa*, a white sheet with coloured corners, was thrown by the man over the widow's head, signifying his acceptance of her as his wife. Symbolically, this gesture brought the widow once again under male protection; she being given "his shelter" or "roof" and receiving colour in her life. There could be certain variations.[2] For example, it could take the form of placing *churis* (glass bangles) on the widow's wrist in full assembly and sometimes even a gold *nath* (nose ring) in her nose and a red sheet over her head with a rupee tied in one of its corners. This could be followed by the distribution of *gur* (jaggery) or sweets. Significantly, this form of remarriage was not accompanied by any kind of religious ceremony, as no woman could be customarily married twice, that is, go through the ceremony of *biah* (religious wedding).

Karewa, as a rule, has been and continues to be primarily a levirate marriage in which the widow is accepted as wife by one of the younger brothers of the deceased husband; failing him, the husband's elder brother; failing him, his agnatic first cousin. Although it is difficult statistically to calculate the number of people who followed this practice, the adherents ranged from the so-called "agriculturist castes" (except the Rajputs)[3] to the low castes known as *achut* and *kamin*. The reports indicate that it was also being followed by the brahmins. The brahmins of this province, who were not a priestly class but were mostly land-owners, followed the dominant social custom of this region in preference to the sanskritic model of the other brahmins who brooked no remarriage at all and upheld *sati* (widow immolation) instead.[4] Among other Hindu castes, the "low grade Khatris" also followed *karewa*, but others, like the bania and kayasth did not do so, nor did the sayyeds among the Muslims.

The popularity of *karewa* among the overwhelming majority of landowning classes emanated, apart from other reasons, out of the need to retain landed property within the family. The main reason for making the marriage arrangements within the family was to transfer control of the deceased husband's land from the widow (who succeeded to a life estate in the absence of male lineal descendants) to his brother or to a patrilineal family member, because a widow who remarried lost all her rights to property, even if she married her husband's brother.[5] Under customary law, as operated by the colonial masters, it was generally assumed that the widow forfeited her right to property after her remarriage, and persons asserting a position to the contrary had to prove the existence of a "special custom".[6] The Sikh Jats of Punjab were by and large able to establish this "special custom" and stay the forfeiture on remarriage. However, even among them the exception was only in relation to the brother; *karewa* with a cousin or a collateral entailed forfeiture.[7] Remarriage, therefore, deprived her of even the limited right to land which she came to possess after her husband's death, that is, only a life interest. Ultimately the property passed to her husband's male line. In case she had children, her sons succeeded to the property and she had a right only to suitable maintenance. Her daughters and their issues had no right to inherit from the father.

However, even this limited right of the widow was seen as a threat, because she could claim a partition of the property on certain grounds, that is, when she could not secure the required maintenance from her husband's heirs. Although the condition of "required maintenance" for claiming partition as voiced by the rural male population was understood by the British to be "a mere expression of opinion as to the custom they would like to enforce, rather than custom itself",[8] it was still accepted as an established custom and became enforceable through the courts. All such attempts of the widows which in fact could be claimed as a matter of right, therefore, came to be challenged in the courts by the collateral (male descendants in different degrees from a common ancestor) and the onus of proof was on her.[9] This meant that the court either implicitly or explicitly took the position that the required maintenance was indeed being granted to her by her deceased husband's agnates. However, the fact that this view was contrary to reality was even acknowledged by the revenue officials. In their considered opinion the widow found it difficult to obtain her "fair share of produce" as long as the holding remained undivided. Moreover, the lower grade revenue officials invariably accepted the rural male assumption that "the widow will only waste the property when she obtains absolute control", and therefore, took the stand that "women are not qualified to manage their land themselves."[10] Although this action was not always considered "groundless", it was still maintained to be "untrue" in the case of "better cultivating castes like the Jats, Sainis, Rais, Kambohs and some others". Only after a great deal of scrutiny regarding the "proper arrangements for the management of holding" were these decisions reversed. There are a few cases in which although the lower courts dismissed the suit of the widow for partition, the divisional judge accepted it on full scrutiny.[11]

While verdicts of the higher court were mixed, the majority of revenue assistants disallowed partition. Their decision was thought to be in keeping with the "very strong feelings among all the tribes against granting a widow separate possession."[12] It was also observed that such claims were made "as a rule at the instigation of her own relatives, who wish to get the management of the land". Separate possession meant that the widow could get it cultivated through someone else as she was customarily not allowed to undertake full agricultural operations herself. Separate possession also produced a fear, "often well founded", that it would lead to an 'attempt to alienate" the property.[13] The widow could alienate the property, though not sell it for her own maintenance, her daughter's wedding or payment of revenue, for reasons dubbed as "strict necessity". That many women had started to utilize this proviso can be seen from the constant appeals made to the Deputy Commissioner, protesting against widows who were accused of alienating their property without necessity.[14] The district level customary law records show extracts of the mutation sheets as well as lists of the details of cases in which widows of different castes commonly mortgaged or alienated the land for considerable sums, all of which were challenged by the reversioners. The decisions of the civil courts were "always against the widows and in favour of reversioners".[15]

The self-assertion by widows in taking control of the economic resources after their husbands' deaths must have assumed such proportions that, for a variety of reasons, government action against it became essential. J.M. Douie, compiler of *The Punjab Law Administration Manual*, advised the revenue officials that the widow's attempts to partition the land "should be disallowed".[16]

However, since legally such advice could not have held much weight, the only solution to the fast growing claims to partition was, according to official instruction, to be sought in "a firm anchoring of the widow in marriage". This, the manual instructed, could be the "only satisfactory arrangement against which she had no appeal".[17]

One of the more revealing accounts, delineating his own role in such marriages came from George Campbell, a British official serving in Punjab in the 1870s:

My trouble was ... to decide adverse claims to women. A special source of dispute was the obligation of widows (under the law, as understood by the men at least), to marry their deceased husbands' brothers. They had a contrary way of asserting their independence by refusing to do so. I am afraid the law that I administered was rather judge made law; my doctrine was that if they refuse they must show reasonable cause. The parties used to come before me with much vociferation on the female side, and I decided whether the excuse was reasonable. But if the man seemed a decent man, and the woman could give no better reason than to say "I don't like him", I said "stuff and nonsense, I can't listen to that—the law must be respected", and I sometimes married them there and then by throwing a sheet over them after the native fashion for second marriages. So far as I could hear those marriages generally lived out very happily.[18]

In their anxiety to encourage widow remarriage in its levirate form alone, the British also favoured its legal regulation through courts to give it validity by awarding damages in favour of the former husband's family "against the stranger who entices the widow away".[19] Such a move was seen to be consistent with the demands of "equity" and with the "custom of many tribes and the idea of the people generally". However, it was soon discovered that the Widow Remarriage Act XV of 1856 would invalidate such a claim if made through the courts, as section Y of the Act took into account the consent of a Hindu widow of full age for remarriage whose marriage had been construed as lawful and valid under the Act.[20] This move had therefore to be dropped. The officials regretfully recorded that this law had given validity to such marriages which would have been "illegal according to native custom" as "the tribal feeling was very strongly in favour of maintaining the power of the husband's family over the action of the widow in this matter."[21] Therefore, fresh instructions were issued, providing administrative guidelines in this connection. The district officials were instructed: "often a young widow will present a petition to the Deputy Commissioner for sanction to marry a man of her choice, but with such application he is wise to have nothing to do."[22]

The fact that the custom of *karewa* snatched away whatever little right of possession women in Haryana-Punjab had come to acquire as widows, was well known to British officials. They were fully aware of the nature and operation of this custom in relation to women. This can be seen from the perceptive observation of Cunningham, a British barrister at law, who compiled a draft gazetteer of Rohtak district between 1870–74. He wrote, "*Karewa* under these conditions may be called remarriage with reference to reasons affecting the women, but such unions often take place for causes which have regard to the men only".[23]

II. Post-colonial situation: inheritance rights for widows

A widow's rights to her life estate in the colonial period for which she had put up a visible fight was to change in the post-colonial period. The independent Indian state directly and positively intervened in the inheritance rights of women to remove the disabilities experienced by them through the enactment of the Hindu Succession Act, which was brought into force on 17th June 1956.[24] This Act amended and codified the law relating to intestate succession among Hindus and brought about fundamental and radical changes in the law of succession in breaking violently with the past. Section 14 of this Act applied to women and granted them equal inheritance rights along with the male members. For the first time the Act enabled daughters, sisters, widows and mothers to inherit land with full proprietary rights to its disposal. The earlier limited ownership right afforded to the widows was converted into full and absolute ownership.

However, cultural and ideological constraints severely militate against a woman claiming her inheritance as a daughter and a sister.[25] Consequently the right to inherit land as a widow, to a large extent, is almost the only way in which a woman can inherit land directly. As a direct and absolute beneficiary, it is the widow, rather than the daughter or sister, who emerges as a major threat in the post-colonial situation. The changed situation was highlighted when a series of court cases were brought by male collaterals challenging the rights of widows on a variety of grounds. The study of a few cases will be illustrative. One such case, Jai Ram Devi vs. Tota Ram, came up for hearing in the Punjab High Court in 1961.[26] the case involved a challenge by reversioners to the mortgage of land in 1959 by Jai Ram Devi, a widow. The case was not found maintainable because the Hindu Succession Act came into force in 1956. The judgment made it clear that where a Hindu widow, a limited owner, is possessed of the property when the Hindu Succession Act 1956 comes into force, she becomes its full owner, by virtue of the provision in Section 14 of that Act. It follows that no reversionary interest remains in that property once the widow becomes its full owner. Hence a suit brought in order to protect his reversionary right by the reversioner, challenging the mortgage executed by the widow as a limited owner, cannot be maintained in a case where the Hindu Succession Act 1956 comes into force pending the suit.

The indications of a sharp breach from the colonial past in the inheritance rights of widows had begun to surface. This position was confirmed in another case, which was initiated in 1961 and decided in 1970, involving the alienation of land by a widow.[27] Uttam Devi, on the death of her husband, came into possession of his estate in 1938. Within a month she gifted the entire estate in equal shares to Daulat Singh and Charan Singh. The gift was challenged on the 19th June 1939 by the reversioners under customary law, pleading that the gift should not affect their reversionary rights. The suit was decided in their favour. Some twenty years later, in 1959, Daulat Singh, one of the donees, gifted back his land gift to the widow Uttam Devi. She sold off this land on 20th October 1959. On 13 March 1961 she died. The reversioners and their heirs filed a suit for possession of all the land, which had formed the subject matter of the 1938 gift. The suit was resisted by the vendees who had bought one half of this land from Uttam Devi in 1959. The suit was decreed in favour of the reversioners by the trial court and the decree confirmed by the lower appellate court. In a regular second appeal filed by the vendee or buyer in 1963, the judgment of the lower court was reversed. The case was then referred on appeal to a full bench who upheld the earlier appeal and maintained that Uttam Devi, who had been gifted back her land on 3rd June 1959, had become a full and absolute owner by virtue of the Hindu Succession Act and therefore had full rights of sale and this sale could not be challenged.

In other cases the question of remarriage was invoked to claim the land of the widows, as had been done in the colonial past. One such case initiated in 1954 involved a Hindu widow, Harnam Kaur, who had come into possession of land belonging to her deceased husband in 1917.[28] The collaterals of her husband brought a suit for possession, saying that since the widow had entered into a *karewa* marriage with one of the collaterals she had lost the right to hold the land of her first husband. The collaterals succeeded in getting the order from the Naib Tehsildar, dated 26th June 1954, and had the land mutated in their favour. Harnam Kaur denied, like many of the widows in colonial times, that she had entered into any *karewa* marriage and instituted a suit claiming possession of the land. While the suit was pending the Hindu Succession Act 1956 came into force and, in 1958, the widow died and her legal representative was brought on record. The Supreme Court held in 1967 that since the land was possessed by Harnam Kaur when she died in 1958, within the meaning of section 14(1) of the 1956 Act, her legal representative must be decreed to have succeeded by those rights.

There were also cases in which widows successfully challenged the right of the male collateral and obtained the property of their deceased husbands. Two cases may be cited in this connection, one decided on the basis of traditional customary rights and the other on the basis of the 1956 Act.

On 29 April 1953, one Mohinder Kaur initiated a suit for the possession of one-fourth share of the agricultural land held by her deceased father-in-law on the ground that as the widow of the pre-deceased son, she was entitled to that share.[29] The agricultural land, however, after the death of her father-in-law in 1951, had been mutated by the revenue authorities in the names of the three surviving sons only. Mohinder Kaur began a suit to claim the share which her husband would have inherited had he been alive. The suit was contested by two of her brothers-in-law on the ground that Mohinder Kaur had married Gurdial Singh, one of the brothers, by *karewa*, and as such her right was forfeited. The trial judge upheld the position of the brothers-in-law and dismissed her claim. Her appeal to the subordinate judge of Ambala was referred to a full bench. The full bench judgement delivered in 1960 settled the matter in favour of the widow saying:

In the case of Jats governed by custom in the matter of succession a widow on remarrying her deceased husband's brother remains entitled to collateral succession in the family.

Clearly, as the matter predated the Act of 1956, the case was decided on the basis of customary practice which prevailed before the Act came into operation. In colonial times, judicial opinion in cases concerning a widow's right to inherit land under customary law, had remained divided, resulting in conflicting decisions being awarded. In the post-colonial period the judges upheld the trend of custom which maintained that the widow did not forfeit her right to land even after her remarriage, where she married the brother of her deceased husband and remained within the family.

One other case which attempted to deny a widow's title to land because she had remarried was decided on the basis of the 1956 Act. According to the facts of this case, after the death of Gulab Singh, a Jat of Muktaar tehsil in the district of Ferozpur, his property was inherited by his five sons in equal shares in January 1932.[30] However, one of the sons, Dalip Singh, died. His widow Sada Kaur, who had no children, remarried in *karewa* form, Chand Singh, who was the real brother of her husband. In the meanwhile, the third brother Sampuran Singh also died leaving two daughters who transferred their father's one-fifth share of land to the surviving three brothers including Chand Singh. The possession of the entire estate, however, continued with the three brothers, though in revenue records Sada Kaur remained as the owner of one-fifth share belonging to her first husband. The court was moved in January 1962 by the remaining two brothers, Bakhteswar Singh and Jit Singh, for a declaration that they were governed by custom, according to which Sada Kaur on her remarriage forfeited the estate inherited by her from Dalip Singh, and the same devolved on her remarriage on the remaining three brothers. Her current husband, Chand Singh, could not have an exclusive use of it. They sought declaration that they were the owners in possession of the two-thirds share of their ancestral land, two of the brothers having already died. The trial court did not grant a declaration to the two brothers on the ground that under the provisions of the Hindu Succession Act 1956, Sada Kaur became the full owner of her share of land which she had inherited in 1932 after the death of her first husband.[31]

Apart from a large number of such cases which firmly established the legal recognition of a widow's claim to inheritance, informal ways of obtaining a recognition of a widow's claim, however minor, also received some support. I came across two cases of elderly widows who appealed to the *biradari* (community) against their sons, alleging ill-treatment. In an informal way they succeeded in getting a fixed monthly income from the sons.[32] The threat of the widows claiming their share of inheritance clearly worked in their favour. Similar cases are also traceable in western Uttar Pradesh.[33]

III. Strengthening of *karewa*

The clarity of the 1956 Act in granting an absolute right of inheritance to widows meant that they could not be deprived of their property by any counter claims. More importantly, as remarriage no longer legally meant that the widow would be deprived of her inheritance, she acquired, superficially at least, a greater freedom to marry outside the former levirate practice. The inheritance rights also increased the value of widows' assets in the remarriage market. Thus, the 1956 Act should have made a great difference to the established practice of *karewa* which had previously been used to control a widow's limited property right. Yet, in reality, the pressure upon widows to enter into a levirate marriage increased, leading to the strengthening of the *karewa* practice in the post-colonial period. The increasing acceptance of *karewa* among castes which earlier frowned upon and made fun of this practice, has been the subject of comment in all the district gazetteers of this region.[34] There are a number of factors responsible for the strengthening of the *karewa* practice, the most significant perhaps being that widows came into possession of a right of absolute inheritance as a result of the 1956 Act. *Karewa* marriages, therefore, have been and continue to be an important way to bring inheritance under male control and dominance.

Another significant factor promoting the levirate form of remarriage has been India's post-colonial military involvements with its neighbours. The widows of military personnel, especially the so-called "war widows" or widows of those who have died in active service, receive a large sum as compensation and are entitled to numerous benefits, both from the Centre as well as the state governments. Thus, such widows are entitled not only to the ordinary family pension, but also a special family pension. Benefits include family pension at the rate of last pay drawn till death or disqualification; family gratuity at specified rates, Army Group insurance benefits and financial benefits under the Army Officers' Benevolent Fund, Army Wives' Welfare Association and the Army Relief Fund. Widows of soldiers killed in action are given "liberalized Special Family Pensionary Awards apart from several other benefits"[35] These "special" benefits have become a lever to reinforce levirate marriages, because they are withdrawn if a widow remarries outside her late husband's family. Instituted by the Ministry of Defence and Finance, this policy was explicitly set out in a letter dated November 24, 1972. In the case of officers, as well as JCOs (Junior Commissioned Officers) and ORS (Other Ranks), if a widow remarries her deceased husband's real brother and continues to live a communal life with and/or contributes to the support of the other living eligible heirs, she will continue to be eligible to the special family pension. On re-marriage with any other person, the widow will forfeit her right to the special family pension, but will be given a pension equal in amount to the ordinary family pension as though the service man had died in normal circumstances.[36] The effects of such a directive in strengthening *karewa* are clear.

The directive also applies to the special assistance provided by different states. Punjab, Bihar, Delhi, Uttar Pradesh and

Rajasthan, for instance have been able to allocate a little surplus land on a priority basis to the war widows. Haryana, on the other hand, which does not have any surplus land to give has given its "war widows" extra financial assistance of Rs. 100 per month, an ex-gratia grant of Rs. 5,000, and additional pension of Rs. 60 per month for each dependant child and Rs. 3,000 as a marriage grant for each daughter.[37] The widows have also been allowed to draw their late husband's salary till the date when he would have retired, after which the family pension begins. This special assistance is stopped if the widow marries outside the family; here remarriage to the real brother alone guarantees its continuation.[38] It is thus clear that the financial attractions, both for men and women contributed to the reinforcement of *karewa* in the rural areas.

The increase in the *karewa* custom has been aggravated by fear and apprehension, in addition to greed. My field work suggests that often the *karewa* is performed in an "indecent hurry".[39] A woman of the village of Jhojho Chamani in the district of Bhiwani was widowed in 1985. Her husband had been a *sipahi* (soldier) in the army and had owned some land in the village. The widow had also received one lakh in cash from the army. These two were attractions enough for the family to get her married to her *dewar* within two weeks of the essential *teravin* (thirteenth day after death ceremony) of her late husband. The family was apprehensive that she might "settle" herself elsewhere. The "exploitation" suffered by the war widows at the hands of their relations and the colleagues of their husbands has been voiced and recorded by the War Widows Guild of India.[40] Quite clearly, it is not land alone which promotes *karewa*, but also other forms of inheritance, be it insurance, pension, or compensation claims.

Instances of *karewa* occurred in the case of the widows of the 1984 riots in Delhi, involving forcible marriages of the widows to their brothers-in-law who were as young as 13–14 years of age.[41] Veena Das's study similarly discloses how, after the Pakistan war of 1971, many of the widows belonging to Punjab were forced to stay with their parents-in-law till their husbands' younger brothers reached a marriageable age.[42] In fact, even now, it is not uncommon for the *karewa* wife to be two to ten years older than her new husband.

With the rising popularity of levirate marriages, the continued threats and even compulsions on a widow to perform levirate are not uncommon. In case of refusal, her marriage elsewhere is made difficult, if not impossible. For example, in the village of Asaudha, in the district of Rohtak, Asha, a nineteen year old girl became a widow.[43] Her in-laws wished to perform *karewa* with her much older *jeth* (elder brother-in-law) estimated to be around fifty years of age with a wife and three children. She did not accept it nor did her father, who settled her marriage elsewhere. Her in-laws, however, refused to allow this and a caste panchayat had to be called. The panchayat sanctioned her marriage elsewhere. But at a crucial juncture the wedding ceremony was forcibly stopped by the in-laws. Even the panchayat decision was not honoured. Asha continues to remain a widow looking after her child.

In such cases, the widow has the right to lease out her land, work at it herself through hired hands or arrive at some agreement with the male members of her former husband's family who may then remit to her a settled share of the profits. Any one of these arrangements may work, depending upon each individual case and family. However, the last option is said to be adopted more often than others, as in the case of Asha, who retains thirty *bighas* of land in her name.

Only when there are no children can an alliance be made outside the conjugal family. Such a remarriage is known as *punar-vivah* which literally means remarriage. In their basic simplicity, the two forms of remarriage, *punar-vivah* and *karewa* resemble each other very closely. The important ceremony in *punar-vivah* is the exchange of *jai malas* (garlands) by the bride and the groom. The performance of *pheras* (religious ceremony) unless the widow is a "virgin" is prohibited. *Punar-vivah* is generally known to have gained popularity among the traditional caste conscious critics like the Rajputs and the Banias, among others. Yet, like the other peasant castes, even in these caste clusters, the first choice in remarriage is *karewa* in its levirate form and only "when none of the brothers accept their widowed sister-in-law as a wife, *punar-vivah* is performed anywhere in their caste". *Punar-vivah* although increasingly accepted still follows a poor second to *karewa* with its basically repressive ingredients and elements of coercion.

Significantly, since the law no longer provides for mere "maintenance" for the widow (as had been the case under the colonial administration) but an absolute right of inheritance, the pressure upon the widow to make a levirate alliance has increased. Consequently there are several cases in which the conjugal family has successfully stalled the wedding plans of the widows.

IV. Fall out effects of *karewa*

The strengthening hold of *karewa* has underlined yet another aspect of conjugality which is also essentially repressive for women. *Karewa* in many cases has actually resulted in polygamy and has therefore been responsible for keeping the institution of polygamy alive, despite the legal requirements of monogamy. This social recognition of polygamy is not only forthcoming in levirate marriages, but also in those situations where the first wife is either barren or has borne only daughters. For a man, polygamy means another hand to work in the fields leading to greater production and property, as well as more children, that is, it is considered a socio-economic necessity. Women therefore continue to be regarded as resources like land, acquired by men. The sons of a polygamous union are inheritors of equal shares of the father's property, either directly through will or by the decision of the village or caste or *kunba panchayat*. The colonial rulers also made no difference between the rights of inheritance of sons of a *phere* (marriage) or a *karewa* marriage.[44]

Polygamy disadvantages both women concerned and, if asked, women freely speak against it. Statistically, a recent study of three villages in Delhi territory overlapping the Haryana state found 75 per cent of the women were opposed to the idea of more than one wife.[45] The other 25 per cent supported it under exceptional circumstances of barrenness of the wife, or a levirate alliance with the deceased husband's brother "to preserve family bonds". The same study also shows that among rural women who favoured widow remarriage, only 13 per cent favoured such remarriage within the family, (that is, with the husband's brother) and the remaining 87 per cent opted for anyone. A very small number even felt that the decision about a new partner should be left to the widows and no force should be applied. Self-made alliances, however, are not readily accepted and some women openly frown upon such an idea. This attitude directly contradicts the increasing cases of elopements.

The disapproval of self-made alliances may very well be due to the negative reactions of men and the negative consequences for women which have followed from such marriages. Indeed conflicts have always arisen whenever the widow has asserted her wishes in a remarriage partnership. For a widow to marry of her own choice, in many instances, still means a run-away marriage. The popular rural belief continues to equate running-away with a *rand* (widow). "*Rand bhaj gai*" (the widow has run away) is a phrase commonly used for any absconding female.[46] It emanates out of the widow's self-assertion in marriage.

There are also certain other restrictions on settling a widow's marriage. Unlike in the colonial period, her partner cannot be a bachelor. The only bachelor she is allowed to remarry with approval is in the levirate marriage. Where a bachelor is involved with a widow, then the opposition from his family members often takes a violent turn. Parents are known to react to such marriages by cutting off all relations with their son, disowning and even disinheriting him.[47]

Many of those widows who have ventured to remarry either on their own or through their parents, have either had to sell their land to their husband's collateral at a minimal price or renounce their claims in property controlled either by the father-in-law or brother-in-law.[48] That is why in the popular perception, notwithstanding the 1956 inheritance law, a remarriage (except in its levirate form) continues to mean what it meant in colonial times, that a widow is deprived of her inheritance.

The *karewa*, apart from granting social and cultural approval and acceptance also allows a woman to remain in the family into which she was married. And even though her *karewa* husband may become the *de facto* owner of land, the land as such remains in her name and she remains on the spot, a full working partner. The pressure upon her to remain assimilated in the family through levirate has not lessened in spite of the property rights she has acquired by virtue of the Hindu Succession Act, 1956. In fact, in some ways the pressure has increased. Given the realities of rural social conditions, levirate also continues to be considered a refuge by the widows for withstanding pressure, threats of violence and sexual abuse from their husbands' male agnates. In addition, the hold they have on their inherited land is tenuous where they have no son. A levirate marriage takes care of all these constraints.

V. Conclusion

In a curious way, therefore, custom, law and the state have all combined successfully to regulate conjugality in safeguarding the patrilineal inheritance interests in vastly differing sociolegal conditions prevalent under the colonial and post-colonial situations. Under the colonial period, the practice of awarding a widow limited property rights was appropriated by her husband's family on his death, by her forceful remarriage to a collateral. The establishment of a widow's right to property during the post-colonial period did not help to arrest the practice. In fact it lead to a strengthening of the practice of *karewa* as there was property at stake over which the husband's family sought to firmly retain its control. Even benefits awarded to war widows by the Indian state, which has been increasingly involved in military activity during the post-colonial period, has only intensified the effort to keep the widow's 'wealth' inside the husband's family.

At the same time as the pressure to perform *karewa* has increased, other laws such as those outlawing polygamy have not been enforced with any rigour, thus legitimizing the practice of *karewa* and the practice of polygamy that has resulted from it. In turn, *karewa* has become a refuge for widows who are otherwise forced to confront threats of violence and sexual abuse from her husband's family and face social ostracism.

Therefore, the role of law in this context has not operated to empower widows, but to further drive them into the folds of their husband's family. There they have found some social protection, but have simultaneously lost control of land rights. In focusing primarily on economic empowerment, the law neglected to address the social and political disempowerment of widows which have effectively undermined their rights.

The issues raised by an examination of the practice of *karewa* under both pre and post colonial rule highlight the limitations of law as a mechanism to liberate oppressed elements in society.

What is the role of law when the rights of a subgroup result in the violation of the rights of some of its individual members, that is, women? How can law ensure the rights of the individual without, at the same time, alienating her from her community? These are questions which must now be addressed by those who create, administer and critique the law.

Notes

[1] *Niyog* was a practice of levirate marriage. Later, as during the Mahabharata times, *niyog* came to signify cohabitation by the wife with men other than her husband under certain specific conditions like impotency of the husband and the "moral and religious duty to beget sons to continue the family line". Eventually, *niyog* was given

up as being inconsistent with increasingly pristinized and Brahmanized standard for marital chastity and devotion. The increasing tendency in the late Dharm Sutras was to proscribe such practices. For details see Gail Hinich Sutherland "Bija (seed) and Ksetra (field): Male Surrogacy or Niyog in the Mahabharata" 24: *Contributions to Indian Sociology*, 77 (Jan–June 1990).

2 For details see C.L. Tupper, 2 *The Punjab Customary Law*, 93, 12 (Calcutta; Govt. Printing, 1881); see also E. Joseph, *Customary Law of the Rohtak District*, 1910, 45 (Lahore: Govt. Printing, 1911).

3 The British under the Punjab Alienation of Land Act, 1900, designated the following as the "agricultural tribes": Jat, Rajput, Pathan, Sayyed, Gujjar, Ahir, Biloch, Ror, Moghal and Mali. By subsequent notifications, Taga, Saini, Chauhan, Arain, Gaud Brahmin and Qureshi were also notified. See *Gazetteer of India*, 1989, part I, the Alienation of Land Bill, 1990.

4 *Census of India, Punjab and Delhi*, 1911, Vol. 17, Part I, Report, p. 219. For a comprehensive account of the low position of Brahmins in Haryana and Punjab see Prem Chowdhry: *The Veiled Women: Shifting Gender Equations in Rural Haryana 1880–1990* (Delhi: Oxford University Press).

5 *Rohtak District Gazetteer*, 1910, III-A, Lahore, Civil and Military Gazette, 1911, at 90. For court decisions leading to the forfeiture of property in cases where the widows remarried see: Parji vs. Mangta I.C. (1931) 767; Hira Singh and Nathu vs. Rami 28 Punjab Record 317 (1893); also Prema vs. Pradhan 18 Punjab Record 414 (1883).

6 *Rohtak District Gazetteer*, 1910, supra note 5, at 90. In certain areas and among specific agricultural castes of Haryana and Punjab different forfeiture customs applied. The customary norm which was to be operative in a particular case had to be decided by the court, on the basis of the custom applicable to the concerned parties. In any case the final result was the same, since the customary law prevailing amongst agricultural castes of Punjab regarded the wife's personal property as merged with that of the husband, who was also deemed entitled to all the wife's earnings and even her ornaments. In other words, the woman both by marriage and by remarriage lost all control over movable and immovable property. See W.M. Rattigan, A *Digest of Civil Law for the Punjab Chiefly Based on the Customary Law as Present Ascertained*, (H.L. Sarin and K.L. Pandit, 2nd ed. 1880) (Reprint, 1960 at 204, 427, 747. Except for the Allahabad and Oudh Courts, the rest, that is Calcutta, Bombay and Punjab, maintained that forfeiture was general. For details of such cases involving lower castes with different customary practices see Lucy Carroll, "Law, Cus-

tom and Statutory Social Reform: The Hindu Widows' Remarriage Act of 1856" 20: 4 *Indian Economic and Social History Review*, (Oct.-Dec. 1983); Parji vs. Mangta, id. at 767–768.

7 18 Punjab Record (1883) Lahore Series 414. Also see Rattigan, supra note 6 at 203–4, 207.

8 A. Kensington, *Customary Law of the Ambala District*, Vol. X, Lahore, Civil and Military Gazette, 1893 at 26.

9 Such cases were very common. For example, see Bhag Bhai vs. Vazir Khan 13, Punjab Record (1912) 375.10 Joseph, supra note 2, at 40.

10 Kensington, supra note 8, at 26.

11 C.C. Garbett, *Riwaj-I-Am of Panipat Tehsil and Karnpal Pargana in the Karnal District*, Lahore, Civil and Military Gazette, 1910, at 12; See Musammat Durgi vs. Shibhu Brahman of Karnal 1900 case no. 348.

12 T. Cordon Walker, *The Customary Law of the Ludhiana District 120* (Calcutta: Central Press Co., 1885).

13 J.M. Douie, *The Punjab Law Administration Manual*, 270–271 (2nd ed. 1908) Reprint, 1971).

14 C.A.H. Townsend, *Customary Law of the Hissar District*, Vol. XXV, 3–34 (Lahore, Punjab Govt. Press, 1913); also H.C. Beadon, *Customary Law of the Delhi District*, Vol. XXII, 32 (Lahore, Civil & Military Gazette, 1892).

15 Joseph, supra note 2, at 70–71.

16 Douie, supra note 13, at 270–271.

17 Id.

18 George Campbell, *Memoirs of My Indian Career*, Vol. I, 83–84 (London: MacMillan and Co., 1893). Interestingly, his observation about having played this role was: "In my business with people my habits were those of extreme patriarchal familiarity". Id. at 84.

19 MSS. Eur. D. 188: "Gurgaon District General Code of Tribal Custom", handwritten by J. Wilson, Assistant Settlement Officer, *India Office Records*, (London, 1879).

20 Id.

21 Walker, supra note 12, at 39–51.

22 *Rohtak District Gazetteer*, 1910, supra note 6, at 90.

23 Cunningham, *Rohtak District Gazetteer*, 1883–84, 51.

24 For details of the Act and its comparison with the earlier situation existing in British India, see the Hindu Succession Act, No. XXX of 1956, in Sunderlal T. Desai, *Mulla Principles of Hindu Law*, (13th ed. 1966) also *Hindu Law*, Vol. II, (3rd ed. 1981).

Attempts to amend the Act of 1956 were made by the Punjab Government in 1977 and by the Haryana Government in 1979 and

1979 and 1989. The amendments sought to prevent the daughter and sister from having inheritance rights in the natal family property. These attempts were subsequently defeated. Yet what is significant is that widows were excluded from all these attempts to constrict the rights. However, as this account will attempt to show, as regards widows, the rights they secured under the Hindu Succession Act have already been greatly compromised in the actual implementation of the Act.

25 This aspect has been fully addressed in Prem Chowdhry, "Culture, Ideology and State: Subverting Female Inheritance (Act of Succession 1956)", *Modern Asian Studies*.

26 A 1961 Punj. 295.

27 Jaga Singh vs. Teja Singh, A 1970 P. & H. 309.

28 Mangal Singh vs. Rattno, A 1967 S.C. 1786.

29 Charan Singh vs. Gurdial Singh, A 1961 Punj. 301.

30 Sada Kumar vs. Bakhtawar Singh, A 1970 P. & H. at 289.

31 An appeal made in 1964, however, recognized the original claim to land made by the two brothers on the basis that the 1956 Act could be applied only in cases in which the widow was actually in physical possession of the land and not in name alone. Obviously, the fears generated by the 1956 Act regarding the possible entitlement of widows to land were genuine and anyone who could anticipate it by exploiting the loopholes existing in its retroactive effects, did it effectively.

32 These cases were brought to my notice by Jasbir Singh Malik, advocate of Gohana village, district Rohtak, 17–18 June 1986 and R.M. Hooda, Advocate, Rohtak, 16 June 1986.

33 A few cases were narrated to me by Girija Devi, a widow from the village of Gandhi in Meerut district. Her two sons have inherited about 200 bighas of land, but refuse to give her any share. She is therefore also considering the idea of moving the court to claim her share, "to teach her sons a lesson". The "shame" she would experience from the publicity, has so far restrained her from taking any action. Interview with Girija Devi, village Gandhi, district Meerut, August 3, 1988.

34 See for example, *Bhiwani District Gazetteer*, 1982, Chandigarh, 1983, at 67.

35 This list of the latest "special awards" was catalogued by the Minister of State for Defence, Raja Ramanna, and was put before the Rajya Sabha on 14th March 1990: see *Hindustan Times*, New Delhi edition, March 15, 1990, at 9.

36 I am grateful to Commander K.P. Kakkar and Shri Chander Bhan of Kendriya Sainik Board, Rama Krishna Puram, New Delhi, for making this information available to me. See letter No. 200847/Pen-C/71, dated November 24, 1972, Kendriya Sainik Board, New Delhi.

37 Information made available by the Kendriya Sainik Board, New Delhi.

38 Nonetheless, despite these benefits the pension continues to remain woefully deficient. The first Defence Pension Adalat (Court) held in Karnal on January 7, 1989, underlined the inadequacies in the pension. *The Tribune*, Chandigarh edition, January 9, 1989, at 16.

39 Interview with Mohran Devi, village Jhojho Chamani, Bhiwani District, January 7, 1990.

40 *The Tribune*, supra note 55.

41 Personal communication from Uma Chakravarti based on unpublished interviews with women activists dealing with the post-1984 riots. Also see Veena Das "Our Work to Cry: Your Work to Listen", in *Mirrors of Violence: Communities, Riots and Survivors in South Asia* (V. Das ed. 1990).

42 Veena Das, "Marriage Among the Hindus" in *Indian Women* (D. Jain ed. New Delhi, Ministry of Information and Broadcasting, Govt. of India, 1975).

43 Interview with Dheer Singh, village Asaudha Todran, district Rohtak, August 8–10, 1990.

44 Douie, supra note 13, at 10.

45 Rekha Bhagat and P.N. Mathur, *Mass Media and Farm Women*, 80–81 (1989).

46 A common observation in all the villages that I visited.

47 Ram Chander's nephew, Gyanendra Singh, married a young widow with two small children in 1986. The family continues to disown him and so far he remains disinherited. Ram Chander, village Bandh, district Karnal, May 20–21, 1988.

48 This reality was common knowledge amongst the men and women who were interviewed or who had gathered together for a conversational session with me.

First published in *National Law School Journal* 1, 1993.

Women, Land and Law: Dispute Resolutions at the Village Level

JAYOTI GUPTA

Introduction

Between 1996–99 a study was carried out in the state of West Bengal to explore the extent of rights women have over the productive forces of society. It analyzed the manner in which the issue of women's rights as individuals and citizens has been addressed by the Left Front government since it came to power in 1977, the impact the government's policies have had on the lives of peasant women, and the legislative complexities that had to be addressed in an effort to reconcile the claims of the individual and those of the collective with reference to land reform in particular and other areas of rights from a gendered perspective. A field survey was carried out in four villages in two districts covering 870 households; several meetings and workshops were held, and individuals from different walks of life equally concerned with the issues taken up by the study were interviewed. Covering a vast canvas of primary and secondary material, important areas of research concerns and spheres where major policy matters are to be rephrased, reworked, and implemented, have been identified. This report will explore these areas of concern by focusing on the way in which the individual and collective interests are being addressed through dispute resolutions at the village level and whether they are being raised at all in this process of mediation popularly called *gram shalishi*. Let me begin by summarizing the demands articulated by the peasant women, reflecting the conditions of life as revealed by the household data, as well as the complexities involved in addressing the question of rights.

What the women demand
A. *To be considered as individuals in their own right*

- Equal rights in inheritance, matrimonial property, and to be recognized as individuals by the State and not as dependents, e.g. mother, wife, daughter, and sister. All the legal restrictions placed on different categories of dependents should be removed.

- Independent ownership of productive resources with or without joint titles, with some of them clearly asking for independent ownership of land and not joint ownership, be it with husband, father, brother or son. This way they felt they could be assured of their independent right to livelihood and could take their own decisions. This feeling was widespread among the younger generation of women, many of whom were unmarried as their parents could not pay the dowry demanded by the boy's family; women who had studied till class eight and above; and deserted and divorced women. While we did not come across instances where there has been a dispute over joint property division, the women themselves articulated the problems as follows:

    (i)   Their husbands still control the lands. Decisions regarding production, credit, and marketing, are mostly taken by their husbands, as they continue to be the owners of other resources such as capital and cash.

    (ii) It is difficult for women to ask for their independent share of the profits from the lands that have joint titles. The earning is perceived as family income. In case of separation/divorce, as the individual share in the joint title to land is not demarcated, it would be difficult to divide title land. At the moment, for lands distributed as joint titles no clarification exists on division of the land if situation demands (sic).

Women pointed out that as there are no laws as yet on equal right to matrimonial property/home, in situations of separation/divorce, they are the ones who have to leave the house. As land is not a moveable property, they have to forego the land. The only option would be for either holder to compensate the other for the half share or for both to sell to a third party. In the former option the compensation would invariably be from the husband to the wife and that would be below the market price. In the case of the latter option, both partners would lose their land. Money cannot compensate for the appreciating value of the land.

B. Property rights

- From their own experience of being denied property rights as daughters by their parents, the women pointed out that the law of complete freedom of testation should be reviewed in order to ensure that even the existing provisions of inheritance as daughters, wives and sisters, are not violated. This is one among many directions in which the demand for equal rights can make a start.

- Equal rights to the homestead of the parents, so that they do not have to feel hesitant to return to their maternal home on being divorced, separated or deserted. Women want their rights to maternal homesteads clearly defined in legal terms as they do not want to be obligated to their brothers for allowing them to return home. The brothers should only be given the usufruct rights of the sister's share of the property in her absence and not ownership rights. Among the peasant women, the issue of Hindu married women under the Hindu Succession Act not having a right to call for partition of the family house was not known and nor did it make much difference to the discussion when the issue was raised. They however insisted on having their share in the maternal home well protected by law. (This came closest to one of the issues to be explored, viz. the legal right of the sister to call for partition of the family home and be independent owner of her share with complete freedom of contract. While the validity of this demand can be circumstantial and judged from case to case, the in-built inequality in the legal provision on partition should be removed.)

- Stricter legislation to deal with multiple marriages and a more transparent enforcement regime to protect the interest of the wife who is left behind to fend for herself. The women suggested expansion of provisions of joint registration of matrimonial property, and securing their rights in the matrimonial home (e.g. shelter, protection from violence by the husband and the in-laws, and a share of and right to matrimonial residence).

C. Dowry

- Government intervention on a war footing to end the menace of dowry. The women as well as the men were aware of the Dowry Prohibition Act and ridiculed it for its provision to punish both the giver and taker of dowry. They felt that the law had failed to grasp the social reality. They also felt that a state wide campaign should begin to address the problem of dowry. They could not however articulate a slogan for the movement and suggest how it is to be taken up. (The activists of the women's movement admitted the rise in incidents of dowry-related matrimonial disputes, deaths and violence. They also admitted, in the course of the investigation, that there was indeed a direct link between the dowry transactions and the pauperization of the land poor, often even resulting in landlessness. They agreed to give some thought to linking the campaign against dowry with changes in land ownership and control in the countryside of West Bengal. The peasants' union was not open to a discussion on this matter.)

D. *Community differences and personal laws*

- The Muslim women expressed deep dissatisfaction with the practice of polygamy. They too were keen to put an end to the system of dowry and felt totally betrayed by the changes in the maintenance provisions for Muslim women. They also complained about the denial of their share of inherited property in practice just as in the case of the women of other communities. The demand for right to independent property in their own names was clearly articulated, and the reasons were the same as indicated in the early part of the report. They demanded recognition of their contribution to agricultural production. As Muslim women (even if they belong to agricultural labourer households) are in general debarred from working as agricultural labourers and from working on their own fields, the demand for independent share of property/land, and equal right to matrimonial property was urgent (there were however no suggestions from the women about lifting the sanction against work outside the house. Under these social conditions, and in a situation where only participation in the sphere of exchange relation is viewed as work, the women's demand to be recognized as individuals in a peasant family context becomes complicated. The situation of the women of the Muslim community is similar to the condition of peasant women of high-ranking castes, not allowed to work in the fields). The women reminded everybody that even when they do not work outside the house, they take on the responsibility of agricultural operations at home. They pointed towards the need to recognize processing of agricultural produce and preparing it for the market as part of social production. In fact, the women raised a very pertinent question. They asked why men who do not work in the fields, who do not plough, are still recognized as cultivators and enjoy independent right to titles. They asked why men at the age of 18 are considered as independent adults (counted as a separate family under the ceiling laws) and unmarried women are not.

- Women did not approve of divisions along religious or community lines in matters of property inheritance, divorce laws, and all the other areas covered by the personal law. In discussions about agricultural land and property one of the issues discussed was that while land reform programmes do not make a distinction between communities in allocation, why are there differences between communities maintained in all matters which involve women's rights?

... Law's tangles: institutional straitjackets
The state of law: formal and informal spheres

The denial of womens' rights as equal citizens of the nation at different levels and spheres lies behind the many contradictory provisions which women have to negotiate in order to establish their rights as individuals. ... A broad analysis of the disputes that have been recorded reveals that while there is a great range of causes of disputes, all related to questions of women's rights and status, there is a greater variation in the laws and acts by which these issues are being interpreted, judged and redressed. The disputes, which have been recorded at the village level and from out-of-court settlements at district legal aid centres run by the women's organizations, show a great variety of causes: bigamy; desertion for not bearing a child; desertion resulting from migration; desertion for lack of dowry; extramarital relationship and physical torture of the first wife; impotency; alchoholism; rape charge against husband; reason for desertion unexplained; torture for non-specific reasons; marital maladjustment; denial of marriage by the boy; early motherhood of unmarried girl; husband threatening wife with remarriage on death of a boy child; and physical torture. Most of such cases are resolved/settled out of court. Of the above issues, the cases of bigamy, dowry demand and physical torture follow that order of priority. There are more transactions of dowry than disputes over non-payment or insufficient payment of dowry. The cases that go to the courts relate primarily to application for a maintenance grant by the wife and not necessarily for divorce.

Of the 1260 cases that have been documented in the course of this study in their various stages of negotiations both for formal and out-of-court settlements, from the districts and from the villages, there were only 23 cases of property dispute in the courts. The data would underscore the trend for the period 1990–1996. The cases which have been compiled from the Law Reports which are at the level of the High Court and above for the period 1940 to 1990 have shown a much higher incidence of property-related cases. Under this head several typologies could be demarcated with distinctive patterns:

The typologies	Year		
	1940–49	50–59	60–69	80–90
Alienation of property		4	–	3
Denial of property by brothers/fathers to sisters/daughters	1	2	–	6
Intestate death with no male child	1	2	3	4
Will contest	3	4	2	4
Misc. property matters involving women	19	20	12	14
Total	24	32	18	31

From the same data source the next highest number of cases relate to bigamy/divorce and maintenance followed by cases of sexual violence.

Lawyers interviewed at the district level pointed out that property inheritance disputes involving the rights of women are on the decline as there has been a decline in the rate of accumulation of real property especially land. This assumption however calls for further investigation and substantiation. Moreover, decline in inheritance-related property disputes does not negate the fact that in the existing state of affairs women are the ultimate losers. However, the present trend of disputes that reach the courts proves that more attention needs to be given to principles of matrimonial property rights for women (especially married women) than to principles of inheritance. But this may be particularly relevant to West Bengal where several restrictions have been placed on accumulation of landed property, and distribution of real property has been carefully implemented even though the authorities have been blind to gender discrimination in the structural sense. It is to be seen whether in other states where land reforms remain an unfinished business, the question of gaining through inheritance rights takes precedence over matrimonial property rights. It is not a question of one or the other, and principles will have to be drawn up for all sources of access to real property and productive resources, and its applicability will depend on the larger social processes at work in the respective contexts. Laws and social processes need to feed each other and benefit from each other. Neither is frozen in time or irreversible or exclusive in its identity.

The present relationship between the formal and the informal legal processes in West Bengal

Apart from the property-related disputes and cases of maintenance that are in the courts, we found the majority of the disputes being resolved and addressed through community participation. However according to the lawyers interviewed, community decisions as a speedier process are not necessarily able to protect the interests of women. This is perhaps because of two reasons. On the one hand, the legal provisions are directly interlinked with the social process and have already had considerable influence in structuring it; on other hand, the formal legal system and its acts and procedures constitute a formidable institutional blockage.

According to one lawyer who is also a leading member of the legal aid cell functioning under the guidance of the women's movement, out-of-court settlements have been the product of an increased participation as well as intervention by the community, the neighbours, and there is a greater sense of social responsibility in society. The separation between the public and the private maintained by the formal structure of law is often bridged in community-based settlements. While this gap has narrowed down in the more democratic atmosphere in the villages of West Bengal, gender discrimination in the existing laws is reflected at the micro level when the participants in a negotiation are divided into male and female support groups. Still, out-of-court settlements have several positive aspects that are restricted by the piecemeal approach within the structure of the formal law courts.

In day to day life the community has begun to play a larger social role. Judgements in the village settlements take into account factors such as a live assessment of the household/ party involved within the village economic and social structure. There is a greater understanding of the exact nature of compulsions of both parties in the dispute and a closer view of the complexities through which relationships are established and broken; several hearings are possible, in which both parties are given enough time to make their representations to the community; the parties feel freer to express themselves sitting among familiar faces and surroundings; there is often a possibility of a balanced mix between the provisions of the formal law and the social reality: formal laws do have a place as they allow the interpreters and arbiters to use them to steer through the myriad issues involved in a dispute, while at the same time the written law does not become restrictive. A greater transparency and reduction of the ambiguities of law can help to bridge the gap between the legal structures, the judiciary and the social reality.

The factors that do not allow the common citizen to make the best use of the formal courts and the law were pointed out as follows:

a. Intimidating procedures and ignorance of procedures.
b. Inability to follow the language of the interpreters of law, i.e. the lawyers as well as the judges, as well as the

language of the judiciary and the interpretations in legal language. (The procedures are conducted in English).

c. The element of time, with repeated 'dates' delaying and complicating the process to the disadvantage of the woman in 99.9 per cent of the cases.

d. Lack of information about dates.

e. Lawyers' fees, court fees and charges.

f. Expenses incurred in travelling to the courts which are situated in the district headquarters.

g. Lack of time for a proper hearing at a stretch as a result of which the arguments become fragmented.

h. The fear that once matters go to the court all options of negotiation are closed.

i. Delay and neglect in implementation of court orders and lack of access to the implementing authorities.

j. The overwhelming number of Acts and procedures that are used to address the issue of rights.

k. The restrictive nature of the personal laws that violate the rights of an individual woman as a citizen and her human rights.

(In village level dispute settlements this last element comes into play with considerable force, as we shall see in later sections of this study.)

The present status gained by *Gram Shalishi*

It would be a hasty conclusion if from a consideration of the formal legal framework one decided that *gram shalishi* as a forum of mediation has been able to address and resolve most of the disabilities built into the structure of the judiciary, the laws, the acts, procedures and interpretations. We need to be cautious at this early stage. We need to understand the way *gram shalishi* has evolved, its role, its strength, its weaknesses, and the place that it has gained before we favour its extension as the main forum for negotiating issues based on individual experience as well as those of a structural nature.

One can begin with the broad composition of gram *shalishi* forums in the present context. A *gram shalishi* body comprises members of the elected panchayat, of women's organizations, of peasants' organizations, members who are functionaries of different political parties (not necessarily as party functionaries but as members of the panchayats; largely elected on party lines the two identities often merged into one), the parties in dispute and their family and friends, and finally, all members of the village community where the *shalishi* takes place—the *shalishi* is an open forum. The formal procedure has to begin with a letter addressed to the secretary of the *gram* committee, who in turn decides on the venue, date and time for the *shalishi*. He/she informs the others who are to participate in an official capacity and the general members of the village community are informed by word of mouth. The secretary of the *gram* committee has an important role to play as the proceedings of the *shalishi* are finally presented by the secretary. ...

Reflecting along with Mafuza Begum

Mafuza Begum, field researcher of this study, belongs to village Paltadanga, of Barasat 2 Block of district North 24 Parganas. Paltadanga was one of the four villages where a household survey was carried out under the earlier project. During the course of that study and subsequently for this study, Mafuza had maintained a diary of *gram shalishi* cases, in which she personally had participated. Mafuza Begum is an activist of a women's organization and belongs to a peasant family. As a responsibility assigned to her by her organization she looks after the work of seven Gram Panchayats (gram panchayats being the second tier of the elected representative body, each gram panchayat represents several villages ranging between ten to twenty-five). Cases also come to Mafuza from areas beyond those assigned to her by the organization. They come to her because they have heard of Mafuza's role in *gram shalishis*—her efficiency; her capability in placing the problem within a perspective that has helped many women; she is a leader of the women's organization and is well known in that area; she is a trusted and a known person; she knows the salient features of the existing laws; she is able to place the law in its context and interpret it well for the protection of the interests of the women; she knows the formal procedures and is able to use the concepts of formal law to serve the demands of the women's movement; she belongs to the area and is considered 'one of us'; and, finally she is also well known for her leadership in many struggles in that area led by the organization she belongs to. Mafuza understands and speaks the language of the people. Interestingly, Mafuza's religion is not a criterion for those who come to her directly or those who meet Mafuza for the first time in a *gram shalishi*.

Speaking on the general trend of disputes that has been addressed by her and those which come for *gram shalishi*, she detailed the following features:

Cases offered for *gram shalishi* are on the rise. All types of cases are handled by *gram shalishi*. Among those which involve questions of women's rights and their violation, there has been an increase in cases of desertion, separation, violence against women and children (irrespective of the sex of the child), abandonment, where the husband disappears for a while leaving the wife and the child behind with his parents, who return the wife to her parents. This last situation develops often in complicity with the parents of the boy, who can marry again, once he has returned the first wife to her parents. There are several cases where the boy has been found to be already married and has entered into a second or even third marriage. Multiple marriages are a common feature in the villages, being resorted to by men of all religious communities. The reasons for such incidents are not always related to dispute over dowry, but it is also a fact today that no marriage takes place without the promise of a dowry. The violence against married women can begin at any point—just after marriage if the dowry has not been up to the expectations of the groom's family; failure to pay the promised amount by the wife's family; failure to comply with repeated demands of the husband and his family years after marriage; when the husband enters into another relationship and uses non-payment of sufficient dowry as an excuse to break away from the marriage; a second marriage entered into as the first wife has not been able to bear a son. These cases when they are discussed before a *gram shalishi* become far more complicated than what the immediate cause of dispute is. It takes several sessions before a case is fully comprehended and before any decision can be arrived at. Apart from cases of marital discord, and marital violence, Mafuza spoke about increasing intervention by *gram shalishi* in cases of denial of the sisters' rightful share of property by brothers. Property cases are more widespread among the Muslim community than among the non-Muslims, for whom most of the cases relate to right to maintenance and return of dowry. Among non-Muslims even the issue of matrimonial property right is not well comprehended, or articulated even in *gram shalishi* if they are to refer to the provisions of the formal law. Mafuza pointed out that among the Muslims, share in parental property (even agricultural land) of the daughters is determined according to well defined principles just as denial of matrimonial property to Muslim women is also worked out on well-defined principles. While intervening in cases of denial of parental property by brothers, *gram shalishis* can adhere to the existing principles in law, be it in relation to Muslim women or non-Muslim women. It is in the areas of denial even in the formal law, that *gram shalishis* play an important role in extending the notion of rights. It is in such instances that factors such as the concern of the village community; the pressure of the village community; elaboration of the concepts of human right, morality, social responsibility; gross violation of standards of what is acceptable and unacceptable by the society; the influence of the women's movement and its perspective on the notion of rights; the perspective of the peasants' organization; the perspective of the *gram* committee secretary, and the gram panchayat member; the socio-economic profile of the parties in dispute; the influence and the status that the parties in dispute have in their respective villages; the extent to which relations of dominance by collectives such as caste, religious groups, powerful families have been democratized; general level of education in the village; history of women's movement; history of social movements—all these come into play and the decision of the *gram shalishi* is often an outcome of the success or failure with which each of these above factors has been correlated.

This framework of functioning adopted by *gram shalishi* makes the notion of 'rights' a variable. It could work in more ways than one and does not necessarily guarantee a predictable outcome of a dispute. The point is that the notion of rights is itself not well defined. What is reflected in the laws is also left to interpretation and is influenced by several macro considerations, e.g. the polity and the economy and the social formation in the making. What I am trying to say is that the notion of rights is still an abstraction and at the moment is concretized only when contextualized. While the formal laws have attempted a broad definition of the concept of rights commensurate with the concept of the family, existing property relations, social relations of labour, accumulation, production, consumption and distribution, and the state, the dynamism observed at the level of reproduction of everyday life deviates from it and sometimes works in conjunction with the wider processes of law and lawmaking. The incompatibility between the formal guidelines for the larger social process and how everyday life patterns reproduce themselves, lead us to conclude that there is enough room for negotiation between the two processes and none is frozen in time. How each sphere is being negotiated with each other and within each other, is evident in the forum of *gram shalishi*. In other situations, contexts and in other states they are in most likelihood played out in the deliberations of *gram sabhas*. Be it the *gram shalishis* of West Bengal or *gram sabhas* in other states, the decisions of these forums would be a reflection of the larger movements within the existing structures of the society, the consolidation of certain patterns and the sites of developing discord. My own position on these forums is that they help to keep alive the written law and feed life into it. They need not be read as romanticized structures of 'community life,' 'people's forum,' or idealized as working towards a homogenized, consensus-based balance of collective community life. They need not also be posed as forums that are exclusive of norms of contract. However two elements dominate the out-of-court settlements, viz. varying forms of conciliation and mediation. Mediation is the manner in which village societies have settled disputes for over centuries. Most private disputes at the village level have been traditionally settled by didactic, or coerced, conciliation as opposed to voluntary conciliation. An insistence upon a clear-cut, all-or-nothing decision in favour of one disputant rather than a compromise settlement in which each disputant conceded something was regarded as inimical to group harmony. There are various theories put forward to account for conciliation. The contrast is posed in terms of individual assertiveness versus group harmony. Whether conciliation has been incorporated in the system of the formal adjudication is yet to be ascertained.

In West Bengal one can see a transitional phase marked by a curious mix of conciliation with decisions in favour of one disputant. The latter is laboriously worked out especially in defence of the rights of the individual against the parameters of social regulation applicable to the collective. Thus while new collectives are in the making (based on class for example), the rights of individuals outside the framework of the collective is often perceived as a divergence from the main site of conflict and its recognition and resolution. A reading of the cases at the village level reveals that protection of individual interests is assured in either/or terms when they do not include matters of property. Property-related disputes that seek individuation of the rights of the women, are not easily resolved at the village level. When they are addressed, an attempt is first made to move it away from the jurisdiction of the women's movement as the main arbiter and take it up as a matter of class conflict to be dealt with by organizations representing 'class'. The separation of issues of violation of equal rights to productive resources and especially land, from issues termed as 'social' across class lines and specific to women and the disabilities that they suffer is a false separation. Mafuza pointed out that the women's organizations are engaged in a struggle to put an end to this separation. She pointed out that whenever a disputant comes with a case involving conflicts around property, and an application is to be prepared requesting convening of *gram shalishi*, the matter is not immediately taken up through village level participation. In such situations elaborate precautions are taken to prevent disputes breaking out in the first place, for instance by making sure that all those affected by a decision are involved in making it and realize its implications. A much quicker action on the part of the *gram* committee is discernible in matters other than property-related disputes. This separation exercised at the village level is only a reflection of the way society is organized through the existing laws that make separate provisions for family laws and general property laws. The general property laws of land for example first address the question of property through collectives of class, maintained through patriarchal interests, in terms of inheritance, caste and religious norms of descent, and even norms of marriage including the practice of dowry and patrilocal residence.

Before a *shalishi* is convened the matter is discussed in detail with either a member of the women's organization or peasants' organization, or a panchayat member. Sometimes a neighbour, or any other member of the village is informed of the situation and he or she then forwards the matter to the collective, i.e. members of organizations/bodies. People do not take up matters spontaneously and mediate such cases. Application is made to the Secretary of the *gram* committee. The official composition of the *gram shalishi* to be convened is decided on the basis of the facts cited in the application. For example in matters such as divorce, desertion, separation, maintenance, in fact, in all the areas that fall under the purview of family law according to the formal legislative framework, members of the women's organization are invited to be the main arbiters. Some cases of denial of property that require extension of the concept of human rights where provisions for such are absent according to the religious codes, are also initiated by the women's organization. In situations where a case calls for a re-definition of the concept of human rights of women as individuals, the women's movement fights hard to claim for itself the main role of arbiter in *gram shalishis*. Even when they succeed, such cases often reach the courts overriding the decision of the *gram shalishi*. In such situations the restrictive and closed provisions of the formal law offer sharp resistance to the demands of the women based on the experience of their own life situations. Cases are often taken to the courts when enforcement of decisions laid down by *gram shalishi* cannot be enforced for some reason or another—here again matters are dragged to the courts to the disadvantage of the women. ...

In twenty years of Mafuza's experience of *gram shalishi*, she has not been called upon to adjudicate a single case of a Hindu woman's claim to right to property. This perhaps corroborates the lawyers' observations that with the decline in landed property of peasant households following the changes in the land reform provisions, there has been a decline in property cases especially at the initiative of women wanting an equal share of parental property. Decline in the patriarchal property structure has been a result of the land reforms in the state; identification of ceiling surplus lands and their takeover by the government followed by their distribution to a large number of households with drastically reduced holdings adequate enough only for subsistence from self-cultivation combined with wage labour, registration of sharecroppers and fixation of share to be paid by the sharecropper to the landlord in favour of the sharecroppers as well as several restrictions that have been placed on the land market and avenues through which land titles can change hands. Land that has been distributed by the government cannot be sold or mortgaged although they can be inherited. Lands that have been distributed but on which titles have not been conferred fall under the category of 'case restrained' (or those that cannot be sold, mortgaged, or even partitioned through the line of inheritance). Land mortgage is no longer officially recognized and even when land is mortgaged it cannot be alienated by the creditor with the help of an official document on the basis of non-payment of interest on the mortgage amount. Lands held by the tribal community cannot be sold or mortgaged by non-tribals, but all other restrictions on land transfers apply to the lands under the control of the tribal population. The tribal population has not been exempted from the provision of ceiling, distribution of surplus, registration of sharecrop legislation, and restrictions on the movement of the lands with government pattas. The decline in the patriarchal property structure is reflected in resistance by both parents as well as by brothers among all religious communities and among the tribals to giving a share in real property to the daughters in the family. The government in their programme of distribution did not provide women clear access to land and real property. As a result while there has been some kind of restructuring of land, reconsolidation of patriarchy and class within all communities is a growing trend; and one of the growing avenues through which this is accomplished is the system of dowry. This process of reconsolidation is combined with the expanding sector of agribusiness where non-landed interest groups are entering the land market largely through the system of lease and even illegal mortgages. As the land is not being purchased by the lessee, it does not come within the purview of land rights accorded to women—women at either end of the transaction—lessors and lessees. Once land is leased out, it is near impossible for women to claim their inheritance to those lands for such a claim would involve negotiating with multiple layers of rights and legalities through the contradictions between the two collectives of lessors and lessees. As a result, establishing women's right to productive resources has become more complicated than before. Decline in property-related cases does not mean that women are not interested in gaining access to their rightful share or are not articulating their rights. At the beginning of this paper, I have listed the demands that have been expressed by peasant women.

While a vibrant land market has developed through the medium of dowry, land is not actually transacted between the dowry giver and the taker, but a parallel land market through the medium of dowry has encouraged the mortgage market and the lease market in agriculture in favour of those who have lost surplus holdings and have lost land under direct cultivation or rent with registration and fixation of share of produce in favour of the sharecroppers. Lands are also being mortgaged to people who do not have large holdings but have earned their capital from business in transport and grain trade and prefer to invest in agriculture as a business proposition. Families who are mortgaging lands are also doing so to be able to reuse the same for the next daughter or other children in the family. Land has become an asset to generate capital not for purposes of agricultural development since the larger part of the sales proceeds goes into unproductive investments. The result is a curious mix of money rent, part capitalist development in agriculture; and a depressed market; and, a further decline in the status of women, with dowry demands reaching frightening proportions. There are cases of parents selling off their homestead too to pay for dowry. The low education level that women are allowed, early marriage with no skill to earn a living independently, denied property as dowry has been paid for her, makes a woman's present life as well as her future more uncertain and insecure. Parents worry what will happen to the daughter in their absence and rush to marry her off. Early marriages are preferred as a lower dowry goes with young age and less education. Parents are yet to start to think that if they could treat their daughters as they treat their sons as future earners and as those who will continue the lineage (read as class, caste as well as religious identity, as male members marrying outside their class, caste and religion can still serve to maintain continuity of the collective structurally which the women cannot as they are married out. In fact women can lose their status if they marry into structures that are lower down the scale in hierarchy), there would be no ground for fear for the daughters' future. This attitudinal change cannot be brought about just by provisions in the formal law but by effective campaign at two levels—a social movement has to begin to address the problem of dowry; formal laws especially those that address questions of real property should be granted less room for interpretation by simplifying the procedures and by making the definitions clearer; by pushing laws to redefine rights of women as individuals, their human rights and by extending their rights as citizens. If these norms are applied both at the level of the social movement as well as in the laws, we can address the social relations detrimental to women, fundamentally tied as they are to the unequal foundation of property relations and proprietorship over women. ...

First published as Occasional Paper 3 by Sachetana Information Centre, Kolkata.

Progressive Land Legislations and Subordination of Women?

K. SARADAMONI

The series of land legislations enacted in Kerala over a period of nearly one hundred years are the outcome of continuous struggles waged by the different sections of the peasantry, who, no doubt, were prompted by the quest for freedom, equality and right to safeguard one's dignity which characterized the late nineteenth and twentieth centuries. However, they remain incomplete and contain contradictions. Above all, they have been a slide-back for the women of the matrilineal communities, and brought meagre benefits to the agricultural labourers who do not have any land to cultivate.[1]

This is a continuation of another paper[2] which pleaded for a fresh study of the matrilineal system as it was prevalent in Kerala. The data presented here was collected for an ICSSR study which has been published.[3] The reason for presenting this paper is to raise some of my doubts regarding the process of law making, especially those legislations which have a bearing on social justice and change. How do laws come to be initiated? What is the mechanism of making the meaning and content of these laws known to the people who are to be affected and their involvement made possible or necessary? Is the impact of the laws studied?

A brief description of the land relations that prevailed in Kerala[4] before British rule was established is necessary here. Nambudiri Brahmins who were at the top of the caste hierarchy were also the principal controllers of land—the *janmis*. They did not engage themselves as cultivators—not even as supervisors of their fields and crop. *That* work was entrusted to *kanakkar*, the principal tenants, most of whom were non-cultivators. Then came various types of sub-tenants—*verunpattakkar*, and the labourer who were the lowest, both in caste and economic hierarchy. *Kanakkar*, who were regarded as "protectors" to the *janmi*'s lands, in early times, came from the tougher ranks of Nayars and castes above them. Ordinary tenants, by the time the British rule began, included lower ranks of Nayars and castes similar to them, Izhars and equivalent castes and Muslims.[5]

William Logan, who was made Special Commissioner to inquire into the land tenures and tenant rights in the 1880s, wrote that prior to British rule, the *janmi* did not own land. According to the customary laws prevalent at that time, the produce of the land was equally divided among the *janmi*, the *kanakkaran* and the *verumpattakkaran*, each taking a one-third share. "The *janmi*, the *kanakkaran* and the peasant shared the produce equally, working out a social equation, on the basis of mutual dependence and reciprocal interests within the confines of a feudal system of exploitation."[6] The first major shake up to this arrangement came with the invasion of the region by the Muslim kings of Mysore, who made a comprehensive land revenue assessment in Kerala and "settlements" with Muslim and other low castes. The British, who soon arrived on the scene, interpreted the rights and interests connected with land with their experience, as well as their needs, in view. They looked upon the *janmi* as "owner" of the soil, and the *kanakkaran* as the owner's lessee, and as such liable to be turned out of the lands, "when the time they leased them for expires". Eviction of tenants and raising of rents were unknown earlier. They became common once the *janmis* became "owners" of lands. These set in motion agrarian unrest and struggles, which by stages continued upto the present century.

Apart from the tenurial arrangements, inheritance laws, marriage practices and the system of *tarawad* or joint family also helped to keep the land holdings intact. Visitors to Kerala were surprised by the *marumakkathayam* (matrilineal) system of inheritance and the *tarawad*, especially of the Nayars. Unfortunately no attempt has been made to study matriliny from the point of view of women and land. The need for such an enquiry is supported by the fact that matriliny was practised by a large section among the cultivating communities. Unlike what is commonly thought, it was not something peculiar to the Nayars. In addition to several Hindu castes—including 17 Nambudiri families in Payyannur in North Malabar Muslims too followed *marumakkathayam.*

Very likely, changes began in the actual functioning of *manumakkathayam* families even before British rule began, and this might have affected different castes differently. Still the place of women in a *tarawad*, and the absence of individual private property, largely continued as Panikkar described it in 1900. He wrote: "The civil law of the land takes cognizance only of relations on the female side".[7] Legally woman was the stock of land title and it was through her that the *tarawad* name was transmitted from one generation to another. She had a birth right over *tarawad* property for maintenance, and this lasted throughout her life. A woman alone was considered progeny and the birth of a baby girl on which depended the continuity of the *tarawad* was a joyous occasion. Even in this century there were *karanavans*—male chiefs of a *tarawad*—who propitiated Gods for a female child when the *tarawad* was threatened with a situation when there was no female issue.

Women under *marumakkathayam* did not depend on husbands for maintenance. They entered into *sambandham* (alliance) with men of their castes or castes above theirs. Children born to them belonged to their caste and to their *tarawad*, where they had the right of maintenance. *Sambandham* was generally effected with mutual consent, but was terminable at the will of either party. A woman who used the freedom to end the alliance was not looked down upon. So were widows, and widow remarriage was accepted.

As already mentioned, one of the serious after-effects of the British interpretation of the customary land laws of Kerala was a series of peasant struggles. By 1850, the government was forced to appoint a Special Commissioner to investigate the matter. The recommendations of the Commissioner were not implemented. The *janmis*, using the new rights they acquired continued to evict tenants, raise rents, and refuse compensation for improvements when a tenure was terminated. While the British gave new rights to the *janmis*, the changed times and compulsions created a new awareness of rights among the tenants. In 1880 another enquiry by William Logan was ordered. In his exhaustive account of the complicated tenurial arrangements of Malabar, Logan touched upon something which is important for our present discussion. In his report, he incorporated "proposals in regard to *marumakkathayam*, the Law of Inheritance (through females) peculiar to the District". Logan emphasized "individual effort", private property and natural affection. They had a corollary—the end of the corporate ownership of property, break-up of joint families and a new relationship between man and woman. These were followed by the Malabar Marriage Act, 1896 which gave legality to the customary marriages.

The compensation for Tenants Improvements Act first passed in 1887 and then raised in 1900 could not do much to appease the tenants. In 1921 a second series of peasant struggles started. In 1924 a Tenancy Bill was presented to the Madras Legislature. It was passed in 1926 after the Select Committee which examined the Bill presented its report. But the Governor refused assent. The Malabar Tenancy Act was passed in 1929. The same period witnessed increasing demands to end *marumakkathayam* and *tarawads*. They were found to have outlived their time and were seen as impediments in the path of economic progress. This idea was spread through newspapers, and even the tenants' organization. On April 19, 1923 *Mathrubhumi* wrote an editorial "Marumakkathayam and Individual Partition of Property". The Secretary of the Tenants'

Organization, which at that time was mainly a body of *kanakkar*, wrote an article (on 19 March 1925) entitled, "Will the Nayars in Malabar wake up at least now?"

It is both interesting and necessary to ask: how did the tenants' struggle against the excessiveness of landlords get linked to the ending of *marumakkathayam*? The tenants wanted a better deal from the *janmis*. They also developed ideas that divisions of property and individual holdings are necessary for individual economic gain. No doubt, these ideas were generated as is evident from what Logan wrote in 1887, by the British rulers, and the ethos of changed times. But, who benefited by these changes? What happened to the women when the *tarawads* which gave them support began to be partitioned? Intervening in the debate on the Madras Marumakkathayam Bill, R.M. Palat, the representative of the Malabar landed interests (*sathani*) pleaded for the exemption of *sthanam* properties from the partition clauses of the Bill, claiming that it was in the interests of the women of those families. By "social usage" they were supposed to marry only higher-caste men when the women's *tarawads* used to maintain (sic). If their property rights were taken away and partition allowed, they would not be able to marry such men and their status and dignity would be affected. (It has to be noted here that the status of the women did not depend upon the status of the husband, but of her *tarawad* property which could establish an alliance with such a man). Regarding women of ordinary *marumakkathayam tarawads*, Palat did not have any such consideration. He said: "It may be asked whether this argument about the diminution of the women's share would not apply equally to ordinary *marumakkathayam tarawads*. To this my answer is that among the general body of the *marumakkathayam* people they marry among themselves, unlike the custom prevalent among the *sthanis* and that what a woman loses in her own *tarawad* she gains from another *tarawad*, through her husband. There is also the moral advantage the non-*sthani* woman gains by having a home and married life of her own and we know the large price which a woman will pay for this and perhaps these reasons account for the absence of protest from non-*sthani* women against partition."[8]

We may not agree with Palat's line of argument, but we have to be thankful to him for putting on record some important points for us to ponder now. Palat, a representative of the landed aristocracy, was keen that the properties of his class were left untouched. For this he used the excuse of the status of that class of women, about whose feelings and reaction we know very little. Palat has again said something of use: "I claim that these families should be preserved on the principle admitted by the government—the principle which has preserved an ancient landed class in Britain and allowed the Impartible Estates Act."[9] About the large majority of non-*sthani* women, we know absolutely nothing about what they knew or felt about what was happening to them. When Logan collected evidence in connection with his enquiry into the land tenures of Malabar, a number of women—mostly Muslim and a small number of Nayar women—had given evidence as tenants. Surprisingly they are absent by the 1930s and 1940s though by the latter period, the whole question of land had taken a more radical tone by the entry of the cultivating tenants to a more active role in the tenants' struggles. There is evidence to show that women directly and indirectly took part in these struggles.[10]

If ordinary *marumakkathayam* women did not react to the above legislations and debates, one reason can be the progressionism that shrouded these laws and the stigma of backwardness and old fashionableness that came to surround the Malabar practices. Just two examples, to illustrate: one Tamil Nadu newspaper wrote on 29 January 1932: "It is the primary duty not only of the wise but also of the government to do away with all foolish practices and customs by means of law. It is urgent that these Bills should be passed into law immediately in view of the welfare and morals of society". Another journal called *Stri Dharma* wrote in December 1932: "We congratulate the Madras council for their almost unanimous support to these two important measures intended to improve the status of women in Malabar". Promoting the sensibility that the practice was out-moded and obsolete about many of the native customs and practices was an achievement for the alien rulers. It is the reason the "masculine legal culture" (I owe this expression to Justice Krishna Iyer) which they unleashed in the country went unquestioned. By their interpretation of the land laws of the region, they were able to create a section of landed interests who were conscious of their class position; they also had a consciousness of male superiority, and became dependable to the rulers. One example of this is contained in the following: "That a man who begets children should be under a legal obligation to maintain them could be hardly disputed as a maxim of justice and sound policy. No man is under an obligation to marry... As the father, more than any one else, is responsible for this multiplication, it can hardly be doubted that the responsibility of providing for the children ought to rest primarily on him. This is a dictate of natural law, and the rank, position or caste of the father ought to make no difference in the case".[11] While these kinds of ideas spread fast, evidence does not show that all men could discharge this new responsibility. Many of them did not have the wherewithal to provide for wife and children. Women's share of the *tarawad* property was often brought to use. But with the rapid division and alienation of property, the individual share of many ordinary women was next to nothing. Large-scale pauperization was a common feature of this period, and women were certainly bigger victims. The *tarawad*, which sheltered them, withered away. For many women from the big landowners' families, the period under discussion offered many new opportunities—education, employment and even political participation—but life for women in the not so well-to-do *tarawads*, which were not only losing property by division and alienation, but were also strife-ridden by litigation and disharmony between members became suffocating. Naturally they had no option other than accepting the protection and guardianship given to them and their children by the newly emerging husbands. This meant that these women got a right to claim maintenance from husbands as well as a share in the latter's self-acquired wealth. This came along with the dissipation of *tarawad* wealth, and women losing a birthright. But this alternative was not a sure guarantee either for material or emotional security.

The Malabar Tenancy (Amendment) Acts of 1951 and 1954 as well as the Agrarian Relations Bill 1959 and later were meant to bring a fair deal to the still lower rungs of the cultivation tenants, and same relief to the agricultural labourers. But this time the landlords and tentans came to be looked upon as two antagonistic categories and all progressive sympathies were with the tenants. Examining the comprehensive land reform legislations Kerala had passed in the 1960s and 1970s from the point of view of women, one is compelled to think that they gave further legal sanction to the protected and secondary role to which the *marumakkathayam* woman was being relegated since British rule and the ideology that accompanied that rule. There was no attempt to examine how the proposed legislation would affect women. This happened even after the governments attention was drawn to the possible hardship that most women who were small landholders and who did not have any other income would face if their interests were not safeguarded. The Bill was given wide publicity to elicit public opinion. Many women responded. Most of them pointed out that they had no source of income, other than the lands entrusted to the tenants for cultivation. They asked for concessions to those who wished to have lands back from tenants for self-cultivation. At least one respondent raised a very valid question as far as women were concerned. Speaking specifically of a Nayar couple, both of whom had inherited *tarawad* property, she wanted to know the guidelines for the retention or surrender of lands of their total holdings exceeded the ceiling limit. She pleaded that the wife be allowed to retain her property as very often the husband would have an independent, regular, non-agricultural income. She even mentioned the possibility of strained relations between the couple, when the wife would be deprived of any economic means if she were to surrender her lands. However, the issues raised by these women did not come up for discussion.

While presenting this paper I am conscious of certain questions that would be posed. Is this not a discussion about women who had some property? How is it relevant when the society is moving towards equality and our major concerns are about the deprived sections. I am also conscious of a charge that would be levelled against the arguments raised here—i.e. it tries to portray a past which met with its natural end.

My plea for a fresh look at *marumakkathayam*, and the process of change is not to glorify it, but it serves as a very good example from recent Indian history to understand the changing status of women. As such, this is more of a specific case for examination. Coming to the other possible questions, the plea is not for retention of private property in the hands of certain people with rights over land. The idea is to see whether questions of fairness and equality between women and men—taking class into account—ever becomes a matter of debate in the process of passing "progressive" legislation. Above all the discussion draws attention to the role of ideas and inculcation of "false consciousness", which is highly relevant even today, especially in the context of women and change. They have a very important role in the institutionalization of relations of power, privilege and status, between classes, regions and countries. The disadvantaged sections, including women, sometimes show an "objectively unfounded faith in the process of law." Malcolm speaking in a different context described this manipulation of consciousness as 'the oppressor's tricknology' which complements but does not moderate the legal system's essentially coercive and alien character".[12] It is necessary for the socially committed scientists and practitioners to understand and explore what concepts like equality, freedom, justice and progress mean in any specific context, to the most disadvantaged, and ask, "equality etc. for whom"?

Notes and References

1. Land reform and its impact on agricultural labour in Kerala has not received sufficient attention. The social and political developments in the State have created a growing sense of awareness among the labourers. While talking about changes over time, they would invariably talk about the fixed hours of work per day, and much less about any economic gains.

2. "Agrarian Struggles and the End of Matriliny: From Common Property Rights to Individual Ownership and the Subordination of Women". Paper submitted to the session 'Women and Social Movement' organized by the Commission on Women at the XI International Congress of Anthropological and Ethnological Sciences; Vancouver, B.C. in August 1983.

3. "Changing Land Relations and Women: A Case Study of Palghat in Women and Rural Transformation." ICSSR-CWDS publication.

4. Land and struggles around land in Kerala have been studied again and again; however no attempt has been made to examine these from a woman's point of view.

5. The number of Muslim tenants increased after the Mysorean conquest of the region.

6. Panickar, K.N. "Peasant Revolts in the Malabar in the Nineteenth and Twentieth Centuries". in A.R. Desai (ed): *Peasant Struggles in India*, 1979, p. 604.

7. Panicker, T.K.G.: *Malabar and Its Folks*, 1900, p. 14.

8. Minutes of Dissent at the Select Committee Report on the *Marumakkathayam* Bill Tamil Nadu Archives. It has to be explored whether it is true that non-*sthani* women did not protest, and if so why.

9. Ibid.

10. There are references to women's part in the peasant struggles in books and pamphlets. See for eg. (in Malayalam) Podural; *Keralathile Karshakaprasthanathinte Oru Laghu Charitram*, pp. 45–8. There is need for a full-lenth study of this topic.

11. A Govinda Pillai (Dewn Peshikar) Trivandrum, to the Malabar Marriage Commission, National Archives of India.

12. Muhammad I Kenyata: "Community Organizing, Client Involvement and Poverty Law", *Monthly Review*, October 1983, p. 20.

Ants in the Pants

MARY ROY

In 1986, the Supreme Court struck down the Travancore Christian Succession Law which stated that:

> A daughter shall inherit one fourth the share of a son or Rs 5000.00 whichever is less.

It was automatically replaced by the Indian Succession Act by which intestate property is equally divided among sons and daughters and the widow inherits a one-third share.

It is extraordinary that in 1995, the Christian male-dominated community in Kerala, assisted by the chauvinistic church and the chauvinistic legislature, continues attempting to water down the Supreme Court judgement and to revalidate and revive the old gender discriminatory law.

At the same time there are demands by women's groups all over India for a Uniform Civil Code, in order to ensure a better deal to women who have been discriminated against by the personal laws of their religions.

In Kerala, there was not a murmur of dissent during the last hundred years when women were cruelly discriminated against. But now, every couple of months, the government is made aware of the "inconvenience" caused to Christian males. In fact, Minister K.M. Mani feels that if legislation is delayed, an ordinance must be passed to revalidate the old Succession Act for a retrospective period of thirty years! The Church is obviously suffering from a bad case of ants in the pants, and Minister Mani feels that his solicitous care of Christian males is necessary to get himself re-elected.

This appeared as a letter to the editor in *Manushi*, 1996: 92–93, p. 5.

Section III

The Tangled Tale of Twisting a Safety Net into a Noose

VEENA TALWAR OLDENBURG

After careful review of the cultural interdict against the Rajputs' and the Khatris' "addiction" to female infanticide—the alleged result of their high-caste custom of hypergamy and the concomitant marriage expenses, presented by Montgomery in his *Minute on Infanticide* in 1852—our own investigations have established that the colonial government's seemingly well-caulked case was deeply problematic. In exploring the cultural construction of the crime of female infanticide, we discovered that caste itself was cut loose from its moorings in politics and its transformation into its colonial image was under way. We also discovered that brideprice-receiving groups such as Jats and Muslims of all classes were at least as culpable as the notoriously targeted high-caste Hindus. In examining the process of collecting knowledge, we also saw how native informants, in an attempt to save themselves from fines and imprisonment, became collaborators in the project of the colonial remaking of Punjabi society.

Now we can take our investigation further and follow the steps taken by the colonial government to eradicate the alleged causes—dowry and wedding expenses—of female infanticide. As the British faltered on causes, their experiments to fix Hindu upper-caste behaviour were bound to be experiments in futility. In any case, the attempt to persuade the upper castes to join in a war against their own constitution makes a very interesting chapter in Punjabi social history, particularly from a feminist perspective. How did the colonialists propose to wean the upper castes of their alleged lethal addiction to "caste pride" and ruinous profligacy at the time of a daughter's wedding, and what social effects might this have produced in the Punjab?

It is important to tease out a baseline in the mid-nineteenth century from which we can begin to track what happened to a variety of marriage expenses, including the vilified "dowry system", over the next century, particularly the way these changed in response to calls for reform from colonial and local leaders. We will also examine how the radical restructuring of land ownership and the revenue system soon after the British take-over, the accelerated monetization of the agrarian economy, urban growth, and emergent middle-class values all worked to transform the dowry system itself ... .

Major H.B. Edwardes, the deputy commissioner of Jullundur, had made it his business to explore the custom of dowry payments in his now-familiar report on female infanticide. After setting out with a very different premise, he had been forced to conclude that, with the exception of the Khatris of Lahore, the custom of dowry among upper-caste Hindus did not appear to be the cause for alarm it was elsewhere in the Indian empire, although wedding expenses certainly were. The most gratifying portion of his report for him was his ability to persuade the people of Jullundur and Rahon to submit voluntarily a schedule of expenses "that was drawn by the people themselves in their own homes, in consultation with the females of their own families, stimulated by the opportunities afforded them by this enquiry" (Edwardes 1852: para. 79). This is probably the first written account of marriage expenses and dowry compiled in the colonial period in the Punjab, and perhaps represented the only time that women's knowledge of such matters was incorporated into a colonial report. The expenses are noted under five heads, with the expenditure on the first or the "lugun" (or *lagan*, literally auspicious date) that "decides the rate of all other expenses". The bride's father usually sends one-third of the value of the gifts in cash, and two-thirds in property such as horses and camels. If a hundred rupees are spent on the *lagan*, then the bride's father customarily spends fifty rupees on the *milni*, the occasion when the bridegroom's procession arrives at the house and the two fathers embrace. The third head of expenditure is the fee of the Brahmin priest, which would be more than the *milni* but would not exceed seventy-five rupees. The fourth is the "Meeta bhat; for two days all sorts of sweetmeats and fruits mixed up together are set before the assembly, and all the neighbours of the same caste come and partake, but it is etiquette to take only a morsel or two". And finally, the "Duheys (*dahej*); or as it is called in the Punjab the 'Khut'. This is one-fourth or one-fifth more than the 'Lugun': and consists of a gift of all household requisites, from water vessels down to a sweeper's broom" (ibid.: para. 81). The average expense for a daughter's wedding would therefore have been within five hundred rupees, a not inconsiderable amount. The informants were Khatris, the educated and wealthier section of the population who had traditionally served the government and the army as officers, and who were also commonly involved in farming, trade, and even shopkeeping and moneylending operations. They were also the community widely accused of committing infanticide in all districts of the Punjab.

This urges us to probe whether a daughter's wedding entailed expenses "ruinous" enough to warrant her elimination in infancy. Were sons so obviously preferred because their weddings cost less? Is this the past we need in order to understand the present?

After fairly exhaustive questioning among his informants, Edwardes asserts that "it is not the general practice, as in Hindoostan (which refers to provinces to the east and south of the Punjab), for the Bridegroom's father to demand a dowry from the father of the Bride, on the contrary whatever the latter chooses to offer, the former is honour bound to accept". The wedding, however, was another matter; the bride's father felt his honour to be at stake and was not past "ruining himself on this occasion. Thus daughters became family calamities, and more than one or two were seldom allowed to live" (Edwardes 1852: paras. 41–42).

We ought to trust what Edwardes's native informants say about dowry and wedding expenses, as little as we trust the just-so story about Bedi infanticides. But there is a significant difference here. In detailing wedding and dowry expenses in 1852 there is no unverifiable past being dredged up, but a workaday report of expenses at that time generated by male householders at home with the help of their wives, mothers, and aunts. Edwardes also makes two telltale distinctions. The first is between Hindustan and the Punjab. Hindustan (literally, "land of Hindus," the name given to the Hindi-speaking regions of north India), where he suggested that dowries could be demanded by the bridetakers, had been under colonial sway for half a century. In Hindustan, dowries were seen as a problem because his bureaucrat forebears had reported them as such. He was quite sure that this was not the case in the recently conquered Punjab, where however little or much the bride's father had to offer, the groom's father was "honour bound to accept" it. Punjabi machismo was deeply intertwined, much like that of the Rajputs of Rajputana or the Pathans of the northwest frontier, with matters of honour.

This is important for the baseline we want to create, because a few decades later, under colonialism, the difference in the attitude toward Punjabi and Hindustani dowries appears not to be remarkable.

Edwardes's observation of this critical difference between the old and new territorial acquisitions of the Raj opens up a new way of thinking about the puzzle of escalating dowries. Did the Raj itself, in its effort to introduce the selected ingredients of capitalist agriculture, alter the economic and cultural chemistry of the regions it brought under its wing and unwittingly change the way dowries were given and received? Edwardes declares that the practice of dowry was bound by rules of honour and mutual respect between bridetakers and bridegivers in the Punjab of the 1850s. This recognition that

Punjabi dowry giving did not induce infanticide is a remarkable internal contradiction of the official case. Does it mean that "problem" dowries were a creeping phenomenon that followed the Raj to the new regions it conquered? Is that why this shift is noticed everywhere today, along with the change from bride-price to dowry?

The second distinction he draws is between dowries and wedding expenses, a distinction that is very real in north India even today. There is no doubt in his mind, after surveying his district and reading the reports of other district officers in the Punjab, that the ruinous expenditure was not dowry but wedding celebrations. And this, as we shall see, applied also to the weddings of sons. This insight is drowned out by the official clamour to establish, as had been done in Hindustan, clear and credible motives for female infanticide. What gained uniform acceptance as the cause for the destruction of infant daughters was the high cost of what a daughter must be given (or what may be demanded) at the time of marriage, and in the annual cycle of festivals and auspicious occasions for the rest of her parents' lives.

One of the critical tasks at hand is to determine whether we are looking only at a steady quantitative change—one that inflation and the burgeoning of consumer goods can explain—or whether there was a real qualitative change in the meaning, function, and composition not only of dowries but also of basal gender relations in the colonial period. There is evidence in the codification of customary law and in the documents generated at meetings held to contain the practice of dowry in 1853 to allow us to discern whether "the people"—those who gave and received dowries—considered it as baneful then as it was perceived to be more than a century later, when the custom was banned in 1961. Amid the din of consultations among prominent local leaders in 1853, and later when inquiries were made during the widespread famines of 1878–1879 and 1899–1900, there are dimly audible voices and opinions of women as mothers, aunts, sisters, and daughters that need to be rescued. These will enable us to disentangle the changing customary and legal constructions of gender at different levels of class and caste in the context of the transition from a subsistence economy to a very curious form of colonial capitalism in the Punjab ... .

The specific agreements signed by the representatives of a wide range of castes and clans—from the Bedis of Dera Baba Nanak, the Rajput princes of Kangra and other hill districts, and the Khatris and Brahmins of a dozen districts in joint agreements with the urban and rural Muslims of Lahore—suggest that no community tried to refute the blanket accusation that wedding expenses and dowry were among the chief causes of infanticide. Rather, they promised to respect the new sumptuary regulations they had expressly gathered to draw up. All of the agreements stipulated that marriage expenses—separated into dowry and wedding celebrations—must be reduced and regulated, but some of the agreements were clearly more negotiated than others. They ranged from curiously perfunctory and spare to highly detailed. Some groups were content to sign agreements that mentioned only the prescribed maximum spending limits, without differentiated allocations imposed on high, middle, and lower classes. The (notorious) Bedis, who had made of Major Edwardes a minor hero and erudite social scientist for the establishment, had already gathered under his auspices at Jullundur and produced the exemplary agreement that was upheld as a model in Amritsar. Higher Khatri tribes agreed to abandon their hypergamous ways and caste pride by pledging to intermarry with the lower ranks of Khatris, including the lowest Bhunjaees. The ceilings adopted for expenses for four classes of weddings were Rs. 500 for the first class, Rs. 200 for the second, Rs. 125 for the third, and a single rupee for the fourth. Other agreements, particularly those authored by Khatris, are obsessively detailed, down to the size and weight of the *pinni* and *laddoo* (sweet balls made from grain, sugar, and *ghi*, or clarified butter) to be distributed on the occasion of the announcement of the wedding. In the clear absence of political power, the princes and chiefs were now forced to quibble over seeming trifles ... .

Another agreement, signed jointly by the "Zemindars and Lumberdars", or small landowners and village heads, of numerous castes of Amritsar district, regulated the expenses of a daughter's wedding fairly simply. "All persons in a low state of life, and not living in easy circumstances, will spend from 1 to 125 rupees; those in easy circumstances and occupying a middle station in life, will incur from 125 to 250 rupees, while all persons of substance and consequence will be at liberty to expend from 250 to 500 rupees, on the marriages of their daughters" (SPCPA 1854: 437). It is interesting that although the British expected the representatives of different castes to consult with their own and conclude caste-specific agreements, the representatives themselves chose to regroup on the basis of class and custom. They preferred to differentiate themselves in two ways: as regional-political elites belonging to a locality or subregion such as Lahore or Amritsar, and as economic elites, falling into three to five income brackets, to determine the outlay for marriage expenses. The ease with which joint agreements were generated and signed points to the possibility that the caste leaders saw this official intervention as an opportunity to restate their own political ranks in relationship to the new rulers.

Information about money actually spent at weddings by the various income groups is sparse or vague, and the agreements do little to tell us precisely, except in one case, what the notions of improvidence or extravagance entailed. There are passing references elsewhere to the exceptional prodigality of 1.7 million rupees (ten rupees were valued at one pound sterling at this time) spent at the marriage of Kunwar Nao Nihal Singh with the daughter of the "Ataree chief", and eight lakhs of rupees (one lakh or lac equals 100,000) at the wedding of the late "Raja of Aloowala".[1] This information, even if accurate, only confused the issue: such vast resources remained only in the hands of the few independent rulers in the Punjab, whose marriages were political alliances, and the money was spent at the weddings of royal children of either sex, not of daughters alone. The British closely monitored the extravagance of independent chieftains, for they perceived it to be an unfailing symptom of misrule. Such big spenders could be forced either into signing subsidiary alliances (defense treaties whereby native rulers underwrote the entire cost of British military protection offered to them) or into having their territories annexed outright. For the preponderance of their subjects, we have to be satisfied with pronouncements such as "[p]eople live to save money to marry their daughters; others impoverish themselves for life to outvie their neighbours" in the very same letter. In actual terms, the entire exercise at Amritsar amounted to reiterating colonial power over Punjabi Hindu and Sikh elite groups and rulers of neighbouring independent kingdoms. As a way of dealing with female infanticide, it did little more than create sumptuary guidelines with prescribed but unenforceable spending limits.

It is possible to extract from these regulations the proportional amounts designated for the dowry, wedding celebrations, and gifts for the groom and his party from the total permitted outlay. Except for Lahore Khatris and Brahmins, most of the castes and classes reckoned marriage expenditures in four discrete clusters. The first was the betrothal *(kurmai* or *dharam sagai)*, an engagement ceremony in which the bridegivers do not accept gifts or cash in consideration for the bride, to be distinguished from the engagement ceremony of those who accept bride-price. The second was the *milni*, or gifts for the close kin of the groom, and the expenses for the hospitality and entertainment of the groom's party at the time of the wedding; the third group was what could be deemed obligatory giving by the bride's parents to their own kin with whom reciprocal arrangements existed, and handouts to various traditional servants, including the *pandit* (Brahmin priest), the barber, and the musicians and professional entertainers (the *bhand, mirasi, bhat,* and others who had formerly been on the village payroll).

The last but not least of the expenses was the *daaj*, the gifts to the bride herself from family and friends. No monetary value or maximum limit was stipulated for the *daaj* in any of the agreements, and it was left entirely up to the means of the bride's family and kin to supply her clothes, jewels, household furnishings, and milch cattle, horses, and camels. The fact that dowry went unregulated after all the fuss made about it tells us that it was a discretionary expense and not the crippling burden that altered attitudes toward female children.

Most of the groups put the entire *daaj* at between 55 and 60 percent of the cost in all classes of weddings. There is a consensus in these documents that household utensils, furniture, apparel, and jewels are the kinds of articles that constitute *daaj*. Cash was not mentioned as a *daaj* item in any of the agreements in 1853. The representatives of the people were willing to compromise and draw up schedules of wedding expenses and gifts given to the groom and his relatives at the time of the betrothal and marriage, but they quietly managed to keep *daaj* as a cluster of items that the bride's parents alone would decide according to their own private means. The Khatris and Brahmins of Lahore seem to have been particularly in favour of keeping this a discretionary and jealously guarded category.

... Dowries might have already cost many times more than all other wedding expenses put together. Why then, in 1853 or later, did the British officials not insist that dowries be regulated just like the expenses associated with the wedding itself, confirmed as they were in their belief in its causal relationship to female infanticide? What might explain this conspicuous omission at a meeting convened expressly to curtail wedding expenses, and therefore dowries, is that both sides had divergent reasons to let the matter go unregulated. For Punjabis, a daughter's *daaj* was simply not negotiable, even for the most pliant and ingratiating subjects. It was where many of the assembled groups drew the line. Marriage was the time for which women aggressively saved and invested. On the British side, it is possible to speculate that it must have been clear to them that the wealthy urban groups and neighbouring princes were the potential consumers of the British-made household goods and textiles, and to limit this consumption, specially in the form of dowries, seemed economically self-defeating. Discretion was certainly the better part of valour here. This conclusion is endorsed by the deliberate vagueness that shrouds the language on *daaj* (compared with the clarity and calculation of all other expenses) in the various agreements of 1853. I was to comb in vain through voluminous documents in search of precise limits set on the values of dowries in these extraordinary agreements that were drawn up expressly to establish those limits in the first place.

These conspicuous lacunae in otherwise purposeful agreements also point to a subtext. They eloquently represent the wisdom and caution of the women who were excluded from attending the deliberations. The men knew that they never determined the selection of clothes, jewels, and household goods unilaterally. At these meetings, they not only debated the minutiae of marriage customs that could be summarily disallowed by English civilians, but also had to bear in mind the interests and dictates of their women—their mothers, grandmothers, wives, and indeed, the daughters themselves—who were the principal actors in questions relating to arranging marriages and weddings. The women might even have foreclosed the possibility of discussions of *daaj* per se, except in the most general terms, since women controlled the decisions regarding the arrangements and expenses of marriages. The men must also have sensed the trap in accepting strict monetary gradations of dowry. It would inevitably have caused disputes about the economic rank of a family and laid it open to the charge that it had given too little (a social embarrassment) or too much (a criminal danger). It would certainly have resulted in unhealthy competition among clan members and imitation by the lower classes of the upper, all ultimately leading to the very escalation in dowries that the restrictions would have sought to avoid.

In the Amritsar agreements of 1853, there is no evidence that bridetakers ever demanded goods or cash above and beyond what the bride's parents presented to them as *milni* gifts and to their daughter as *daaj*. There is no mention of curbing demands by bridetakers, only curbs on the voluntary spending by bridegivers. This is critical information for the baseline that I am trying to establish, because it makes it possible to assert that until the middle of the nineteenth century dowry was not a bargaining chip in the negotiations to arrange a marriage. Although it is fair to assume that dowries are not actively bargained for by the vast majority of Punjabi Khatris and Brahmins even today, there is a growing minority of bridetakers among these groups who actually demand bigger dowries than the bride's parents can comfortably give. The gradual mutation of dowry into a social pathogen is complex. It entails not only the interaction between bridegivers and bridetakers but also colonial social and economic interventions. The late nineteenth century presents a different picture.

The Amritsar covenants are the place to look for some of the earliest clues to this transition. They reflect at least three areas in which *daaj* could easily have gone on to become a far larger proportion of marriage expenses than hitherto. ... the expenditure on the distribution of sweets and presents to the groom's party on the second day of the wedding (called *vadhai* and *beyee vadhai*, or congratulatory gifts), valued at three times the gifts made for the *milni* on the first day, was a custom that many did not observe any longer, choosing "in lieu of the presents made on the occasion. . . [to] give [more] jewels to the Bride on marriage" (SPCPA 1854: 440–43). This suggests that if the government did not want bridegivers to squander large sums of money on gifts for their wedding guests, this customary allocation could best be diverted into the bride's *daaj* itself, for which no limit had been proposed. This impetus to increase the *daaj* probably came from both sides—from the bride's mother, who was always looking for ways to increase her daughter's *daaj*, and from her in-laws, who would rather have the resources reallocated to the bride than miss out altogether.

A standard feature of weddings today is the colourful presence of the groom's female relatives and large entourages that have to be entertained, feasted, and housed for the two to three days of the wedding ceremonies, and who also have to be received with welcoming *milni* gifts. This was obviously not the case in 1853, when *milni* gifts were described in almost all the agreements as rather small cash tokens for the male relatives of the groom who actually attended the wedding, ranging from five to twenty rupees. Women relatives of the groom customarily stayed at home, where they feasted and made merry while waiting for the *baraat* or the groom's party to return with the bride. What changed the symbolic welcoming gesture of *milni* into an elaborate gift-giving occasion by the bride's male and female relatives to their counterparts in the groom's family can be traced to the gradual inclusion of women in the *baraat*, as conditions of travel eased and women could no longer be denied the pleasure. The number of relatives who attended the ceremonies appeared to grow as travel became cheaper and easier with the coming of the railways in the last quarter of the nineteenth century, raising proportionately the expense for hospitality borne by the bride's family. If the groom's female relatives and fictive kin accompanied him to the wedding celebrations, it was only natural that they should also be welcomed with saffronstained envelopes of money and enjoy the hospitality of the bride's family and village. Although this added considerably to the wedding expenses, it must have also have happened at the urging of women themselves. From early in the twentieth century, a set of clothes and jewels was added to the *milni* for the principal female kin of the groom (such as his mother and sisters), and clothes or cash for other women relatives became customary.

Today *milni* gifts can be a major wedding expense, sometimes bargained for in advance between the two parties—an escalation that is more material than cultural. Sometimes, of course, *milni* can become the occasion for mounting greed. The cash and clothes for the *milni* may almost rival the bride's trousseau, as the bridetakers assemble all their surviving kin for the ceremony. ... we see that in one case the demand for a set of jewels for a *milni* for a deceased mother-in- law nearly brought the betrothal to an end. In cities, the gift giving is now staged at the beginning of the festivities as an important theatrical moment watched by the wide-ranging circle of friends and officials who attend the wedding. The sumptuary regulations of 1853 had little effect on containing costs; on the contrary, outlays for token and auspicious giving have steadily ballooned in Punjabi families that now equate status with material gifts.

The only area in which a reduction was actually achieved appears to be the traditional dues paid to the *pandit* or priest, and to *bhands*, *mirasis*, beggars, and *hijras* (groups of transvestites who sing and dance at weddings, births, and other auspicious occasions). The *purohit* or *pandit* (always a Brahmin) who is the ritual specialist for performing the wedding found his fees sharply reduced as time went on, and today it is a negligible fraction of the cost of the wedding. Recall that the British disapproved of paying for what they considered to be the noisy and meaningless activity of idle rascals—the many drummers, dancers, and singers who traditionally received small amounts of cash and partook of the wedding feast after the wedding guests had eaten. Although this expense was not proportionately a large one, a utilitarian and austere-minded officialdom strongly urged that it be discontinued entirely as one of the appropriate places to trim waste. Over time, the presence of such traditional performers tailed off, but the expense of entertaining the *baraat* has gone up considerably. The far more expensive English-style brass bands, often rented from the army or the police forces, began to replace local traditional musicians.

The British also wanted the wedding feast to include only the kin and affines of the bride rather than all village artisans, the poor, and the menials. "Another large item of expense, that of the *Bhajee Kurahhee*, or food distributed occasionally to the whole village has been reduced to the proper limits and the relations and more intimate friends of the two families only be entitled to partake. The *Nurizee*, a distribution of food and money to bramins [*sic*], has been suppressed, as regards the poorer classes, and greatly reduced as regards richer people."[2] The entitlements of village servants, too, were gradually eroded until these functionaries were regarded more as criminals to be dealt with by the police than welcome and necessary adjuncts. Again the modest success at excising traditional generosity to village servants to reduce marriage expenses was more than offset by the far greater expenditure on nonvegetarian food and European spirits (scotch whisky, rum, beer, and wine) the British introduced into Punjabi society.

... What these agreements did not acknowledge was the existence of customary giving, which distributed the "burden" of wedding expenses throughout a web of reciprocal relationships. Most of the gifts for the bride were also collected over time by the bride's own family, particularly the mother, who, virtually from the day a daughter was born began to collect clothes and jewels that the daughter would take with her to her new home. The dowry did not have to wait to be bought until the profit from the last harvest, salary, or trade was available; it was, and to some extent still is, accumulated gradually and rather less painfully, in the course of the young girl's maidenhood. The bride's mother—in consultation with elder female kin and affines, particularly her own mother, aunts, and mother-in-law—was and is the principal decision maker, economic manager, and actor in putting the *daaj* together. In fact, among families with even small surpluses the strategy is to fill the *pitara* (a wooden chest, often carved and with ornamental brass trimmings and latch, in which *daaj* was given), continually over the twelve to fifteen years from the time a daughter is born, with the clothes, bedding, and utensils that she will eventually receive. Today the receptacles may be suitcases and tin trunks or modern steel almirahs, but there is not a Punjabi household of some means where children are being raised where a hope chest for a daughter and a *vari* (the gift to the bride from the groom's family) for a daughter-in-law are not being accumulated or set aside. Only uncustomary demands can actually transmogrify a daughter's wedding, the most anticipated event in a parent's life, into a nightmare.

Neonda (also *neondra*) or the premise of reciprocity came into play on all ritual and social occasions, and still does in some parts of the Punjab, at all levels and across religions in Punjabi villages and towns alike. [3] All life-cycle events, including births, tonsure and circumcision ceremonies, betrothals, birthdays, funerals, and local Hindu festivals such as Diwali, activated the network of reciprocities among villagers and city dwellers alike, but the centerpiece of social and political transactions was the marriage of sons and daughters, and the gifts given on such occasions reflected the status of the giver and his relationship to the recipient. This elaborate web of social giving was never casual. A *behi khata,* or account book of what was received and from whom, was maintained by every family, because proper reciprocity involved calculating not just the market value of the gift but also the status of the giver, the number of sons and daughters in his family, and the degree of the relationship. [4]

Once the custom of *neonda* is factored in, and its nature as a dependable resource at the time of marriage understood, the financial impact of dowry giving on the family is greatly diluted. The anthropologist's diagram with arrows representing the flow of gifts in dowry-giving families appears hopelessly unidirectional, but the sources are wider than the illustration indicates. What goes on is complex and burdened with emotional and gendered meaning, with mutual and unequal obligations that shape the nature of kinship and affinal connection. Hershman observes that "[t]raditionally a great deal of the money towards the bride's dowry and also towards the entertainment of the marriage party was collected through the institution of *ninda* (a linguistic variant of *neonda*) amongst the *biradari* of the bride"; and he defines *biradari* to mean "an agnatic *rites de passage* group" (Hershman 1981: 202). He defines dowry quite properly as the "money (and goods) collected by the institution of *ninda*" and "contributions from the bride's father, brothers, mother's brother, mother's sister's husband, etc." The nucleus of the bride's jewellery comes from her mother's own *daaj* and *vari*, and the grandmothers and aunts from both sides supplement these ornaments. Among Khatris and Brahmins, a ceremony called the *chura* ceremony is designed to bring together all the bride's gift-giving relatives to give the bride and her parents the gifts intended for her and other gifts and cash to help defray the costs of the wedding itself. This occurs only a day before the wedding, although what is going to be given by the close kin is already clear by the rules of reciprocity from the day a daughter is born. The wife's mother's brother *(mama)* leads off the ceremony by presenting the *nanki bhat* (gifts from the bride's mother's family, especially the bride's maternal grandparents and uncles). The *mama's* own gift varies in value according to his circumstances, but minimally consists of the *chura*—a set of ivory bangles embossed and dyed in red—and the set of clothes and jewellery the bride will wear for the wedding ceremony. The cumulative, and assuredly intended, effect of the system was to benefit all; it made events such as a daughter's wedding a shared responsibility and far less a burden than the British believed it to be, because much of the dowry and the provisions for the feasts were contributed by the direct kin and the fictive family in the village.

The principle of reciprocity defined the bounds of this group to include maternal and paternal kin, fictive kin, and virtually all other residents of the village, who may have been members of other castes. Even estranged kin had to be invited to attend a girl's wedding so that they could be given the opportunity to reciprocate in terms of gifts; to fail to do so was a moral lapse. The parents of the bride coordinated and arranged these matters well in advance—and these traditions greatly reduced the need for loans even if the season was a bad one. This premise of reciprocity surely weakens the logic that wedding expenses were the cause for the killing of female infants; if anything, it supports the view that dowry was the collectively woven traditional safety net for the bride for her future away from the natal village.

... *Neonda*, it can be argued, was the key to understanding the social relationships and status markers in a village with all its layering and stratification. In 1853 however these subtleties, reciprocities, and customs totally escaped the British, and they defined dowry as a direct, almost individual burden for the bride's father that they believed encouraged female infanticide. These traditional networks were, in fact, tested and weakened or even destroyed when peasants became individual owners of land that was once communally held, and when indebtedness, famine, or a loss of income foreclosed social giving.

It appears from the caveats at the end of some of the *ikrar nameh* that most of the middling and lower-income families spent well below the new scale of wedding expenses, because it was suggested that they should continue to do so without their "suffering in repute". The unspoken fear, of course, was that in trying to curb the few extravagant families by setting limits, the British might push the average sensible families, who married their daughters within their means, into an officially approved and publicly endorsed spiral of escalating costs, causing them to go into debt. In other words, these agreements might not have checked the offenders for whom they were intended, but instead made nonoffenders vulnerable to social pressures or the temptation to aspire to higher status by spending more money to make a "third-class" or "second-class" wedding into a "first-class" one.

Notes

[1] Letter No. 458, from P. Melville, Secretary of the Chief Commissioner of Punjab, to the Officiating Secretary to the Government of India, dated Lahore, July 1853. Proceedings, Home Department. National Archives of India.

2   Report by J.R. Carnac, Deputy Commissioner Rawal Pindee District, 10 Edward Thornton, Commissioner and Superintendent. Jhelum Division; dated Camp Husun Abdal, 15 February 1854. This is a report on one of the many meetings modelled on the Amritsar meeting; this one was held to induce the Hindu communities, particularly the Brahmins and Khatris, of the Rawalpindi and Jhelum districts to sign similar engagements. These were competently obtained in a brief three-hour meeting at which the Brahmins and the Khatris signed, as was noted above, joint agreements. Only two hundred families of these two castes were suspected of committing female infanticide. The Muslims of Rawalpindi, an overwhelming majority in this district were not subjected to a census to determine how many girl children survived, nor was it considered necessary to invite them to the meeting.

3   As with much else in this chapter, it is difficult to decide whether to refer to *neonda* in the present or the past tense. The latter would imply that the practice has died out completely, whereas it in fact survives, vestigially in some places but strongly in most others. Anthropologists (Sharma 1980: 40–41, Hershman 1981: 202) testify to its decline by barely mentioning it as a traditional practice in the villages they studied, whereas Alavi (1972: 1–27) reports its robust survival. Based on my own observation of some fifty weddings of well-to-do Punjabis in Lucknow and Delhi, the practice is certainly alive, but has a very different form. I therefore want to show how this premise of reciprocity was impaired over time.

4   Women generally kept this type of account book, so a literate woman would often lend her services to those who were not. My paternal great-grandmother, Lajwanti, for example, who died in 1972 at the age of eighty-six, was the keeper of the book in our family and had kept the books for many families in Chakwal in pre-Partition Punjab. She read and wrote three scripts—Urdu, Gurmukhi, and English—and was married two years before she would have finished high school. Many women who came to Saheli, a women's resource center where I did research for ten months, showed me such account books kept by their mothers to prove the existence of gifts given as dowry. These notebooks were often entered as evidence in court cases to retrieve the dowry given to a daughter.

The calculation of reciprocal obligation was complex. For example, if A, who has three daughters, receives from B a gift of Rs. 50 for one of his daughter's weddings, he is expected to give a gift of nearly three times that value when B's only daughter weds. However, if A is much poorer than B and his status in the village or town is perceived to be much lower, he may not be expected even to match the gift, and would give only a token sum of, say, eleven rupees. These variables are expertly and sensitively juggled to produce the encoded gift that in turn reinforces the connection between the two families. This system, as we shall see in chapter 4, was impaired as the British revenue system made peasant indebtedness chronic in many parts of the Punjab.

Excerpted from Veena Talwar Oldenburg, 2002. *Dowry Murder: The Imperial Origins of a Cultural Crime*, New York: Oxford University Press.

The Political Economy of Dowry

RANJANA SHEEL

RANJANA SHEEL

... The Dowry Prohibition Act, 1961

The Dowry Prohibition Act of 1961 too symbolizes the failure of the state, as is evident in its dithering on the Hindu Code Bill, to bring about transformation in women's status. As noted earlier, the obdurate attitude of the state regarding women's rights witnessed further expansion of the practice of dowry in post-Independence Indian society. The Act, promulgated as an acknowledgement of dowry as a major social evil, was an attempt to deal with the problem separately from other issues pertaining to women.

The lack of the state's commitment to the principle of equal inheritance rights for women provides, to a large extent, the contextual background and perspective for the problem of dowry. The most notable and perceptible effort in this respect, as we shall see, is to strengthen women's *stridhana* as her property through dowry. Even in the modern context, in upholding the concept of *stridhana* as an integral part of the patrilineal system, the state's approach and objectives have been largely to leave it undisturbed. It thereby assumes that a woman loses the membership of her parental family after marriage. It reiterates the traditional linkages of property, patriliny and marriage. The inherent contradiction in the state's posture is thus evident. It, on the one hand, seeks to dispense equal inheritance rights—although limited in scope, and on the other, it promotes the concept of *stridhana* as a separate property. This concept was central to the arguments that favoured gift-giving to the bride at the time of marriage in debates in the Lok Sabha preceding the Dowry Prohibition Act of 1961.

These debates divulge disparate opinions on dowry—its definition, nature, and remedial measures. The consensus was on abolition of the 'social evil which we have to fight in the name of transforming our society' (LSD 1959: 4436). Speeches of the Members of Parliament manifest that dowry was an all-pervasive phenomenon. The scenario appears similar to the one seen now three–and–a–half decades later, that speaks of spate of suicides, last minute dowry demands resulting in cancellation of a marriage, the trauma faced by the bride and her parents in not being able to fulfil demands, and above all the imperative of arranging a marriage of a girl at all costs. ...

(a) The debates on the bill presented prior to the Dowry Prohibition Act, 1961
(i) Justifications for the Bill

The purpose of the legislation to prohibit dowry was spelt out by the then Law Minister, A.K. Sen. He emphasized that 'we are all agreed that the evil should be eradicated wholly by law, nevertheless the law is necessary, if not for anything else, at least for declaring to the whole country the social consciousness of the nation, expressed by the voice of the House. That itself has an effect in weakening the impact and the incidence of the evil.' He further added that:

> No drafting, no device which we may think of here, is going to improve the situation. It is only the consciousness of the evil, armed with the powers granted under the Act, which alone can eradicate the evil altogether ... . We can only think of introducing such improvement as may be necessary in order, first of all, to understand for ourselves, and for also carrying that understanding to the country as a whole, what the evil is, and how this House sought to tackle it ... and as an expression of the unanimous will of this House. (XXXVI Lok Sabha Debates 1959: 4009)

Armed with the above formidable purposes, it is not surprising that most of the debates preceding the DPA (1961) in the Lok Sabha, centered around the justification for the bill and definition of dowry. One member even termed it as the 'soul' of the Bill. The understanding of the 'evil' varied and consequently the solutions also differed. That the 'evil' had become all pervasive is reflected in the speeches of the members belonging to different states.

Most of the members in the debate accepted the fact that dowry had pervaded almost all sections of the society and was no longer limited to only the upper classes or some particular states of the country. They also agreed that the bride and her natal family were being increasingly victimized by the rampant growth of the dowry practice. Narayanankutty Menon of Mukundapuram asserted that 'giving or taking dowry is taken as a matter of fact in every society' in spite of the fact that everybody considers it 'an anti-social evil' (LSD: 3237). Dowry was also seen as not being only an urban phenomenon. Satyabhama Devi of Navada, Bihar, indicated its practice among all castes and classes in both rural and urban areas of Bihar. So much so that the girls in the villages of Bihar were unable to find suitable grooms (LSD: 3709). Its prevalence in many Indian villages was also testified by Sri Jadhav (LSD: 3730).

Linkages of dowry with growing complexities in Hindu marriages as well as with violence on the girl/bride was thus completely recognized. Ila Palchoudhury (LSD: 3437) noted the growing complexities in the performance of Hindu marriages. Instances of the bridegroom leaving the marriage pandal on account of some of his demands not being honoured had become quite 'common'. These demands often included financing a foreign trip for the groom to enhance his educational qualifications. As a result, she added, suicides had become quite widespread among girls who could not bear to see their parents suffer on account of heavy dowry demands. Prakash Vir Shastri of Gurgaon (LSD: 3478) and Parvati Krishnan (LSD: 3696) both mentioned cases of young girls either committing suicide or being discarded by their husbands who remarried for additional dowry. Subhadra Joshi of Ambala cited the case of a girl from Punjab pleading with her father to send a radio demanded by her in-laws if he valued her life (LSD: 3705). Similar cases of the untold misery of the daughters and the bankruptcy of the father occur throughout the debates.

In fact, the Parliament members pointed out various dimensions of dowry as practised all over India. It could be seen as an extravagant marriage expenditure; Pandit Thakur Das Bhargava of Hissar provided an example of a marriage in which demands included hospitality for the groom's party (*baraat*) at an expensive hotel, the reservation of a room costing Rs. 250 per day for the groom, the presentation of silver plates, bowls and glasses to all the *baraatis*, and fireworks worth thousands of rupees to accompany the procession (LSD: 3446). The bankruptcy of the father of the bride was inevitable in such circumstances.

Dowry also provided an occasion for demand for gold or other precious items. Renu Chakravarty informed the House that the offer of gold was especially 'prevalent' in the villages where utensils and furniture were becoming less common as items in dowry among the average middle class families. She said that 'they extort gold, because gold is the medium of wealth. They demand it in the form of jewellery for the daughter,' thus exposing a large number of middle and lower middle class girls 'to a lot of suffering' (LSD: 3712–16). Demands for gold and ornaments, as Parvati Krishnan pointed out, arose out of a need to establish the grooms' families' 'social status', thus causing the demand for the diamond earrings for the bride and 'many sovereigns worth gold jewellery and so on' (LSD: 3991). Even working women with B.A. and B.T. degrees had to pay such dowries to get suitable choice in grooms (LSD: 3715–16).

Linkages of hypergamous marriages with dowry were also unmasked. Jadhav, for example, noted that while the upper class families were able to meet dowry demands with offers of money, car, furniture, etc., to the groom at the time of marriage, its impact on the middle classes, the peasants, and the labour class was significant. These classes too tried to encash their son's marriage, especially the one with some educational attainments (LSD: 3728–9). For some, it was a pure and simple exploitation of the urgent need of a father to find a suitable husband for his daughter. Those who attained a certain status during the colonial period or earlier as Zamindars, Amins or Patils extracted dowry on account of their social status. Similar commanding position was being enjoyed by newly appointed MPs, MLAs and other influential members of the ruling party. Dowry thus increased with enhancement of one's position or status in society (LSD: 3740–2). Elaborating further, Lakshmi Bai of Vikarabad said that ministers in Andhra Pradesh demanded between Rs. 50,000–70,000 before marriage. The villagers tended to emulate these important public men (LSD: 3760). In fact, 'well-educated persons who take medical degrees, engineering degrees—law graduates are not very much wanted now—demand the highest prize' (Achar in LSD: 3753). Both at the individual and caste levels, e.g., activities of such caste-based association as the Kayastha Sabha and the Brahmin Sabha, attempts to curb dowry evils had been unsuccessful primarily because members and office-bearers themselves broke the rules in their personal lives (LSD: 3769).

(ii) Discussion on definition of dowry

The Joint Committee's Report on dowry that was placed before the House on 3 December 1959 contained the following clause:

> In the opinion of the committee, the fixing of a limit of Rs. 2000 for presents, ornaments, clothes etc. made at the time of marriage to either party thereto may have the effect of legalizing dowry upto that amount and encouraging the giving or taking of dowry into that limit. This would be defeating the very object of the Act, namely, to do away with the system of dowry. They therefore, feel that item (II) may be omitted. Presents worth Re.1 would also constitute an offence.

This attempt to de-link gift-giving with marriage, thereby cutting at the roots of dowry, elicited vehement opposition from most members. In fact, the proposal of the Joint Committee to make all gift-giving an offence was spurned by '99 per cent of the participating MPs' (LSD: 3441). Their response provides valuable insights into their understanding of dowry and its implications on the finalization of the Act. This also illuminates two issues: Which facets of the system of dowry did the legislators wish to retain and which did they consider objectionable? What was their understanding of the 'evil' of dowry?

Emphasizing the widespread criticisms that the proposed Bill by the Joint Committee on dowry received, Menon quoted the initial reactions to the Bill from a Bombay journal that described it as 'social reforms running amuck'. The journal pointed out that if a father-in-law gave even a coat to his son-in-law at the time of marriage he could be hauled up before a court of law and the magistrate would have to pass a sentence of imprisonment on him. Thus, such a Bill on dowry would bring about 'many a difficulty and also outrage upon the well-settled conscience of certain sections of society' (LSD: 3239). Menon, however, deliberated that since this piece of legislation was one step forward into a new type of society, such 'a sort of anachronism, difficulties and even outrages upon the conscience are inevitable' and it thereby 'expresses the earnest desire of the country to check this pernicious system'.

The 'plight' and the 'untold misery' of young girls, some members observed, underlined and justified the need for gift-giving or dowry which protected the interests of girls all over the country. In fact, Pandit Thakur Das Bhargava of Hissar (LSD: 3441) demanded the abolition of the Bill if its intentions were to abolish the system of dowry itself. Other members[1] regarded dowry as 'an ancient custom' which had provided 'security' and 'protection' to women. As such it was a mark of affection for the daughter. Thus it was 'not always an unmitigated evil'. What made this custom objectionable was the recently introduced 'new phenomenon' of dowry demands. The Speaker of the House excluded the *stridhana* which was given out of love and affection to the daughter from dowry, 'the evil'. What was demanded or given as 'consideration of marriage' was dowry, the 'evil'. If the daughter, having no other provision, was not provided with the dowry as *stridhana*, it would cut at 'the root of even such provision for daughters' (LSD: 3446). While a son was provided education, property rights and family acquisitions, the daughter, if not given dowry, would be totally deprived, for her marriage severed her connections with her parental family. Dowry as such was not an evil till the demands went 'beyond the reasonable financial competence of the other party or any other person on behalf of such other party' (LSD: 3445–51). The 'unreasonability' of the demands thus depended upon the financial competence of the bride's family. No radical reform was apparently acceptable to the members.

Recurring references to the moral stance as well as natural love and affection emerge as the justification of providing for a girl who has no other means of support. Marriage, which is 'the starting point' for a girl's life, must thus be accompanied by gift-giving (LSD: 3454). The *shastric* recommendation of the high spiritual merit of *kanyadana* in a Hindu marriage which required the bride to be properly ornamented and clad in riches was also brought into the discussion to justify dowry (LSD: 3451). Thus, 'voluntary gifts to any extent, in any form, are outside the scope of the Bill. It is only when the money is extorted, or any property is extorted as a consideration', then it would come under the purview of the Bill.[2] Definitions of dowry which thus emerged followed the above line of thinking. For instance, Hem Barua defined dowry as 'a gift or a present which is not a voluntary present or a gift, but a present that is extorted under compulsion' (LSD: 3474). Manjula Devi (Gopalpara) defended the voluntary gift of *stridhana*/dowry at the time of marriage on the ground of its ensuring the daughter's 'economic independence and security in life' (LSD: 3702).

But the predicament of a distinction between conditionality in payment and giving out of love and affection was pointed out too, especially by the women members. Parvati Krishnan cautioned that such endorsement of gift-giving at the time of marriage perpetuated dowry as 'one of the most abominable social evils in this country' (LSD: 3695). She questioned the very need for giving—whether due to social sanction or love and affection—at the time of marriage. 'If the parents wish to give their daughter something they can do it at any time from birth till the time of her death' (LSD: 3698). She criticized the suggestion of one of the members that dowry could be based on the affordability of the person concerned as an 'extraordinary' attempt 'to legalize dowry on the same slab system as the income-tax and we will have the same sort of evasion here also' (LSD: 3699).

Subhadra Joshi too demanded the de-linking of marriage with gift-giving in order to end the exploitation of women. To support dowry in order to uphold a certain tradition which was no longer favourable would only amount to accepting 'a chronic illness for oneself without attempting to cure it'. Such a tradition, she asserted, should be destroyed from its roots (LSD: 3708–9). As a result, whatever has to be given to the girl must be done outside the framework of the marriage ceremonies as it was difficult to ascertain the nature of gift-giving at that time (LSD: 3706–7). Renu Chakravarty justified this on the grounds that 'in a majority of cases, when a young bride goes to the house of the bridegroom, most of the property—money cash jewellery, etc., is actually in the control of the father-in-law or somebody else in the husband's family. Often times, the daughter-in-law is not even able to see the jewellery later on, if she needs it' (LSD: 3710–11). Therefore, the concept that at the time of the marriage of a daughter Rs. 25,000 or Rs. 50,000 will be settled to lend her security be changed drastically. In fact, setting any limit for gift-giving would only 'legalize' dowry (LSD: 3712). Women members thus questioned the daughter/woman's power to control dowry offered to her as gift or *stridhana,* a point discussed later as a theoretical issue in Ursula Sharma's study on dowry (Sharma 1984). They thus also exposed the futility of the discussion of dowry within the framework of gift-giving.

(iii) Discussions on the scope of dowry

Another aspect of the discussion preceding the DPA (1961) was that most members focused on the scope of dowry or on what was permissible. In spite of some, and especially women members' objections, the definition of dowry elicited broad acceptance of its equation with gift-giving. What was then needed was not to totally declare dowry as an illegal custom but to determine the extent of its scope. Thus, there were many suggestions to limit the value of 'customary presentations' made at the time of marriage to the bride and the groom.

Such limits proposed for dowry ranged from a gift of *mangalasutra* and clothes for the bride and the groom worth Rs. 100 (Jadhav in LSD: 3724); or Rs. 500 (Bhakt Darshan in LSD: 3728); or a security or property up to Rs. 2000 (Patel in LSD: 3724), to property, gifts or ornaments, and entertainment expenses to any extent provided these were not given for the purpose of procuring a consideration for marriage and not 'beyond the reasonable financial competence' of the party concerned (Bhargava in LSD: 3725-6). More specifically, Manabendra Shah (of Tehri Garhwal) suggested that the aggregate value of presents must not exceed: '(a) in the case of persons paying income tax upto 2% of their wealth; and (b) in other cases upto five hundred rupees'[3] (LSD: 3727).

Clearly, the debate centred around 'extortion' of dowry and the unfairness of dowry demands except for a few arguments to the contrary. To distinguish between gifts given voluntarily and those in consideration of marriage, limits were prescribed. But if dowry provided security to the girl as she stepped into her new life, why was there the need for such drastic limits?

The state's position on the scope of dowry was represented in Clause 2, as moved by Hajarnavis, Deputy Minister of Law, on 7 December 1959. After defining dowry, it explained that:

For the removal of doubts, it is hereby declared that any presents made at the time of a marriage to either party to the marriage in the form of cash, ornaments, clothes of other articles, which by custom or usage are made at the time of a marriage by any person to either party to the marriage, shall not be deemed to be dowry within the meaning of this section, unless they are made as consideration for the betrothal or marriage of the said parties. (LSD: 3731–2)

The validity accorded to custom in defining the scope of dowry was an implicit acceptance of the system itself. Menon thus correctly forewarned that nothing would be 'prevented by this legislation'. He doubted whether the minister was really keen 'to check this pernicious system of dowry' (3964). To permit gift-giving according to custom would only legalize dowry. 'In exercise of the right of this custom', the grooms and their families would demand dowry with impunity. With its teeth extracted, the Bill was an innocuous document and Menon suggested it be withdrawn from consideration.

The Speaker as well as A.K. Sen, the Law Minister, on the other hand, endorsed the giving of customary ornaments or gifts as 'absolutely obligatory' gift-giving and not 'dowry' (LSD: 3966–7). The Speaker insisted that the intention of the Bill was to restrict and avoid anything being given by way of extortion, at the same time, excluding the smaller ones which, by custom and habit, will form a necessary part of the marriage ceremony (LSD: 3968).

While one member suggested that a schedule be prepared of the customary gifts of different regions (cf. Jadhav), Menon cautioned against the use of the word 'custom' as it was difficult to prove what it sanctioned (LSD: 3968). He pointed out the inherent danger in keeping presents up to Rs. 2000 as the limit of exemption from the penal provision of the Bill. 'In almost all middle class families the system of dowry will continue' (3970) and the government's above quoted explanation would provide 'a blanket moratorium to pay dowry, to get dowry and to ask for dowry' (LSD: 3971). Nathwani felt that the explanation was unnecessary as 'custom or usage may be interpreted or construed as dowry which is also customary, which also obtains as a practice in many parts' (LSD: 3972). Krishnan denounced the efforts on the part of some members of the House to take advantage of the sentiments of people through talk of 'spirit of joyousness' at the time of marriage, that people were happy and be allowed to give 'presents' that they naturally wanted to give. But this, according to her, would be used in 'an invidious way to avoid the very spirit' of the measure and would make the Bill 'a dead letter' even before it became an Act (LSD: 3993). Chakravarty also warned that 'custom and usage' will allow all sorts of 'blackmail dowry' to go through (LSD: 3993) and could be easily manipulated.

Summing up the argument regarding the definition of dowry, T.D. Bhargava distinguished between dowry and *stridhana*. The latter must be permitted because it was traditionally offered to the daughter at the time of marriage and was never given as a consideration for marriage. 'Dowry' is only 'what the father of the bridegroom gets in order to induce his son to marry. And it is there that we want to eliminate the element of extortion. We do not want to eliminate all sorts of gifts. We only want to see that at the time of marriage, persons do not come with bloated faces, almost in sorrow, without any happiness and without any sort of gifts' (LSD: 3981).

To demarcate the line between customary gift and 'conditional' payment he suggested that (i) The court must ascertain the 'reasonable financial competence' of the person concerned; and (ii) It should also verify the presents' customary nature. He further explained that if a marriage is cancelled on account of the question of presents then it is payment *as consideration*, but if it is performed without consideration of presents then these amount to only 'incidental' or customary gifts (LSD: 3983-

4). He also pleaded for exemption of gifts given from husband to wife or *vice-versa* from the purview of the Act (LSD: 3984-5 and 3987). Hajarnavis also reiterated that voluntary gifts to any extent, whatever may be the reason for the offer—it may be affection, it may be because the parents feel that they are bound by custom or it may be because usage dictates so, are not dowry. The term 'extortion' implies that 'but for a promise to pay that sum the marriage would not come of'. Obviously no shades of grey were evident to these honourable members. It was a case of love or affection on the part of parents vs. extortion which may stall the marriage.

Questions then naturally arose on the line of demarcation between voluntary gift-giving or legalized customary presents and dowry given out of consideration.[4] To guard against exploitation on grounds of custom, members suggested placing limits on the value of gifts in order to make the Bill more practical and 'workable'.[5] C.K. Bhattacharya explained that the sacramental customary nature of the Hindu marriage necessitated giving of gift to the daughter and the groom. The ritual of *kanyadana* in which the Hindu father sits 'with all the things that he considers holy in life—first, the holy water, the god head represented by Saligram and other things' and says 'I give away my daughter to you properly ornamented and in the name of God' and the ritual of *vara dakshina* to the groom, were some of the customs that had to be considered (LSD: 4004). Besides, no father would like to call gifts given to his daughter as compulsory; it will always be treated as voluntary. So a more realistic solution would be to limit the gift of presents and other things at the time of marriage to a certain valuation (also Shah in LSD: 4006).

The Law Minister, A.K. Sen, justified gift-giving to the bride at the time of her marriage as the only way by which 'our women used to acquire *stridhana*'. Although the Hindu Succession Act granted women the right to property, it could be defected by a will or by testamentary or non-testamentary desposition. The 'surest way' in which women can still acquire property was what was given to them by their parents and relatives at the time of marriage (LSD: 4011). Therefore, he asserted, there was no 'evil' in dowry, unless extorted. It was a 'pure transaction' (LSD: 4012–13).

Finally, Clause 2, i.e. the definition of dowry—as present in the DPA (1961), was passed with 183 members approving and 40 voting against it. According to the definition, any property or valuable security given directly or indirectly, before or during or after marriage as consideration for the marriage was to be considered 'dowry'. In Explanation I, it was declared that presents in the form of cash, ornaments, clothes or other articles were not 'dowry, the evil' unless given as consideration of marriage. Thus, gift-giving upto any amount was legalized by this act if given voluntarily. Despite the warning by members that such a definition of dowry would legalize it, the legislators paid little attention to it and bowed down to the traditional approach of the 'necessity' of gift-giving. Some members had also warned against difficulty in distinguishing between voluntary giving and extortion, yet the Clause remained. As later developments were to show, it was practically impossible to prove that any 'gift' was given in consideration of marriage. This proved to be the major lacuna in the Act. Members especially opposed Explanation I as 'throwing the door wide open' (Menon); 'all dowry is legalized' (Chakravarty); and some even sarcastically commented that the word 'prohibition' be dropped from the title of the Bill (LSD: 4016). Renu Chakravarty and other Members left the House in protest at what they called the 'nullification' of the whole object of the Bill (LSD: 4209).

(iv) Discussion on other clauses of the Dowry Prohibition Bill

Parliamentary discussions on other sections of the Bill did not receive as much attention as the one dealing with the definition of dowry. An overview of these discussions point out once again to the state's stance to maintain the low profile of the

Prohibition Act and prevent any radical change. With dowry being in a sense legalized by legitimization of the custom, and by anachronistic interpretation of customary norms and practices, it is not surprising to observe similar effort to keep other clauses as ineffective and vague as possible. As noted earlier, the state's major aim and objectives in the presentation of the Dowry Prohibition Act was not the complete abolition of the practice but to maintain it within tolerable limits in the patriarchal social structure, of which the state itself was an integral part.

The debate on Clause 8 to consider whether or not the dowry offence be considered cognizable provoked much response. A large number of members opposed the move to make the offence of demanding or giving dowry cognizable. Their apprehensions included fear of police entering 'every aspect of our private lives' and disturbing 'the sanctity, sacramental quality and beauty' of marriage as well as simply a lack of faith in the police force.[6] Ila Palchoudhury also opposed cognizance and, instead, emphasized changing of public conscience as a corrective measure (LSD: 4246). Several members on the other hand pressed to make the offence cognizable in order to increase its effectiveness.[7] They held that an old custom like dowry could not be abolished by mild legislative measures. The gravity of the offence committed under the Dowry Act exceeded the act of murder and it should thus be made 'cognizable and non-bailable' (LSD: 4241). Without the state taking responsibility of implementation of the Act through high level police officials, the Act would remain a dead letter and would abet dowry rather than curb it. The raising of social consciousness against dowry would not alone solve the problem (LSD: 4247). The Deputy Minister of Law, however, echoed the sentiments of the majority and ruled out the need for making the Act cognizable.[8] He contended that wider powers to the police would only 'entail invasion of liberty of an individual', without any 'corresponding gain to the state' (LSD: 4248). Clause

8 was finally adopted as part of the Bill. It left the dowry offence as non-cognizable, bailable and non-compoundable.

The above debate indicates that the legislators, many of whom were prominent lawyers, always stopped short of assuaging or arousing public disapproval in spite of the DPA's professed aim of providing advantage to the public by making it more practical. It was therefore alleged that the government, while having accepted changes in the Bill as proposed by the Select Committee, adopted a different course and continuously shifted its attitudes.[9] To pass the onus of inefficiency on the police was to skirt the real issue, i.e. how far was it willing to make the legislation an effective one? Moreover, as pointed out earlier, making the offence cognizable was an evidence of the realization that the problem was grave and required urgent and effective reform. Unwilling to interfere in the patriarchal family 'privacy', the government obviously thought otherwise despite strong protests.

The discussion on Clause 3 pertained to the penalty for giving and taking of dowry. Both the Minister and the Deputy Minister of Law proposed that the giver, the taker, and the abetter of dowry be declared guilty and punished in order to make the Bill a healthy measure.[10] Most members agreed to this. Yet they disagreed on the amount of fine. It was felt that since dowry was a 'social evil' compulsory jail sentence would turn it into a criminal offence. A heavy fine was enough as exemplary punishment.[11] Bhakt Darshan (LSD: 3744) especially pleaded for avoiding force or stringent punishment as it would ward off complainants and would also be difficult to enforce. The emphasis was instead placed on moulding the public opinion against dowry.[12] Some members forewarned that such moves would render the legislation 'lame', 'toothless', and 'ineffective'. One member for instance, pointed out that there was no distinction between a social and any other crime and accordingly no leverage was required for the former in terms of punishment or seeking evidence (LSD: 3745).

In all, 11 members spoke on Clause 3. The government, as pointed out by A.K. Sen, was in favour of including the giver of dowry within the ambit of the offence so as not to make the bill 'shorn of its value'. Only 39 members voted for excluding the giver of dowry while 141 voted for inclusion of all—the giver, the abetter and the taker of dowry in the ambit of punishment (LSD: 3960). The punishment recommended by the Joint Committee (i.e. a fine of Rs. 5000 and/or the imprisonment upto six months) was not accepted. Those who voted for either imprisonment or fine or both according to the decision of the magistrate based on the gravity and significance of the offence numbered 153 while 22 members voted against (LSD: 3956) stringent punishment. Clause 3 was thus adopted in the Bill. On the one hand, the giver, abetter, and the taker of dowry were all brought within the ambit of punishment, on the other, members were hesitant to impose compulsory imprisonment along with fine on those committing the offence. The nature of punishment was to be concurrent with the size of the dowry exchanged. One could infer that some dowry was acceptable, and required little or no punishment. The magistrate was to evaluate whether the acceptable size of dowry payment had been exceeded.

Clauses 4, 5 and 6 did not elicit lengthy discussion and were approved almost as presented. They respectively concerned the penalty for demanding dowry, illegality of any agreement on dowry, and benefit of dowry to the wife and her heirs. The penalty for demanding dowry was fixed to be a fine of Rs. 5000 and/or imprisonment upto 6 months. It was similar to the one accepted for the giver, taker and abetter of dowry as in Clause 3 (LSD: 4210). Clause 5 affirmed that the state did not provide recognition to any agreement made for the exchange of dowry. The next clause fixed the same punishment as the two earlier clauses for the person who failed to transfer the dowry to the bride within one year of marriage. If the woman died before receiving the amount, her heirs would be the claimants to such property. According to Paras Diwan, this section has made even extorted dowry into *stridhana*, thereby changing the nature of *stridhana* which customarily consisted only of voluntarily given gifts (Diwan 1987: 171).

Clause 7 pertained to the cognizance of dowry offence and the discussion revolved around the best method to implement the Act and to make it really effective. Patel's amendment suggested that a person convicted of dowry offence be not allowed to continue in his service or to improve his status because the ascending social status was linked to the escalation of dowry demands (LSD: 4215–17). Such exemplary punishment would convey to the people that dowry is a social evil and whoever demands it shall have no special status. This amendment was vehemently opposed by several members including the Law Minister for being too severe. Pattabhi Raman commented that this would turn 'most marriages, Hindu marriages in particular, into funeral occasions by terrorizing family members on a festive occasion. People would take advantage of this measure to settle scores out of spite' (LSD: 4224). The Law Minister dismissed the suggested amendment as an 'outmoded' one, similar to the 'attitude of the law-makers in the medieval ages and also of the seventeenth and eighteenth centuries when they thought that crime can best be met by making the law rigorous so that if the punishment is very extreme it is the best deterrent against crime. It would be similar to taking a dowry-taker to his death sentence'. A wide social conscience was a more viable remedy than rigorous punishment through law. It was the system that encouraged dowry which required tackling and not 'individual delinquents'. He further said that 'I do not claim—none of us can claim—that just by passing this law we are going to completely eradicate dowry. We are not; I am perfectly sure we are not' (LSD: 4237–8). Patel's amendment was thus defeated.

Another amendment called for permission to only 'the aggrieved person' or a social organization to report dowry related offences in order to forestall false complaints and harassment due to caste or family feuds.[13] The Law Minister, in spite of the members' objections, encouraged the approach of depending upon the boldness of an individual who will voluntarily go to a court to lay a complaint when he thinks that a crime has been committed against the society (LSD: 4240). In this case, Sen felt it appropriate to discount the factor of social reality even though many members pointed out that the 'social conscience' or 'selfless motive' of people had not reached such a stage that a person could report about a crime committed against society.[14]

Clause 7 when adopted thus accordingly provided that the Courts of Metropolitan or First Class Judicial Magistrates could alone take cognizance of the offence under the Act. The complaint had to be made within one year from the date of the offence. No specifications were provided as to who were authorized to lodge the complaint. It was left to the aggrieved party to do so, which was unpractical and unrealistic. They were unwilling to lodge a complaint for fear of it affecting their daughter adversely.

Clauses 9 and 10 were added to the Bill without discussion and these provided for the central and the state governments to make rules for the purposes of the Act. There was a sense of hurriedness and urgency in completing the proceedings related to the Bill. The Government was not interested in adopting the suggestions of the Joint Committee on vital issues like the definition of dowry or the nature of punishment. The aim of the Bill, as the government accepted, was 'to create public opinion' (LSD: 3748–54).[15] The Bill was finally considered at the Joint Sitting of both the Houses of Parliament held on 6 and 9 May 1961, and was passed. The said Act, namely, the Dowry Prohibition Act, 1961 came into force from 1 July 1961 (Diwan 1987: 315). Members had a mixed opinion about the Act. Ila Palchoudhury, for instance, felt that such a legislation focused public attention on the dowry issue as well as provided 'a channel through which one could protest when necessary'. Others, however, believed in the need for a 'powerful movement', 'a resurgent or a generating force', 'arousal of social conscience through education' before the legislative measure could become effective. The task of moulding public opinion could be undertaken either by political parties or through social organization. Little faith was expressed in government machinery. "The keepers of the law are mainly the breakers of the law, i.e. the police. Nobody, trusts them", Renu Chakravarty said (LSD: 3715). Instead, "an awakened social conscience and a strong public opinion could prevent the law from becoming 'infructuous'." Yet, on the whole, despite the large number of legal enactments being executed, most members expressed little faith in the Bill. "No amount of legislation", Patel remarked, "will cure this disease". It would only serve as "balm to the uneasy conscience" of some social reformers as "the remedy is worse than the disease" (LSD: 3742, 3748, 4249) ... .

Excerpted from Ranjana Sheel, 1999, *The Political Economy of Dowry*. Delhi: Manohar Publishers.

Beginning with Our Own Lives:
A Call for Dowry Boycott

MADHU KISHWAR & FIVE OTHERS

Though we feel very encouraged by the fact that over the past year, many more individual women, women's groups and organizations have become activized around the issue of dowry and dowry murders, we have noticed with concern a rather disappointing trend. Many of us see our role as that of women 'activists' mobilizing 'other' women in protest action against atrocities like dowry murders. Many, who take upon ourselves the task of changing society's attitudes, continue to live our own lives almost untouched by the ideas with which we seek to influence others.

We, at *Manushi*, feel that initiating any kind of social and political action is meaningless unless it begins with our own lives, that those of us who assume the role of the mobilizers, lead protest marches and speak or write against dowry, owe it to ourselves and to all those whom we try to draw into collective action not to, in any way, be party to such crimes as the giving and taking of dowry. We have no moral right to shout slogans like '*Dahej mat do, dahej mat lo*' ('Do not give dowry, do not take dowry') if we privately continue to participate in marriages where dowry is given or taken. If we do not dare to boycott the marriage ceremony of even our own brothers or sisters where lavish dowry is given, if we do not start the campaign in our own homes, what moral right have we to preach to others? We are not for a moment suggesting that every woman who participates in a protest action or starts getting involved in the campaign should be called upon to make such a commitment. We are referring only to those who take upon themselves the task of mobilization or consciousness-raising with other women, those who see themselves as leading the anti-dowry movement.

It is unfortunate that the viciousness of the dowry custom comes to be noticed only when a woman is murdered for it. We feel that all those who give and take dowry or participate in this ritual are also responsible for making such murders possible. Are they not helping perpetuate a vicious custom which reduces women to articles of sale and barter? Why cannot a protest or public meeting begin or end with the organizers making a commitment that they will not be a party to dowry giving or taking in any form, that they will boycott all dowry marriages?

We, therefore, appeal to all women's groups and organizations to ensure that the movement begins with our own lives, that all of us be prepared to pay the price of our convictions. At least the women actively involved in taking up any issue should seriously discuss how it touches their lives and make commitments to personally and collectively battle against it.

Some of us have been practising this form of boycott for a while. But now we publicly affirm that:

1. We will not attend, or in any way, participate in a marriage where dowry is either given or taken in however veiled a form (as gifts, trousseau, or as money deposited in a bank in the girl's name at the time of marriage), even if the marriage be that of a close relative or a dear friend. We will openly make known our reasons for boycotting such marriages, rather than just quietly staying away from the ceremony. We will also boycott all rituals wherein dowry continues to be given after marriage such as customary gifts to the son-in-law's relatives at festivals and childbirth.

2. We will henceforth not confine protest actions to dowry murders but will also protest when dowry is given at extravagant marriage ceremonies.

3. We will not attend marriages in which the woman has no active choice in deciding whether she wants to get married at all or in choosing the person to whom she is to be married.

By protesting only when murders take place, we are keeping our own homes untouched, because dowry murders, for all their frequency, are still rare as compared to the high frequency of dowry giving and taking. Almost all of us participate in, or connive with, the giving and taking of dowry—not just in the form of cash, jewellery, household goods, and gifts to the husband's family on every conceivable occasion—but the various bribes that the woman's family is forced to continue offering so that she may not be taunted and maltreated.

Only when dowry itself is attacked in all its forms and manifestations does the battleground shift to our own homes and personal lives. It is there that the real struggle begins.

*First published in *Manushi*, No. 5, May–June 1980.

Rethinking Dowry Boycott

MADHU KISHWAR

For years now, we have participated in the common refrain that dowry is a social evil. Slogans have been raised against it; politicians have condemned it from public platforms; Parliament has legislated against it. Some of us at *Manushi* were also caught up in the euphoria and took a pledge in 1980 not to attend any dowry weddings.

This pledge was prompted by the fact that almost everyone, including those who are at the forefront of anti-dowry campaigns, continues to give and take dowry. We hoped that the refusal, even by a few people, to attend dowry weddings, would build pressure within their families and communities against the practice, and that the boycott would spread.

However, the pledge did not have the desired effect, nor has it borne fruit even when taken on a larger scale, in the course of campaigns by other organizations. Very few, even from amongst *Manushi* readers, responded when we gave a call for more signatories. Amongst my family, friends, and neighbours, my stand was viewed with respect, even appreciation. But it did not lead anyone (except my two brothers) to refrain from taking (or giving) dowry, even though some were apologetic about their compulsions.

All these years. I have adhered to the pledge, even at the cost of annoying many friends and relatives. Simultaneously, however, I have also been forced to re-examine the question, given that most young women, for whose benefit we wish to

268

'abolish' dowry, are not willing to give it up. This raises a political and ethical question—do we, as self-appointed social reformers, have the right to promulgate measures for the supposed welfare of any group when that group itself does not perceive the reform as being in its interest?

Instead of dismissing the refusal of young women to say 'no' to dowry, as being a sign of their 'low consciousness' or lack of awareness, we would do better to examine why they are not willing to give it up. The answer is simple. Under the existing family structure, giving up dowry does not entail any alternative advantage for a woman. She loses the little she would get, and gains literally nothing. And yet, we, the social reformers, have shied away from this simple answer, and have continued to demand that women, as proof of their 'liberated' thinking, should refuse to take dowry.

Most women see their dowry as the only share they will get in their parental property. In a situation where women do not have effective inheritance rights, dowry is the only wealth to which they can lay claim. To suggest that women refuse dowry and go empty-handed to their marital homes is to suggest that they make even greater martyrs of themselves than society makes of them. Until we can ensure inheritance rights for daughters, we have no right to ask them to sacrifice the inadequate compensation they get by way of dowry.

The few women who, motivated by idealism, do not claim what society recognizes to be their due—a dowry—are rarely able to enforce their claim to inheritance rights since society does not recognize this as their due (regardless of what the law may say). Take the example of a colleague of mine, who is the only woman in her family to have built a career and stayed unmarried. She abstained from taking her share of her mother's jewels when it was offered to her because she does not like wearing jewels. Nor did she get a dowry or its equivalent. The result is that while her brother's son inherited the ancestral house and business, and her brother's daughters got huge dowries in cash and kind (much of it of their own selection), she had to start from scratch to build her own assets, and is not sure of where she will live after retirement. Needless to say, no one in the family expects her to demand her share in the family house. If she were to do so, it is likely to lead to a complete rupture with the family. So she ends up staying briefly in what should be equally her house, but is viewed as a semi-dependent of her nephew.

While in some cases the woman is not allowed to enjoy her dowry, in many other cases she is able to exercise control, partial or total, over it. To go dowryless is to be deprived of even this chance. Hence, women's commonsense desire for a dowry.

Her wedding is the one occasion when a daughter is specially indulged and made much of. She has, to some extent, the chance to select clothes and jewels, to demand and to get. This is a valuable experience for most girls, given that, in general, a daughter's desires are much less indulged by parents than a son's. Further, a woman never knows whether, after marriage, she will be given any money to spend on her own needs or will be provided with clothes or jewels. We have heard many women complain that for years after marriage, they were not given money by their in-laws to buy a new blouse or pair of slippers, and continued wearing what they had received in dowry or what their parents continued to give them from time to time—part of an extended dowry. In many cases, therefore, dowry is a woman's lifeline. To ask her to do without it is like asking workers to protest against wage-slavery by working for free and abstaining from taking their wages.

What is dowry? The transfer of wealth at the time of marriage. In itself, this is neither good nor evil. In many societies, marriage payments have been made in different forms. The practice of giving the daughter wealth of some kind—in the form of a settlement or a trousseau or family jewels passed from mother to daughter—has been prevalent in many societies, including throughout Europe until very recently. While this system prompted men to look for women with bigger fortunes, there is no evidence that this always, in all societies, led to the woman's maltreatment. It may even have enhanced her status under certain circumstances.

The harassment of wives is related to the utterly dependent and powerless position of women in our present family structure which concentrates economic and decision-making power in the hands of men. What we need to fight is not a phoney symbol such as dowry but the power relations within the family. Not giving dowry will not, by itself, alter the fact that property control is in the hands of men and that women are deprived of it.

Social and political activists have tended to single out dowry as the prime cause of maltreatment of wives, and have attributed increase in dowry demands and payments to growing greed and materialism in our society. In an earlier article, 'Dowry: To Ensure Her Happiness or to Disinherit Her?' (*Manushi*, No. 34, 1986), I tried to demonstrate how this analysis is extremely misleading, if not useless, in combatting dowry. Yet this analysis continues to be popular because it is relatively easier to give sermons to people to be less greedy than to work out ways to actually restructure relations, even within our own families, in such a way that power and property control is redistributed.

There is also a widespread tendency amongst activists to confuse the issues by condemning lavish and ostentatious weddings and gift-giving as somehow evil and harmful to women. A critique of waste and ostentation should not be confused with a critique of what goes specifically against women's interests. The pressure to make a lavish display is not confined to daughters' weddings, or even to weddings alone. To take just one example, there is great pressure amongst the middle and upper-classes in urban areas to make increasingly lavish displays—more recurrent than weddings—on children's birthdays. Parents do complain even while they comply, but the pressure certainly does not lead them to harass or kill their children. Nor does it act as a deterrent to having children. Therefore, we should take with a pinch of salt the argument that it is only the fear of having to give dowry and arrange ostentatious weddings which makes people prefer sons to daughters, or makes them neglect their daughters.

When, in the late 1970s, it was discovered that many of the deaths of married women which used to pass off as accidents were in fact suicides or wife-murders, women's organizations and the press too quickly assumed that the main cause of these deaths was the greed for dowry. One possible reason why this happened is that when the woman's parents narrated the story, they always projected dowry demands as the most torturous part of the harassment inflicted by her husband and in-laws.

To the woman's parents, dowry demands loom largest because this is the one form of harassment which has to be borne by them. All the other forms of torture have to be borne by the woman alone. If she is taunted for her looks, culinary or house-keeping skills, mannerisms, inability to bear a son or inability to 'please' her husband, as almost every woman in such a situation is, the near invariable response of her parents is to tell her to try to improve herself, to 'adjust' and 'mould' herself to her marital family's requirements. But when the taunt relates to dowry the woman's natal family, especially the men, find themselves in the dock. No adjustment on the woman's part will do—it is her father who has to adjust to the demands for more wealth. That is why this particular aspect of the harassment pinches the woman's family most, and eclipses all else in their minds.

If the woman is killed or thrown out by her husband, her parents have yet another reason to project dowry demands as the primary or only cause of harassment—they hope to get the dowry back. Even if the woman is alive, it is relatively easier to get part of the dowry back than to ensure that the woman can live with dignity in her in-laws' home.

When the woman is dead, it is always her parents or brothers who bring the case to public attention; even when she is alive, she is almost invariably accompanied to the police station or the social organization by her father or brother because she badly needs their support. In most cases, the father or brother is the one to draft the complaint and narrate it to the authorities.

In this narrative to the police and the social workers, the parents, or even the woman herself is usually compelled to highlight dowry demands and to downplay other problems because today, dowry demands are perhaps the only form of harassment which will be unequivocally condemned, even by the police. Other forms of harassment, including even wife-beating, are much more likely to be condoned. When told that the husband berates or beats his wife, the police tend to ask why he does so, implying that she must be provoking him. That under no circumstances should a man beat his wife is not yet universally accepted in the way that it is accepted that dowry demands are wrong. So, highlighting dowry demands is one of the simplest ways to get a complaint to be taken seriously and registered as a criminal case. In the process, it comes to be projected as the main cause of harassment. The downplaying of other forms of harassment tends to draw public attention away from the inherent powerlessness of women in the existing family structure.

If one listens closely to the narratives of women, a number of elements recur as regularly as do dowry demands. One such recurrent element is the flinging of insulting remarks about her family, ancestry and upbringing. Another is the strict control over her movements, contacts, associations and expenditure. After years of listening to the detailed narratives of harassed wives, and working to provide legal advice to such women, I have realized that it is a fallacy to see dowry as the root cause of the harassment of wives. I have not come across a single case amongst the hundreds I have heard, read about or dealt with, where the husband and in-laws harassed the woman because of dowry alone, and were, in all other respects, satisfied with her. Dissatisfaction is expressed, not only with the quality and quantity of the dowry but equally with the woman herself. She is told that the husband could have got not just a better dowry but also a better wife. Criticizing the dowry, like criticizing her family, is a way of criticizing her and the package deal that she represents. This is one reason why meeting dowry demands almost never induces husband or in-laws to view with greater favour a woman whom they otherwise view with contempt.

It is highly significant that it is not only when the dowry is considered inadequate that a woman will be harassed; this can happen equally if the dowry is considered large and ostentatious. She may be accused of arrogance, of trying to show her in-laws up and dazzle them with her parental affluence. In the same way, great beauty is made a pretext for humiliation just as much as its lack; high educational qualifications or a good job become a pretext for taunting just as much as lack of education or her unemployability. If a woman's parents are loving towards her, this can become an occasion for insult; so can their being neglectful.

There is almost no attribute—negative or positive—which a woman may possess, which cannot be used against her if her husband and in-laws so wish. Clearly, what requires rectification are not her attributes or possessions but her position of dependence and helplessness which forces her to put up with harassment and violence. To expect that harassment will stop if she is dowryless, is like advising a wife to give up her job because her violent husband resents her having a better job than he does.

Dowry is only one among many pretexts used by in-laws to legitimize abuse. A certain degree of ill-treatment is built into the subservient and dependent status of a wife in the existing family structure. This ill-treatment only comes to public notice when it crosses certain limits. In those cases where a woman is not maltreated, this is because her in-laws refrain from using their power. But the fact of their having the power still remains.

Dowry in itself does not always and under all circumstances lead to blackmail. In several cases, harassment and violence occur without any relation to dowry. In the few cases where the woman is in a strong position because of her independent earnings, profession and status in society, and has managed to acquire self-confidence, gifts given by her parents, whether or not they are termed 'dowry', do not make an appreciable difference either way.

The real problem lies not in the wealth itself—the furniture or gadgets or vehicles or clothes or jewels, however abundant or expensive—but in who controls them. In our society today, women are not expected to control wealth but to surrender it—in favour of brothers or husband. A wife is treated not as an individual who controls her own life and assets but as herself an asset who must perform several functions. One function is to bring wealth just as another function is to provide services of various kinds, and yet another to provide a male heir.

She is usually unable to resist this role because her parents have not treated her differently. Even as unmarried daughters, most girls are made to live a narrowly confined and dependent life. Most parents do not allow daughters to have money or other assets in their own name or to learn to manage family property. In rural areas, where the overwhelming majority of Indian women live, they may toil on the family farm but are seldom given the right to inherit it, as sons are. Even among non-agricultural families and in urban areas, daughters' education is not taken as seriously as that of sons'. Frequently, daughters are actively deterred from taking up paid employment. A life of economic independence tends to be seen as almost a stigma for a woman.

A girl who has been crippled on the pretext of being 'sheltered' is not likely to be less helpless just because no dowry is given at her wedding. The well-being of such a girl is at the mercy of chance—whether her husband and in-laws are good enough to refrain from exercising the arbitrary power they have over her life. If they decide to be nasty, no amount of dowry or lack of it can help her. Most women realize this. That is why they are not convinced by the argument that to refuse dowry would be to ensure their own welfare. They are aware that as their lives are structured today, the chance of getting a kindly disposed husband will play a more important role in their welfare than anything they can do.

If, on the other hand, a woman is equipped to take care of herself and of what belongs to her, her having a dowry will be no disadvantage. If ill treated, she will know how to resist, how to guard her interests, and how, if necessary, to walk out, taking her dowry with her. It is in this context that the recent Supreme Court judgement defining dowry as *stridhan* is important. Changing a name does not make a social evil a social good. What the judgement stresses is that shifting control of the assets would render them advantageous to women, whereas today they can be used to her disadvantage.

Today, I find it irrelevant to talk of abolishing dowry. Instead, we should single-mindedly work to ensure effective inheritance rights for women—but not on paper alone. We should forget the slogan '*Dahej mat do, dahej mat lo*' ('Do not give dowry; do not take dowry') and raise the slogan '*Betiyon ko virasat do, Betiyan, apni virasat lo*' ('Daughters must be given property rights; daughters must claim inheritance rights').

A number of steps need to be taken to facilitate this:
1. Any will which disinherits daughters should be considered invalid.
2. All land, property and succession related laws, including land ceiling laws, should be amended to ensure equal rights to women, particularly over immovable property such as housing and land.
3. Any document whereby a woman surrenders her right in favour of her brothers husband or in-laws, should be considered invalid.
4. A woman should not be able to pass on to her husband or in-laws property inherited from her parents. If she dies childless or under suspicious circumstances, the property should revert to her natal family. This would ensure that her inheritance does not become an incentive for her husband and in-laws to kill her. Her inherited property should be inherited by her adult children or, if

she is childless and dies a natural death many years after marriage, it may be inherited by her husband, as his would be inherited by her under the same circumstances.

If women's inheritance rights were to become real, dowry in its present form would almost certainly disappear. Gifts at a son's or daughter's wedding could not then be at all objectionable, even if termed 'dowry'. Equal inheritance rights would also ensure that a woman who does not marry does not end up empty-handed.

We should work to equip women with the resources and abilities to define, control and guard their own interests and their own lives. Whether or not they are given dowry will then become irrelevant to their essential well-being.

Is dowry the real killer?

We made a count of all marital violence cases mentioned in *Manushi* from No. 1, 1979, to No. 50, 1989, in order to see what pattern of causality, if any, emerged. We included here only cases where physical violence was used against the woman by her husband or in-laws. The cases are described in varying degrees of detail, from a paragraph to several pages, in the form of reports by activists, victims or their families, letters from readers, interviews, and interview- or survey-based articles.

A pattern we noticed in the reporting was that when the woman spoke or wrote about the violence she suffered, dowry was almost never mentioned as the sole cause and, further, that most of the reasons were merely pretexts, the violence being actually irrational and causeless, a straightforward expression of power. When a third person who was not a continuous witness to the violence, such as the woman's parent, sibling, other relative, or an activist, reported the case, the description tended to be briefer and more unidimensional, and more frequently focused on dowry as the only or primary cause of violence.

This pattern is evident from the fact that in cases where the woman had died, and had left no account of her suffering, about half the cases (reported by others) were ascribed simply to dowry (36 out of 79). But in cases of torture or attempted murder where the woman either reported herself or would have spoken to the person reporting, only 14.7 per cent of the cases cited dowry as the sole cause; 13.2 per cent cited other causes as primary while mentioning dowry, and 72 per cent cited other causes (or none) and did not even mention dowry. It is noteworthy that the violence in these cases was not of a negligible kind, ranging from being attacked with an axe, or having her nose chopped off, to repeated rape by father-in-law, severe battering and sadistic torture.

*First published in *Manushi*, No. 48, Sept–Oct 1988.

Reaffirming the Anti-Dowry Struggle

RAJNI PALRIWALA

Mental acrobatics may leave the writer and readers gasping—with wonder at one's own daring or with amazement at the distortions of peripheral vision. Thus it is so with Madhu Kishwar's pronouncements on dowry [Kishwar, 1988]. Rather than a rethinking of issues which have been central to the women's movement Kishwar constructs straw models of the anti-dowry struggle to knock down. In her search for *apparently* 'independent thought and creativity', she isolates elements of social reality in a manner in which no person directly involved in the struggle could. Thus for her dowry is the "transfer of wealth at the time of marriage. In itself, this is neither good nor evil" (Kishwar, 1988: 10). I wish to present here a very condensed analysis of some aspects of dowry in India and of the anti-dowry movement which I think are necessary to clarify the issues which Kishwar's 'argument' has obfuscated. This analysis is based on participatory research and on written and oral documents of the movement as well as secondary material.

Why did dowry become such a 'burning' issue at the end of the 1970s? Why did it bring women on to the streets in various forms of collective protest, establishing in the process the basis for a renewed women's movement in Delhi? Dowry, after all, is not a new practice. But the increased incidence of what are acknowledged to be dowry related murders was. It was this, rather than the dowry system itself, which spurred the movement. Kishwar argues that the harassment and murder of young brides had little to do with dowry. I argue that this intensification of homicidal violence against wives was a consequence of changes in dowry practices due to social and economic changes resulting from the colonial and post-colonial capitalist development in India. This is premised on the understanding that dowry, and indeed most forms of "transfer of wealth at marriage", cannot be understood "in itself".

In the feudal society of pre-colonial India, land and caste defined the parameters of power. Marriage was central to social strategy and an important instrument of social control. Dowry highlighted and cemented marriage alliances between landed, high status and powerful families. Although according to Manu, dowry was the lawful form of marriage presentations for Brahmins only, it was in fact associated as much if not more with castes such as the Rajputs. Dowry and hypergamy were practised only by 'high' or 'middle' ranking and upwardly mobile castes even during the colonial period, for restrictions were placed on 'lower' caste emulation of the customs and ritual of the 'high' castes (Srinivas, 1984). Hypergamy, the marriage of a woman into a family belonging to a clan or a sub-caste of slightly 'higher' status than her own, was an important feature of this complex (Srinivas, 1984; Das 1975; Committee on the Status of Women in India, 1974). The ideology of hypergamy, tied to the caste system, meant status asymmetry between the affinal groups, such that the relation between dowry and hypergamy may be seen as an exchange of goods for an increase in the status of the bride's family. Dowry and hypergamy were also tied to the 'upper' caste ideology which entailed seclusion of women, their exclusion from productive work, their categorisation as economic burdens as well as status asymmetry between husband and wife. Dowry helped 'ease' the entry of women into their marital homes (Das 1975). While in material form and content, as well as the social groups among whom it is found, dowry has changed radically, it continues to carry with it this ideological complex.

Changed practices

A number of anthropologists have discussed dowry in terms of *stridhana* (Das, 1976), female property (Tambiah, 1973) or pre-mortem inheritance (Goody, 1976), (the last especially where there has been an attempt to construct a category of Eurasian societies which Kishwar seems keen to do). Contemporary dowry not only has little to do in form and content with the classical *stridhana* (Srinivas, 1984), evidence indicates the lack of control by the bride over a major portion of 'her' dowry in earlier times too (Tambiah, 1973; Desai, 1957; Altekar, 1956). This was not a case of reality diverging from the ideal. Rather, as is true today also, normatively a substantial part of the dowry was not meant for her or her husband, but for the latter's kin. Furthermore, in north India, land was not given in dowry. In the context of patrilineal inheritance and the exclusion of daughters from ancestral property, this ensured the separation of the outgoing woman from the material symbol of the preeminent social group, the family, as well as from the most valuable economic resource. The linkage between dowry and hypergamy also points to an inherent tendency, intensified in later periods, of continuous inflation in the amount of dowry, and of the possibility that the demands of the bridegroom's family rather than custom determined the amount and kind of gifts to be given. Thus while dowry was an indication of the status of the families uniting in marriage, it was also symptomatic of the control and dependence of 'high' caste women.

As Srinivas notes, contemporary dowry practices are quite different from earlier patterns. Five dimensions of this change may be noted. First, dowry has spread to all castes, communities, religions and regions. It is practised in all classes to varying degrees. Second, the 'voluntary' character of the 'gifts' is disappearing. The 'gifts' are dictated by the demands of the groom's family as well as the status symbols of the groups within which the natal and marital family wish to project themselves, rather than 'tradition'. Indulgence of the bride and her choice has little to do with the dowry 'gifts', except among upper class and upper middle class households. Third, the money value of dowry has increased and there has been a qualitative change in the goods given, following on from the above. Often the dowry is worth significantly more than a daughter's equal share in her father's property, leading to resentment on the part of the other members of the family and a disinclination for further support. The inflationary cycle continues as families are pressured to recuperate economically from a daughter's dowry through the marriage of a son. Fourth, dowry has come to encompass the entire marital relationship and customary gift exchange between affines. Truly there is 'extended dowry' (Kishwar, 1988: 10)! Demands begin at the engagement and may continue at frequent intervals and on special occasions during the life of the marriage. Gifts given directly to the married daughter are but a portion of what is transferred. The women's parents comply with the continuing demands—made on the grounds of alleged inadequacy in the dowry at the wedding—in the hope of 'saving their daughter's home'. Finally, while the extent to which women ever have had control of the major portion of their dowries is questionable, their lack of control in contemporary times has been intensified. This has been a result both of the changing nature of gifts, its rising value and, more significantly, the overall change in women's position.

The imposition of a market economy and capitalist development during the colonial period and its spread in independent India has loosened, but not wholly transformed, earlier patterns of feudal land control and has increased liquid forms of wealth. New groups joined the elite and new avenues for economic and social mobility opened up, particularly after 1947. However, increasing economic differentiation accompanied these processes. While intra-caste and intra-kin economic heterogeneity deepened, caste and kinship have remained central to social life, but with a new freedom for 'lower' castes to emulate the behaviour of 'high' castes. Norms of 'high' traditionality in pre-colonial India—dowry, ritual expenditure, conspicuous consumption—are now being adopted by 'lower' castes, non-Hindu groups and middle and low income groups. It may be true to say "a critique of waste and ostentation should not be confused with a critique of what goes specially against women's interests" (Kishwar, 1988: 11). However, not to see the link between conspicuous consumption and the spread of dowry as status symbols in contemporary India is to miss the wood for the trees. After all, despite the ideology of patrilineality, the mother's natal family may make a substantial contribution to the child's birthday party, held at the mother's marital home, as part of extended dowry!

In addition with rising costs of living and increasing unemployment, dowry has become a means of obtaining the necessities of life and achieving upward economic mobility for the husband's family. The dowry is to provide the in-laws of the bride the capital for a business investment, the fee to be paid to a broker for a job for the young man, the gifts to be given to the husband's sister, publicly and ostentatiously, or the bicycle, television or house for their own use. Further, the need to accumulate a daughter's dowry is often given as the reason why an individual starts accepting bribes.

The spread of dowry is crucially linked to the devaluation of women in latter-day India. Women of the 'lower' castes were increasingly eliminated from their traditional areas of production (Mitra, 1979; Mitra, Srimany and Pathak, 1979). As new opportunities were closed to them, they became confined to jobs in the most menial and lowpaid sectors. Increasing economic dependence reinforced the traditional dependence of women on kin and marriage, emphasising the idea that women were an economic burden for which their in-laws must be compensated. Sharma postulates that the "expansion of dowry has been accompanied by a decline in women's capacity to contribute to household income *compared with that of men*, even though there has been no absolute diminution of women's economic activities" (1984: 67–68). As money has become a measure of value, women's declining ability to bring in cash has led to a devaluation of women.

Anti-dowry movement

The above analysis was reflected in the anti-dowry movement. The Dahej Virodhi Chetna Manch (DVCM), the co-ordinating forum of a range of organisations involved the anti-dowry movement, said that dowry cannot be viewed as an 'isolated phenomenon'. In its August 1982 memorandum it stated that dowry was "linked with the entire gamut of inferior female condition. Its increasing incidence is symptomatic of the continuing erosion of women's status and devaluation of female life in independent India. It is equally related to the worsening socio-economic crisis within which structural inequalities have accentuated and black money power grown to fuel greater human oppression". Thus the DVCM did not see dowry as the root cause of the harassment of women, which Kishwar may once have seen it as, but as symptomatic of many causes. Dowry was and is no phoney symbol. Dowry and harassment and murder for dowry are the most immediate and inhuman expression of the coalescence of those processes and relationships which are objectifying and degrading women, turning them into commodities and into means for commodities, in the context of a largely patrilineal, patri-virilocal society.

The spread of dowry is not the spread of a practice of the transfer of wealth at marriage 'in itself'. It indicates the commercialisation of the marriage relationship in addition to its earlier importance in terms of establishing alliances between elite families. But most importantly it meant the equation of the woman with the dowry. Thus, unmarried working class and educated middle class women work to accumulate their dowry. Rural women in Rajasthan working on family farms are seen as contributing to 'their' dowry or to their daughter's 'extended dowry', not to the family in terms of basic subsistence or surplus accumulation. Daughters indeed grow up looking forward to their marriage, to being 'adult', to having a husband and children. They look forward to the wedding when they will be the centre of attention and, among the middle class, to the nice clothes and the 'wealth' they will be given. Marriage is essential to attain social adulthood, but problems of accumulating the dowry can delay the marriage. Young girls grow up sensitive to this and sensitive to the fact that their marriage can mean the ruin of their natal family. The psychological traumas that are generated were sharply forced on all of us in the suicide pact of the three young sisters in Kanpur. Soon after marriage a significant enough number of brides who had looked forward to being recipients of 'gifts' find they have little control over, or access to, their 'gifts'. They find that the dowry given is taken as a measure of the affection their parents hold them in and the esteem of their in-laws. Kishwar says that "dissatisfaction is expressed not only with the quality and quantity of the dowry, but equally with the woman herself" (Kishwar, 1988: 12). Yes, for the woman is the dowry and the dowry is the woman. Much before the anti-dowry movement it could be observed how in urban middle class households and among rural peasants, criticism of a daughter was seen by her, her parents and neighbours to relate to the dowry she had not brought or the post-wedding gifts with which she did not return from her natal home. One can understand Kishwar's reluctance to accept that there is a social equation between the woman and her dowry, for it is indeed bitter and inhuman. But even more important, Kishwar's framework, where it is paramount that one accepts the socially constructed desires of some sections of women as what they 'truly' want, as the basis of struggle, would imply also accepting this equation.

Kishwar tells us that dowry was highlighted in the cases of harassment and murder which came to women's organisations because the bride's father and brother were interested only in dowry-related harassment since it directly affected them, while other abuses affected only the daughter. (Kishwar confuses forms of harassment with reasons for abuse so that one is left wondering if there are particularities in the forms of abuse for dowry related reasons as against for other reasons.) What happened to kill the love and affection in which they held the girls and which allowed them to "indulge and make much of her" at her wedding (Kishwar, 1988: 10)? Anyone who has been involved in some minimum counselling or engaged in intensive fieldwork will know that a constant topic of conversation among those with recently married daughters or daughters who are harassed, is the latter's situation in their marital homes. Parents agonise over it, bemoan their inability to do much, discuss their advice to their daughters to 'adjust'. What are the options before them? They can bribe their daughter's in-laws into treating their daughters better. They can leave her alone to 'adjust'. Or they can bring her back, with all possibility that this will mean the end of the marriage. Economic dependence of the woman, the expenses incurred on her marriage and the social stigma attached to a woman with a broken marriage reinforce her natal family's and her own desire that she remain with her husband. In addition there is her fear that she will lose her children if she leaves her husband. The social obligation on the bride to 'adjust' and the acceptance that once she enters her in-laws' home, she will leave it permanently only on her funeral bier is reinforced by the fact that she has become her dowry, not only for her in-laws, but for her parents too. Dowry as a social fact cannot be treated in isolation, but it is increasingly isolating the woman from her own kin, constraining the bonds of affection and the tie of support. The prescription for continuing gifts, whether a family can afford them or not, adds to the resentment of the woman's natal kin and her own insecurity. She hears people say of another woman "She works there [in her *sastra*] and consumes here [in her *peehar*]". Her in-laws tell her, "Don't expect that just because you live here we have to keep you—your parents cannot even give us what self-respect demands" (clothes for the woman and her husband and his kin). Just as neither marriage nor dowry were issues of individual choice in pre-colonial India, they remain instruments of social control, of women and of their families too.

After the anti-dowry movement, a fourth option has emerged for her and her parents. A women's organisation may be asked to intercede on the woman's behalf, so that the in-laws are pressured into treating the woman better, in the process reducing the isolation of the woman. Kishwar of course sees another possibility, of the woman's parents single-handedly changing socially constructed relationships in the same manner in which she wished to end dowry with her boycott.

Many forms of struggle

Many trends of thinking and consciousness made up the anti-dowry movement. It ran at many levels and through various forms of struggle ranging from legal action, seminars and corner meetings, neighbourhood demonstrations, *dharnas* and public marches. The agreement within the Dahej Virodhi Chetna Manch was that despite differences on particular points the Joint Select Committee report and recommendations would be taken as the consensus. The recommendations included suggestions for comprehensive legal reform, not only of the Dowry Prohibition Act, 1961, but also on inheritance rights for daughters, registration of marriages and all gifts given at marriage, custody of children, family courts, legal aid and a common civil code. Other recommendations were on the use of mass media and school textbooks for public education, the establishment of vigilance committees with representatives of women's organisations as members, dowry prohibition officers and a national commission on women. The understanding was clearly that dowry cannot be fought in isolation. As a fight against dowry it was not a call for dowry boycott by itself, but raised a gamut of issues related to women's economic dependence and their legal and social rights in both their natal and marital homes. With the further specification which one finds in the August 1982 memorandum of the DVCM, the first three demands in the section on legal action related to women's rights in property. These included demands for amendments to provide equal property rights for women under all prevailing laws, a compulsory share for a daughter in a testator's property and a half share for the wife in all assets acquired by the couple after marriage. In 1983, the anti-dowry movement's concern with women's dependent status continued in the focus on the issue of women's employment by women's organisations on March 8, International Women's Day.

Activists had found that the inadequacies in the law and the collusion and connivance of the police and local administration added to the problems of dowry harassment. However, for many sections in the anti-dowry movement, legal changes were viewed only as an instrument of social change. Thus the emphasis was on public campaigns in order to build the necessary political and social will to ensure action that would be effective in eradicating dowry and the increasing harassment of brides. Included in the written list of slogans circulated and raised at meetings and marches were "*parivar mein rishta vaisa ho, bahu-beti samaan ho*" (relatiohships within the family should be such that the daughter and the daughter-in-law are treated the same) and "*stri par na ho atyachar, ham parosi hain zimmedar*" (we neighbours are responsible that women are not abused).

Hindsight can and must clarify and sharpen our understanding, must aid activists in correcting mistakes, in rethinking issues and future struggles; and it must be based on the concrete experience of struggle. In relooking at the anti-dowry movement and examining the developments of the last few years, the essential understanding of the anti-dowry movement is reaffirmed. The experience of the participating organisations and women made it clear that it was not a question of dowry first or inheritance first, but that both struggles have to take place together. Simultaneously, immediate and urgent measures were needed—legal, social and administrative—to tackle the harassment and murder of women for dowry. Whatever Kishwar may argue, dowry did not, and does not, give women much in material terms, while as a social phenomenon it takes away their very right to humanity and to life. The continuation of dowry acts as a justification for the daughter's exclusion from her father's property, leave alone devaluing her and her economic contribution to her family. Being attached to dowry and excluded from property, she can never be a full member of any family, where no family wants the complete responsibility for her or can give her a share in their unity, their property. If, socially, women are to be accepted as complete persons, in their self-conception as well as the perception of society at large, the equation of women with dowry has to be broken and they have to become equal members, equal shareholders in the family property. The fight for the latter has to be in conjunction with the fight against dowry. Kishwar's argument for first one and then the other is as mechanical as was the idea that dowry boycott would by itself end dowry. In conclusion I would like to quote a slogan which the anti-dowry movement can take much of the credit for popularising: *"jo aurat ko hak de na sake, woh samaj badalna hai"*—we must transform that society which cannot give women their due.

References

Altekar, A.S. 1956: *The Position of Women in Hindu Civilisation from Pre-Historic Times to the Present Day*, Banares, Motilal Banarsidass.

Committee on the Status of Women in India 1974: *Towards Equality*, New Delhi, Department of Social Welfare, GOI.

Das, V. 1975: 'Marriage among the Hindus' in D Jain (ed), *Indian Women*, New Delhi, Publications Division, GOI.

—— 1976: 'Indian Women Work Power and Status' in B.R. Nanda (ed), *Indian Women: From Purdah to Modernity*, New Delhi: Nehru Memorial Museum and Library.

Desai, N. 1957: *Women in Modern India*, Bombay, Vora and Co.

Goody, J. 1976: *Production and Reproduction: A Comparative Study of the Domestic Domain*, Cambridge, Cambridge University Press.

Kishwar, M. 1988: 'Rethinking Dowry Boycott', *Manushi*, 48: 10–13.

Mitra, A. 1979: *Implications of Declining Sex Ratio in India's Population*, ICSSR Programme of Women's Studies I, Bombay, Allied.

Mitra, A., A.K. Srimany and L.P. Pathak 1979: *The Status of Women: Household and Non-Household Economic Activity*, ICSSR Programme of Women's Studies III, Bombay, Allied.

Sharma, U. 1984: 'Dowry in North India: Its Consequences for Women' in R. Hirchon (ed), *Women and Property, Women as Property*, London, Croom Helm. (Reproduced in this volume.)

Srinivas, M.N. 1984: *Some Reflections on Dowry*, Delhi, Oxford University Press. (Reproduced in this volume.)

Tambiah, S.J. 1973: 'Dowry and Bridewealth and the Property Rights of Women in South Asia' in J. Goody and S.J. Tambiah, *Bridewealth and Dowry*, Cambridge, Cambridge University Press.

First published in *The Economic and Political Weekly*, April 29, 1989.

On Kidneys and Dowry

C.S. LAKSHMI

A young cousin of the family, aged 14, needed a kidney transplant recently. The donor whose blood and tissue group agreed with hers was a supervisor in a factory. His monthly income was Rs 2,000. Asked why he wanted to donate a kidney, he said that he had three daughters and that he needed money for their dowry. He wanted Rs 10,000 deposited in the bank in each of his daughters' names. The daughters were 6, 4 and 3 years old. He said that the money in the bank will take care of their dowry when they grow up. On the day of the operation, when his kidney was removed, one of the attendants came to the waiting room and told his wife, "It has been removed successfully". "Removed? Removed?", she asked in a choking voice, turned towards the wall, put one end of her saree over her face and began to weep quietly. That is what dowry means to most and not a "share in the property" as Madhu Kishwar, the editor of *Manushi*, seems to think.

In her article in the latest issue of *Manushi*, Madhu Kishwar talks of women wanting dowry to be given as a share in the property and also of dowry giving them a certain status. So long as women want it this way, others cannot impose changes upon them, she feels. She seems to think that these women who feel this way have thought about marriage and status in a mental island unaffected by the values in the society. These women are those who are influenced by material values which say that a colour TV and video give you status in the society. They are part of a consumer society where status comes with the number of kitchen gadgets and electronic items a person owns. To agree with these women and say that dowry is a share in the property, and dowry gives status will be to support those very values and to find nothing basically wrong with them. It will be an act of supporting corrupt values of a consumer society that has turned marriage into a market place. Women who want their parents to give dowry want it in the mistaken notion that it ensures a comfortable future. The boy's parents look upon it as a 'price' to be paid for a husband who earns well. Do we bless these transactions and call it marriage and sit back and say "this is what they want, so let them have it their way"? This is not a feminist viewpoint or any kind of intelligent viewpoint. This is the viewpoint of someone who has confused several separate issues like marriage, status, property and dowry as being one issue.

Definition of women's status

Underlying this kind of argument are some dangerous definitions of a woman's status. If we go along with this line of thinking it would mean accepting the fact that a woman's status is linked to marriage. Not only that. The question of a share in the property is also linked to her marriage. Even worse, it would mean that status within a marital system has nothing to do with the individuals, it has to do with goods and property. A woman inherits property by being the child of parents who own property. Whether married or unmarried, she has a right to this property. Whether divorced or widowed, she has a right to this property. Dowry cannot be termed this property because dowry is a price demanded for the boy and has nothing to do with the girl's right to inherit. If one argues that dowry and dowry items are the girl's share of the property and that a woman's status depends on the quantity and amount of this, then one has to accept all the other notions that go with that kind of statement: notions that a woman "goes away from her parental home into her home" and that her legitimate status comes only when she is in her husband's house; notions that a girl becomes somebody else's belonging the moment she marries; notions that a single woman does not have any status, nor does she have a legitimate occasion like marriage to demand her share of the property; notions that once a woman enters her husband's home only her ashes can come out of it; notions that marriage is for those women who can afford it; notions that the dignity and status of a woman depend on who she marries; notions that it is the duty of parents to educate, pamper and find a husband for the daughter at whatever cost; notions that not love, warmth, understanding, sharing and empathy make a marriage work but that a transistor, cycle, scooter or Maruti car is the foundation of a happy marriage. Unfortunately, women who get burnt or young girls who hang themselves are not those who come from families where there is any property that a girl can demand as her share. Very often fathers and brothers have to work hard or pay off debts all their lives or demand dowries from girls who come into their families. Or the woman herself works and earns her dowry. Sister Subbalakshmi, the well known social reformer and educationist was once asked what will happen if women can't get married because they refuse to give dowry and she said, "Then women must have the dignity and courage to remain single". It is a pity that after all these years we are still debating what a woman's dignity entails.

Many years before Madhu Kishwar's good conscience began asking her the wrong questions, the dowry question was discussed by many women in the early Sixties and family women who were directly affected by it had some firm opinions. I give below two excerpts from articles written by women in 1960 in a Tamil magazine:

> ... Dowry is the money given by the girl's people to the boy's family. The girl's people give not according to what they want to give but according to the *demands* of the boy's family. In the name of 'dakshina' for the boy, the boy's people have made marriage a market and are making a business of it... Accepting bribes is ille-

gal. Whether it is in the form of money or gifts it is considered a bribe. Likewise, giving dowry in the form of money or household goods should still be a crime... Some people ask who else will help the boy and the girl to set themsleves up if not their parents—it is a biased opinion to say that only the girl's parents are responsible for this. Why can't both the families help them?...

* * *

Twenty five years ago what a person could save on a salary of Rs 50 one is not able to do today with a salary of Rs 300. Nowadays girls are educated in schools and colleges according to the financial capabilities of the family. They are also taught music and dance... Women have begun to work now, in a period of fifteen years it will be common to find both husband and wife working... How many families can afford to educate a daughter and also give dowry items and dowry? ...

Cultural chauvinism

For the record, let us set some facts about dowry and related issues straight. What was given as *kanya shulka* in very early times is not dowry. That was given as a gesture of affection from kinsmen and family to indicate that she had a family to fall back on. What exactly the *shulka* should be was a matter of individual choice and convenience. It was more of a symbolic gesture. Even now in marriages in the South, there is an occasion when relatives of the bride and the groom would offer money-gifts. It can be anything, even a rupee. But the priest who would sanctify it with an announcement would declare each amount to be "a thousand crores of gold coins" equalising all the money that is given. By the nineteenth century one finds two customs operating simultaneously. One is that of the boy's family offering money to the girl's family. The amount was fixed by the girl's family. The other was that of *stridhan* or bridewealth. Those who had property, chose this occasion to write a piece of land in the name of the girl because she did not have rights of inheritance. Both these customs are linked with several factors that formed the basis of existence. The first practice has embedded in it the idea of 'giving away' a girl and 'buying' her off. "To give a girl to a family and to take a girl from a family" are common ways of talking. Marriage generally meant a lot of work, responsibility and sacrifice. The girl had to work in large households with some lands, cows and numerous dependants whom she had to take care of. It was not easy to find intelligent, hard-working women. However, there was no fixed price attached to a girl. Very often, the boy's family, or the boy in some communities, would offer money as a symbolic gesture. There are also several instances of a boy's family or a man wanting to marry a girl much younger than him running into debts to get married. But both *stridhan* and brideprice were not *conditions* to a marriage. The amount, quantity or the nature were not rigidly defined or categorised. Sometimes only the symbolic gesture was adhered to. However, *stridhan* made it very clear that the unmarried daughter will remain a dependant. *Stridhan* was not property a daughter could claim as a matter of right but property that was given to her with marriage as a primary condition.

The practice of dowry, which is not to be confused with *stridhan*, from what I have understood while researching into the social history of women in the southern region, began when more and more boys went in for English education to be part of the bureaucracy, which meant, for one thing, a steady income unlike the insecure life attached to landed property or other activities to eke out a living. This happened around the latter half of the nineteenth century. Western educated boys working in offices and earning well, meant a less exacting life for girls they choose to marry. This tempted slightly well-to-do parents to offer to educate the boys themselves or to pay the parents the amount invested in their education. This was done with the idea that the girl will lead a comfortable life in future. But this led to a situation where the boy's family began to lay down conditions and get the upper hand. Not long after, dowry itself became one of the primary conditions for marriage, whatever the qualification of the boy. For just being a man who can marry a woman and give her a status, money had to be paid. The practice has spread to many other communities like the Nadar Christians, Syrian Christians and Tamil Muslims. One incident in the Twenties, that shocked people out of their complacent acceptance of this state of affairs was the suicide of Snehlata, a Bengali girl. Snehlata burnt herself because she did not want her father to sell the only house he owned to celebrate her marriage. Snehlata became a household name everywhere. People realised that what at one time were a few symbolic gifts like lamps, new pots and mats given to a girl to herald her life as a householder had now got transformed into specific items like furniture, bed, mattress, silver, brass and steel vessels and vehicles. Gone were the times when even these symbolic gifts were not compulsory and when poor parents could say that they would place flowers in the place of gold and conduct the marriage and when marriage expenses would be borne by both the families. The death of Snehlata sparked off a series of reactions that formed a firm basis for anti-dowry activities. It also led to a lot of questioning of the nature of the institution of marriage. Snehlata's death acted as a catalyst to give more strength to activities already set in motion. Obviously, we are more thick-skinned or worldly-wise for the suicide of four sisters in two different parts of the country has only led to this polemic on what dowry means to a woman.

Some western scholars have now begun to say that dowry is a colonialist construction and that, in reality, it is the woman's share in property and that those who look upon dowry as an evil are those who are influenced by imperialist notions, with no understanding of the values and strengths of their own culture. Arguments such as these are put forth by those scholars in the name of objectively viewing a given culture in terms which fall within the framework of that culture and in the name of judging a culture for what it is with academic objectivity. While, on the face of it, this argument seems like a noncolonial one with no Katherine Mayo kind of biases, it is deep within a very dangerous argument which actually says that nothing in a given culture needs change; all it needs is understanding. It also stresses the notion that everything in a given culture is there because it needs to be there. There is nothing to question or alter; those who question are traitors to that culture. This line of thinking, in the long run, will lead to a situation of deep fundamentalism presented as pride in one's culture and rigid prejudices practised as being 'true' to one's culture. It will also lead to a situation when each culture will become a chauvinistic island of its own, burying its neck deep into its own sand, not attempting to criticise, judge or take a stand on anything happening anywhere else. Such a state of affairs will help those who benefit from other cultures remaining stagnant; those who we term imperialists.

First published in *The Economic and Political Weekly*, January 28 1989.

Dowry and Inheritance Rights

MADHU KISHWAR

It is puzzling that *EPW* should think fit to publish such a confused diatribe as C.S. Lakshmi's 'On Kidneys and Dowry' (January 28).

Nowhere in any of my writings have I argued that "dowry items are the girl's share of the property" as Lakshmi fantasises I have argued. On the contrary, the thrust of my argument was that it is women's lack of inheritance rights which forces them mistakenly to continue viewing dowry as some sort of inadequate compensation for the denial to them of an equal share in parental property.

My article in *Manushi* (No. 48, 1988) was an inquiry into why anti-dowry campaigns, despite their stridency, have been so ineffective. Dowry continues to be practiced near-universally and most women continue to participate in it. Is this because most women are fools, or is it possible that approach leads us away from comprehending their limited alternatives?

Reflecting on my experience of actively participating in anti-dowry campaigns for 10 years, of having personally implemented a strict boycott of all dowry weddings, and of providing legal aid through *Manushi* to hundreds of women in distress, besides reading the narratives of hundreds more that came to us from different parts of the country, I came to the conclusion that one of the key reasons anti-dowry campaigns have been ineffective is that they were not accompanied by concerted efforts to make effective women's legal right to equal inheritance.

Lakshmi pompously misses the point when she declaims: "A woman inherits property by being the child of parents who own property. Whether married or unmarried, she has a right to this property. Whether divorced or widowed, she has a right to this property". If, instead of relying on the deceptive authority of paper laws which bestow such rights (although only partially) on women, Lakshmi were to look at actual women's lives, she would find it far more accurate to say that most women do not inherit property, even if they belong to propertied families. Whether married or unmarried, most women have not been able to establish their right to parental property. Whether widowed or divorced, women have not obtained rights to this property. Income generating assets, whether in the form of land, house, apartment, shop, factory or vehicle are almost always passed from father to son. When there are no sons, land is often passed to brothers' sons rather than to daughters. Women are made to sign away their rights in favour of their brothers in the overwhelming number of cases where any question arises about who are to be the rightful inheritors.

Having no secure foothold in her natal home, no economic base she can call her own, and for other reasons, most women have little choice but to see their marital home as the only place where they must try to belong, and so see their status as deriving from their husbands'. These are not "notions" as Lakshmi would have it, not myths deriving from false consciousness, but unfortunate actualities deriving from women's disinherited, dependent position in our society.

In this situation, dowry is the crumb given to the slave deprived of choice. Given a choice between a piece of land in her own name versus saris or furniture, few women would choose the latter. But to expect her to refuse the latter when the former is not on the agenda, is to ask her to become a martyr to a cause invented by social reformers, which will bring her no real advantage. How would it alter her powerless position in the marital home to marry dowryless when she will get nothing else either? It is like asking slaves to refrain from eating the only food provided by the master because accepting it would be degrading. Campaigners who suggest such a method of fighting slavery should not be surprised if their campaigns prove ineffective because slaves want to eat in order to stay alive. Unless they see some way of obtaining their freedom by effective actions to overturn the system, they will take what they can get. Some women do choose not to marry at all. But this society has a multitude of ways to discourage free choice of that option, as I have discussed in many other articles.

Lakshmi makes the sweeping statement that "women who get burnt or young girls who hang themselves are not those who come from families where there is any property that a girl can demand as her share". Anyone who has worked with women victims of marital violence and their families will confirm that this is an absurd and false generalization. A large number of women who are murdered or driven to suicide in their marital homes are daughters of businessmen, shopkeepers, landed peasants. Many of them die because their father and brothers, despite having adequate means to support them, despite owning a house or other property, refuse to give them shelter when they seek protection from a violent marriage. The men fear that the daughter will become a 'burden' on them, that is, will become, or make some sort of, claim on the property.

The culture of disinheritance of daughters, bred by hegemonic groups who own income generating assets, spreads to other groups as well. However, when we talk of dowry we are not primarily talking of the destitute poor but of those who have some economic assets or creditworthiness to encash.

Lakshmi has nothing but contempt for "women who want their parents to give dowry... in the mistaken notion that it ensures a comfortable future". She dismisses "these women" as "influenced by material values". Unfortunately, I cannot be as loftily dismissive of "material values" after listening to scores of women narrate how they were denied a new blouse or a pair of slippers or even bus fare for years after marriage, and had to go through the humiliation of drawing on what their parental family had given or continued to give them. The humiliation of asking their natal or marital family for personal expenses can only be obviated when women have an independent survival base which includes not just an independent income but the right to decide how it is spent.

As long as women continue to be in a powerless position in the marital family, a position which is crucially linked to disinheritance in the natal family, doing without dowry will certainly not empower women. To ask for abolition of dowry is to start at the wrong end. Instead, we should single-mindedly work to ensure effective inheritance rights for women as well as to ensure that women are not made mere vehicles for transfer of property. Once inheritance rights become a reality, dowry in its present form is almost certain to disappear.

Lakshmi accuses me of accepting that "status within a marital system has nothing to do with the individuals, it has to do with goods and property". She, on the contrary, thinks that only "love, warmth, understanding, sharing and empathy make a marriage work". She will find many supporters of the Hindi filmi, or rather Mills and Boon, view of marriage in all those who advise women to reform their husbands by 'love' and 'understanding' to 'empathise' with the problems that lead men to batter their wives and to make the marriage work by sharing the husband's problems. I have no hesitation in differing from this view of the marriage and family system. Why Lakshmi deserts her presumed Marxist orientation for romantic idealism is not clear. Perhaps she can afford to do so because she may have arranged other supports in her marital life that are not available to most women. Suggesting that married women and those considering marriage should ignore their economic survival interests in favour of total reliance on 'love', understanding, sharing and empathy seems very much at variance with any sensible woman's analysis of her options. Most women who act on such self-denying promises increase their chances of being victimised.

This is because men control decision-making and own most of the income generating property in our society and have owned it for generations; they are the decision-makers not only for themselves but for women and children too. Men's economic, social and political power tilts the balance overwhelmingly in their favour in marriage and leads to their dominance over women's lives. And this is no new phenomenon. It is certainly not the "corrupt values of a consumer society that has turned marriage into a market place", as Lakshmi moralistically claims. Marriage was not a romantic idyll before the advent of the consumer society. As an institution, marriage is a social and economic arrangement which has inequality built into it because of the unequal property control and power contribution between men and women. Lakshmi need not trouble herself to read Engels to understand this. Nineteenth century Indian literature, eighteenth century European literature, even ancient Greek drama, will make it clear to her, if she can manage to look beyond the 'goodness' and 'badness', the 'material' and 'non-material' values of individuals to the power relations between them, determined not by their 'notions' but by their actual situation.

Since Lakshmi concludes by accusing me of not wanting to "question or alter" anthing in our society or to "take a stand on anything", she naturally cannot afford to address my stand on inheritance rights, which is central to my argument and which she chooses to ignore. I had concluded my article by stressing the need to empower women by giving them an independent base. I reproduce that conclusion here:

"1. Any will which disinherits daughters should be considered invalid.

"2. All land, property, and succession related laws, including land selling laws, should be amended to ensure equal rights to women, particularly over immovable property such as housing and land.

"3.   Any document whereby a woman surrenders her right in favour of her brothers, husband or in-laws should be considered invalid.

"4.   A woman should not be able to pass on to her husband or in-laws any property inherited from her parents. If she dies childless or under suspicious circumstances, the property should revert to her natal family. This will ensure that her inheritance does not become an incentive for her husband and in-laws to kill her. Her inherited property should be inherited by her adult children or, if she is childless and dies a natural death many years after marriage, it may be inherited by her husband, as his would be inherited by her under the same circumstances ...

"We should work to equip women with the resources and abilities to define, control and guard their own interests and their own lives. Whether or not they are given dowry will then become irrelevant to their essential well being".

First published in *The Economic and Political Weekly*, March 18, 1989.

Bibliography

Aaby, P. 1977. "Engels and Women" *Critique of Anthropology* 3.9–10: pp. 25–53.

Agnes, Flavia. 2000. "Women, Marriage, and the Subordination of Rights" in *Community, Gender and Violence: Subaltern Studies No. 11*, ed. Partha Chatterjee and Pradeep Jeganathan, pp. 106–137. New York: Columbia University Press.

AIDWA (All India Democratic Women's Association). 2002. *The Practice of Dowry Itself is a Crime, Not Just its Excesses: A Report on the National Workshop on Expanding Dimensions of Dowry*. New Delhi, 1-2 September.

Alavi, Hamza. 1972. "Kinship in West Punjabi Villages" *Contributions to Indian Sociology New Series* 6: 1–27.

Aziz, Abdul. 1983. "Economics of Brideprice and Dowry." *Economic and Political Weekly* 9 April: 603-604.

Agarwal, Bina. 1994. *A Field of One's Own : Gender and Land Rights in South Asia*. Cambridge: Cambridge University Press.

Barrett, M. 1980. *Women's Oppression Today: The Marxist/Feminist Encounter*. London: Verso Books.

——. 1985. "Introduction" in F.A. Engels *The Origin of the Family, Private Property and the State*. Hammondsworth: Penguin Books.

Basch, Norma. 1986. "The Emerging Legal History of Women in the United States: Property, Divorce and the Constitution" *Signs* 12.1: pp. 97–117.

Basu, Srimati. 1999. *She Comes to Take Her Rights: Indian Women, Property and Propriety*. Albany: State University of New York Press.

Berreman, G. 1972. "Social Categories and Social Interaction in Urban India" *American Anthropologist* 74: 567–86.

Bhachu, Parminder. 1993. "Identities Constructed and Reconstructed: Representations of Indian Women in Britain" in *Migrant Women: Crossing Boundaries and Changing Identities*, ed. Gina Buijs, pp. 99–117. Oxford: Berg

Bhattacharji, Sukumari. 1991. "Economic Rights of Ancient Indian Women." *Economic and Political Weekly* March 2–9: pp. 507–512.

Bhattacharya, Malini. 1996. "The Monkey Dance: A Playscript" *Seagull Theater Quarterly* 9: pp. 37–40.

Bleie, T. 1987. "Gender Relations among Oraons in Bangladesh: Continutity and Change" *Economic and Political Weekly* 25 April.

Bloch, Maurice. 1978. "Marriage Amongst Equals: An Analysis of the Marriage Ceremony of the Merina of Madagascar." *Man (New Series)* 13.1: pp. 21–33.

Billig, Michael S. 1991. "The Marriage Squeeze on High-Caste Rajasthani Women." *Journal of Asian Studies* 50.2: pp. 341–360.

Boserup, Esther. 1993 (1973). Women's Role in Economic Development. London: Earthscan Publishers.

Bourdieu, P. 1984. *Distinctions*. Cambridge, MA: Harvard University Press.

Bradford, Nicholas. 1985. "From Bridewealth to Groom-Fee: Transformed Marriage Customs and and Socioeconomic Polarization Among Lingayats" *Contributions to Indian Sociology* 19.2: pp. 269–302.

Bossen, Laurel. 1988. "Toward a Theory of Marriage: The Economic Anthropology of Marriage Transactions" *Ethnology* 27.2: pp. 127–144.

Caplan, Lionel. 1984. "Bridegroom Price in Urban India: Class, caste and 'Dowry Evil' Among Christians in Madras". *Man (New Series)* 19.2: pp. 216–233.

Cassia, Paul Sant. 1982. "Property in Greek Cypriot Marriage Strategies, 1920–1980." *Man (New Series)* 17.4: pp. 643–663.

Chowdhry, Prem. 1993. "Conjugality, Law and State: Inheritance Rights as Pivot of Control in Northern India" *National Law School Journal* 1: pp. 95–116.

Chen, Martha, ed. 1998. *Widows in India: Social Neglect and Public Action*. New Delhi: Sage.

Comaroff, J. 1980. *The Meaning of Marriage Payments*. London: Academic Press.

Committee on the Status of Women in India. 1975. *Towards Equality: Report of the Committee on the Status of Women in India*. New Delhi: Government of India Ministry of Education and Social Welfare.

Coward, R. 1983. *Patriarchal Precedents: Sexuality and Social Relations*. London: Routledge and Kegan Paul.

Delmar, R. 1976. "Looking Again at Engels' Origin of the Family, Private Property and the State" in *The Rights and Wrongs of Women*, ed. J. Mitchell and A. Oakley. Hammondsworth: Penguin Books.

Delphy, C. 1977. *The Main Enemy: A Materialist Analysis of Women's Oppression*. London: Women's Research and Resources Centre.

Deolalikar, Anil B. and Vijayendra Rao. 1998. "The Demand for Dowries and Bride Characteristics in Marriage: Empirical Estimates for Rural South Central India" in *Gender, Population and Development*, ed. Ratna Sudarshan. New Delhi: Oxford University Press. pp. 122–140.

Department of Women and Child Development. *National Perspective Plan for Women, 1988–2000*. New Delhi: Ministry of Human Resource Development.

Dixon, R. 1978. *Rural Women at Work: Strategies for Development in South Asia*. Baltimore, MD and London: Johns Hopkins University Press.

Dowry Prohibition (Amendment) Bill. 1984. *Lok Sabha Debates Seventh Series*. 15 Session. L.19: pp. 271–301.

Eglar, Z. 1960. *A Punjabi Village in Pakistan*. New York: University of Columbia Press.

Epstein, T. Scarlett. 1973. *South India Yesterday, Today and Tomorrow: Mysore Villages Revisited*. London: Macmillan.

Firestone, S. 1970. *The Dialectic of Sex: The Case for Feminist Revolution*. New York: Bantam Books.

Franco, Fernando, Jyotsna Macwan and Suguna Ramanathan. 2000. *The Silken Swing: The Cultural Universe of Dalit Women*. Calcutta: Stree.

Frankel, F. 1978. *India's Political Economy, 1947–1977: The Gradual Revolution*. Delhi: Oxford University Press.

Friedl, E. Vasilika. 1976 (1962). "Kinship, Class and Selective Migration" in *Mediterranean Family Structures* J.G. Peristiany (ed.) Cambridge: Cambridge University Press.

Fruzzetti, Lina M. 1990 (1982). *The Gift of a Virgin: Women, Marriage and Ritual in a Bengali Society*. Delhi: Oxford University Press.

Gangoli, Gitanjali. 2000. "'Dowry' Revisited: Refocus on a Vexed Problem" *Economic and Political Weekly* December 30: pp. 4624–25.

Gautam, D.N. and B.V. Trivedi. 1986. *Unnatural Deaths of Married Women with Special Reference to Dowry Deaths: A Sample Study of Delhi*. New Delhi: Bureau of Police and Research and Development, Ministry of Home Affairs.

Gellner, David N. 1991. "Hinduism, Tribalism and the Position of Women: The Problem of Newar Identity" *Man (New Series)* 26.1: pp. 105–125.

Ginsberg, Faye and Rayna Rapp. 1991. "The Politics of Reproduction." *Annual Review of Anthropology* 20: pp. 311–343.

Goody, Jack. 1990. *The Oriental, the Ancient, and the Primitive: Systems of Marriage and the Family in the Pre-industrial Societies of Eurasia*. Cambridge: Cambridge University Press.

Goody, Jack and S.J. Tambiah. 1973. *Bridewealth and Dowry*. Cambridge: Cambridge University Press.

Gulati, Mitu and Leela Gulati. 1993. "Remnants of Matriliny: Widows of Two Kerala Villages" *Manushi* 76: pp. 32–34.

Harrell, S. and S.A. Dickey. 1985. "Dowry Systems in Complex Societies" *Ethnology* 24: pp. 105–120.

Hartung, John. 1982. "Polygyny and Inheritance of Wealth." *Current Anthropology* 23.1: pp. 1–12.

Hershman, Paul. 1981. *Punjabi Kinship and Marriage*. Delhi: Hindustan.

Heyer, Judith. 1992. "The Role of Dowries and Daughters' Marriages in the Accumulation and Distribution of Capital in a South Indian Community" *Journal of International Development* 4.4: pp. 419–436.

Hirschon, Renee, ed. 1984. *Women and Property–Women as Property*. London: Croom Helm.

Jaising, Indira (ed.). 1996. *Justice for Women: Personal Laws, Women's Rights and Law Reforms*. Mapusa, Goa: The Other India Press.

Jethmalani, Rani, ed. 1995. *Kali's Yug: Empowerment, Law, and Dowry Deaths*. New Delhi : Har-Anand Publications.

—— 1985. "Dowry and the Law–Subversion of Human Rights" in *Social Action Through Law* ed. P.K. Gandhi, pp. 114–126. New Delhi: Concept Publishers.

Jethmalani, Rani and P.K. Dey. 1995. "Dowry Deaths and Access to Justice" in *Kali's Yug : Empowerment, Law, and Dowry Deaths*, ed. Rani Jethmalani, pp. 36–78. New Delhi: Har-Anand Publications.

Jhutti, Jagbir. 1998. "Dowry Among Sikhs in Britain" in *South Asians and the Dowry Problem* ed. Werner Menski, pp. 175–198. New Delhi: Vistaar.

Kapadia, Karin. 1993. "Marrying Money: Changing Social Preference and Practice in a Tamil Marriage" *Contributions to Indian Sociology: New Series* 27.1: pp. 25–51.

Kaplan, Marion, ed. 1985. *The Marriage Bargain: Women and Dowries in European History. Women and History #10.* New York: Haworth.

Kapur, Ratna and Brenda Cossman. 1996. *Subversive Sites: Feminist Engagements with Law in India.* New Delhi: Sage.

Kelkar, Govind. 1993. "Women, Land and Agrarian Reform: Issues of Gender and Class in Improving Women's Effective Access to Land." *National Law School Journal* 1: pp. 117–141.

Khan, M.Z and Ramji Ray. 1984. "Dowry Death" *The Indian Journal of Social Work* 45.3: pp. 303–315.

Khare, R.S. 1972. "Hierarchy and Hypergamy: Some Interrelated Aspects among the Kanya-Kubja Brahmans" *American Anthropology* 74.

Kishwar, Madhu. 1999. *Off the Beaten Track: Rethinking Gender Justice for Indian Women.* New Delhi : Oxford University Press.

—— 1989. "Dowry and Inheritance Rights." *Economic and Political Weekly* 24 (18 March): pp. 587–588.

—— 1987. "Toiling Without Rights: Ho Women of Singbhum" *Economic and Political Weekly* 22: pp. 95–101, 149–155, 194–200.

Kressel, Gideon M. 1977. "Bride-Price Reconsidered." *Current Anthropology* 18.3: pp. 441–458.

Kumar, Dharma. 1998. *Colonialism, Property and the State.* New Delhi: Oxford University Press.

Kumar, K. and Punam Rani. "Dowry and Dowry Related Crimes" Offences Against Women pp. 180–194.

Kumar, Radha. 1993. "The Campaign Against Dowry" In *The History of Doing: An Illustrated Account of Movements for Women's Rights and Feminism in India, 1800–1990.* London: Verso. pp. 115–127.

Kumari, Ranjana. 1989. *Brides Are Not for Burning: Dowry Victims in India.* New Delhi: Radiant.

Levi-Strauss, Claude. 1969 (1949). *The Elementary Structures of Kinship.* London: Eyre and Spottiswoode.

Levine, Nancy E. 1987. "Fathers and Sons: Kinship Value and Validation in Tibetan Polyandry." *Man (New Series)* 22.2: pp. 267–286.

Luthra, Arati. 1983. "Dowry Among the Urban Poor: Perception and Practice" *Social Action* 33.2: pp. 194–216.

MacKinnon, C. 1989. *Towards a Feminist Theory of the State*. Cambridge, MA: Harvard University Press.

Madan, T.N. 1975. "Structural Implications of Marriage in North India: Wife-Givers and Wife-Takers Among the Pandits of Kashmir" *Contributions to Indian Sociology n.s.* 9: pp. 217–243.

Manimala. 1983. "*Zameen Kenkar? Jote Onkar!*: Women's Participation in the Bodhgaya Land Struggle" *Manushi* 14 (Jan–Feb): pp. 2–16.

Mauss, Marcel. 1967. *The Gift: Forms and Functions of Exchange in Archaic Societies*. Trans. Ian Cunnison. New York: Norton.

Menon, Nivedita. 1999. "Embodying the Self: Feminism, Sexual Violence and the Law" in *Community, Gender and Violence: Subaltern Studies No. 11*, ed. Partha Chatterjee and Pradeep Jeganathan, pp. 66–105. New York: Columbia University Press.

Menski, Werner, ed. 1999. *South Asians and the Dowry Problem*. New Delhi: Vistaar.

Miller, Barbara D. 1981. *The Endangered Sex: Neglect of Female Children in Rural North India*. Ithaca: Cornell University Press.

Millett, K. 1970. *Sexual Politics*. New York: Doubleday

Molyneux, M. 1981. "Socialist Societies Old and New: Progress Towards Women's Emancipation" *Feminist Review* 8: 1–34.

Monsoor, Taslima. 1998. "In Search of Security and Poverty Alleviation: Women's Inheritable Entitlements to Land, the Untapped Resources." *Journal of International Affairs*. 4.2: pp. 42–56.

Moors, Annelies. 1995. *Women, Property and Islam: Palestinian Experiences, 1920–1990*. Cambridge: Cambridge University Press.

Mulder, Monique Berghoff. 1995. Bridewealth and its Correlates: Quantifying Changes Over Time" *Current Anthropology* 36.4: pp. 573–603.

Mukund, Kanaklatha. 1990. Turmeric Land: Women's Property Rights in Tamil Society Since Early Medieval Times" *Economic and Political Weekly* April 25.

Murickan, J. 1975. "Women in Kerala: Changing Socioeconomic Status and Self Image" in *Women in Contemporary India* ed. A. de Souza. New Delhi: Manohar.

Narayan, Uma. 1997. *Dislocating Cultures: Identitites, Traditions and Third-World Feminism.* New York: Routledge.

Nazzari, Muriel. 1991. *Disappearance of the Dowry: Women, Families and Social Change in Sao Paolo, Brazil (1600–1900).* Stanford: Stanford University Press.

Nongbri, Tiplut. 1988. "Gender and the Khasi Family Structure" *Sociological Bulletin* 37.1–2: pp. 71–82.

Omvedt, Gail. 1993. *Reinventing Revolution: New Social Movements and the Socialist Tradition in India.* Armonk, New York: M.E. Sharpe.

—— 1990. "Women, Zilla Parishads and Panchayat Raj: Chandwad to Vitner" *Economic and Political Weekly* 4 August: pp. 1687–1690.

Ortner, S.B. and Whitehead, H. 1981. *Sexual Meanings: The Cultural Construction of Gender and Sexuality.* Cambridge: Cambridge University Press.

Palriwala, R. 1989. "Reaffirming the Anti-Dowry Struggle" *Economic and Political Weekly* 29 April: pp. 942–944.

Papps, Ivy. 1983. "The Role and Determinants of Bride-Price: The Case of a Palestinian Village." *Current Anthropology* 24.2: pp. 203–215.

Parashar, Archana. 1992. *Women and Family Law Reform in India: Uniform Civil Code and Gender Equality.* New Delhi: Sage Publications.

Parry, J.P. 1979. *Caste and Kinship in Kangra.* London: Routledge and Kegan Paul.

Pati, Biswamoy. 1993. "Face of Dowry in Orissa" *Economic and Political Weekly* May 22: pp. 1020–22.

Paul, Madan C. 1993. *Dowry and Position of Women in India: A Study of Delhi Metropolis.* New Delhi: Inter-India.

Peletz, Michael G. 1995. "Kinship Studies in Late Twentieth Century Anthropology" *Annual Review of Anthropology* 24: pp. 343–72.

Rajan, Rajeswari Sunder. 1993. *Real and Imagined Women: Gender, Culture and Postcolonialism*. London: Routledge.

Rajaraman, Indira. 1983. "The Economics of Brideprice and Dowry." *Economic and Political Weekly* 13: 275–80.

Ram, Kalpana. 1992. *Mukkuvar Women : Gender, Hegemony, and Capitalist Transformation in a South Indian Fishing Community*. New Delhi : Kali for Women.

Randeria, Shalini and Leela Visaria. 1984. "Sociology of Bride Price and Dowry." *Economic and Political Weekly* 14: pp. 648–52.

Reiter, R.R. 1977. "The Search for Origins: Unravelling the Threads of Gender Hierarchy" *Critique of Anthropology* 3.9–10: pp. 15–25.

Rubin, Gayle. 1997 [1984]. "The Traffic in Women" in *The Second Wave: A Reader in Feminist Theory*, ed. Linda Nicholson, pp. 27–62. New York: Routledge.

Sacks, K. 1975. "Engels Revisited: Women, the Organization of Production and Private Property" in *Toward an Anthropology of Women*, ed. R. Reiter. New York: Monthly Review Press.

Sambrani, Rita Bhandari and Shreekant Sambrani. 1983. "Economics of Brideprice and Dowry." *Economic and Political Weekly* 18.15 April 9: pp. 601–603.

Saradamoni, K. 1999. *Matriliny Transformed: Family, Law, and Ideology in Twentieth Century Travancore*. New Delhi: Sage Publications.

Sayers, J., M. Evans and N. Redclift, eds. 1987. *Engels Revisited: New Feminist Essays*. London: Tavistock Publications.

Schlegel, A. and R. Eloul. 1988. "Marriage Transactions: Labour, Property and Status" *American Anthropologist* 90: pp. 291–309.

Selwyn, Tom. 1979. "Images of Reproduction: An Analysis of a Hindu Marriage Ceremony" *Man (New Series)* 14.4: pp. 684–698.

Shah, A.M. 1982. "Division and Hierarchy: An Overview of Caste in Gujarat" *Contributions to Indian Sociology* 16: 1–33.

Shanley, Mary Lyndon. 1989. *Feminism, Marriage and the Law in Victorian England, 1850–1895.* Princeton: Princeton University Press.

Sharma, Ursula. 1980. *Women, Work and Property in North-West India.* London: Tavistock.

Sheel, Ranjana. 1999. *The Political Economy of Dowry: Institutionalization and Expansion in North India.* New Delhi: Manohar.

Srinivas, M.N. 1984. *Some Reflections on Dowry.* New Delhi: Oxford University Press.

Tambiah, Stanley J. 1989. "Bridewealth and Dowry Revisited: The Position of Women in Sub-Saharan Africa and North India" *Current Anthropology* 30.4: pp. 413–435.

Thapar, Romila. 1987."Traditions versus Misconceptions: Status of Women and Dowry." *Manushi* 42–49.

Uberoi, Patricia. 1996. "When is a Marriage not a Marriage? Sex, Sacrament and Contract in Hindu Marriage" In *Social Reform, Sexuality, and the State,* ed. Patricia Uberoi. New Delhi: Sage Publications. pp. 319–345.

Umar, Mohammad. 1998. *Bride Burning in India: A SocioLegal Study.* New Delhi : A.P.H. Pub. Corp.

Unnithan-Kumar, Maya. 1997. "Girasia Brideprice and the Politics of Marriage Payments" in *Identity, Gender and Poverty: New Perspectives on Caste and Tribe in Rajasthan.* Oxford: Berghahn Books. pp. 189–214.

Vander Veen, Klaas W. 1972. *I Give Thee My Daughter: A Study of Marriage and Hierarchy among the Anavil Brahmans of South Gujarat.* Assen: Van Gocum and Company NV.

Vatuk, Sylvia. 1975. "Gifts and Affines in North India." *Contributions to Indian Sociology n.s.* 9: pp. 155–96.

———. 1972. *Kinship and Urbanization.* Berkeley: University of California Press.

Visvanathan, Susan. 1989. "Marriage, Birth and Death: Property Rights and Domestic Relationships of the Orthodox/ Jacobite Syrian Christians of Kerala. *Economic and Political Weekly* June 17: pp. 1341–46.

Watson, Rubie S. 1981. "Class Differences and Affinal Relations in South China." *Man (New Series)* 16.4: pp. 593–615.

Werbner, Pnina. 1990. "Economic Rationality and Hierarchical Gift Economies: Value and Ranking among British Pakistanis." *Man (New Series)* 25.2: pp. 266–285.

Wolff, R. and S. Resnick. 1989. "Power, Property and Class" Discussion Paper No. 21, Association of Economic and Social Analysis, Department of Economics, University of Massachusetts, Amherst, MA.

Contributors

BINA AGARWAL is Professor of Economics at the Institute of Economic Growth, University of Delhi. Among her extensive publications are several books including: *A Field of One's Own: Gender and Legal Rights in South Asia* (1994) and *Cold Hearths and Barren Slopes: The Woodfuel Crisis in the Third World* (1986). She is currently working on the theme of gender, environment and collective action in India and Nepal.

C.S. LAKSHMI has been doing research in the field of women's studies for the past 30 years and has published several articles on the subject. She writes Tamil fiction, using the nom de plume Ambai. She is founder trustee and currently Director of SPARROW (Sound and Picture Archive for Research on Women) in Mumbai. She is the author of *The Singer & the Song: Conversations with Women Musicians* (2000) and *Mirrors & Gestures: Conversations with Women Dancers* (2003) Her most recent work is *The Unhurried City: Writings on Chennai* (2004).

D.N. SANDANSHIV was on the Law Commission, and has worked with Women's Action Research and Legal Action for Women (WARLAW). He is presently an independent legal consultant.

ENAKSHI GANGULI-THUKRAL has been involved for over 10 years in research and advocacy on issues concerning displacement and rehabilitation, women and children. Currently she is working on a project on advocacy for reproductive rights at the Population Council.

INDIRA RAJARAMAN currently holds the RBI Chair at the National Institute of Public Finance and Policy, Delhi. From 1976 to 1994 she was on the faculty of the Indian Institute of Management in Bangalore. Her research interests broadly cover macro policy and transition issues in the developing world.

INDU AGNIHOTRI is a Senior Fellow at the Centre for Women's Development Studies, New Delhi. She has written extensively on the women's movement in India.

JAYOTI GUPTA is at the Centre for Studies in Social Sciences, Kolkata. Her research interests include the land market in West Bengal, bonded labour in India, women and inheritance, and the informal sector.

JOLLY MATHEW worked as legal coordinator for Women's Action Research and Legal Action for Women. She has since been a model for Pierre Cardin and Cartier, among other famous international brands.

K. SARADAMONI is a senior social scientist based in Trivandrum. Among her published works are *Family, Law and Ideology in the Twentieth Century* (1999) and *Finding the Household: Conceptual and Methodological Issues* (1992).

LEELA VISARIA has conducted research in historical demography, and has also been involved in field-based studies on problems of health, family planning, education and demographic transition. She has co-authored *Contraceptive Use and Fertility in India: A Case Study of Gujarat* (1995) and has co-edited *Maternal Education and Child Survival: Pathways and Evidence* (1997). With Tim Dyson and Robert Cassen, both of the London School of Economics, she has recently co-edited *Twenty-First Century India: Population, Economy, Human Development and the Environment* (2004). Since 1996 she has served as coordinator of a network of non-governmental organisations and researchers, known as HealthWatch.

M.N. SRINIVAS (1916–1999) helped found the Department of Sociology at the Delhi School of Economics. Among his many awards is the Padma Shree from the President of India. Among his works are *Religion and Society Among the Coorgs of South India* (1952) and *A Remembered Village* (1976).

MADHU KISHWAR is founder-editor of the journal *Manushi*, and Fellow at the Centre for the Study of Developing Societies, Delhi. Among her published works are *In Search of Answers: Indian Women's Voices* (co-authored with Ruth Vanita, 1984) and *Off the Beaten Track: Rethinking Gender Justice for Indian Women* (1999).

MARY ROY is Principal of Corpus Christi School, Kottayam. In 1986, she successfully petitioned the Supreme Court of India against discriminatory inheritance laws among Syrian Christians in Kerala. The case made for a landmark judgement in favour of Syrian Christian women.

MAYA UNNITHAN-KUMAR is Senior Lecturer in the Department of Social Anthropology, School of Oriental and African Studies, University of Sussex. Her research in the early 1990s focused on kinship and gender relations in northwest India and appeared as *Identity, Gender and Poverty* (1997). Most recently, she has authored *Reproductive Agency, Medicine and the State: Cultural Transformations in Childbearing* (2004).

PREM CHOWDHRY is Professorial Fellow at the Centre of Contemporary Studies, Nehru Memorial Museum and Library, New Delhi. She is the author of *Colonial India and the Making of Empire Cinema: Image, Ideology and Identity* (2000), *The Veiled Women: Shifting Gender Equations in Rural Haryana, 1880–1990* and *Punjab Politics* (1984). Her research interests include politics, society, culture and gender in colonial and contemporary India. She is currently engaged in exploring different aspects of popular culture and cultural practice in north India. Her forthcoming work is titled *Dangerous Liaisons: Contentious Marriages in Northern India.*

RAJNI PALRIWALA is Professor of Sociology at the University of Delhi and has been teaching, researching and writing on various themes, particularly in the areas of gender and kinship, women's work and women's movements. She is the author of *Changing Kinship, Family, and Gender Relations in South Asia: Processes, Trends and Issues* (1994), *Shifting Circles of Support: Contextualising Kinship and Gender Relations in South Asia and Sub-Saharan Africa* (1996, co-edited with Carla Risseeuw) and *Structures and Strategies: Women, Work and Family in Asia* (1990, co-edited with Leela Dube). She is currently completing an ethnography on single parents and the welfare state in The Netherlands.

317

RANJANA SHEEL is with the Centre for Women's Studies, Banaras Hindu University. Among her published works is *The Political Economy of Dowry: Institutionalization and Expansion in North India* (1999).

SEEMA MISRA is a lawyer by training. She is a Senior Programme Officer in the Legal Literacy Programme of the Multiple Action Research Group (MARG). She has written two manuals: *The Inter-State Migrant Workmen and their Rights* and *The Law on Compensation for Motor Accident Victims*, both published by MARG.

SHALINI RANDERIA received a Ph.D. in ethnology at the University of Oxford and is currently working with the Institute of Sociology, Free University of Berlin. Her fields of research are cultural anthropology, political anthropology, population policy and sociology of development. Her present research focuses on "Legal Pluralism: Gender, Community and Justice". She has been an activist of and a consultant for NGOs for human rights and women's empowerment in India.

SRIMATI BASU teaches anthropology, women's studies and Asian Studies at DePauw University, USA. She has been involved with community work and research in the areas of feminist jurisprudence, violence against women and development. She is the author of *She Comes to Take Her Rights: Indian Women, Property and Propriety* (1999).

URSULA SHARMA trained as an anthropologist, and has conducted fieldwork in India and Britain. She has held posts at the University of Delhi and at Keele University, teaching sociology and social anthropology. She is currently Professor of Comparative Sociology at the University of Derby.

VEENA TALWAR OLDENBURG is Professor of History at Baruch College and The Graduate Center of the City University of New York. She is the author of several scholarly articles and of *The Making of Colonial Lucknow* (1984) and *Dowry Murder: The Imperial Origins of a Cultural Crime* (2002).